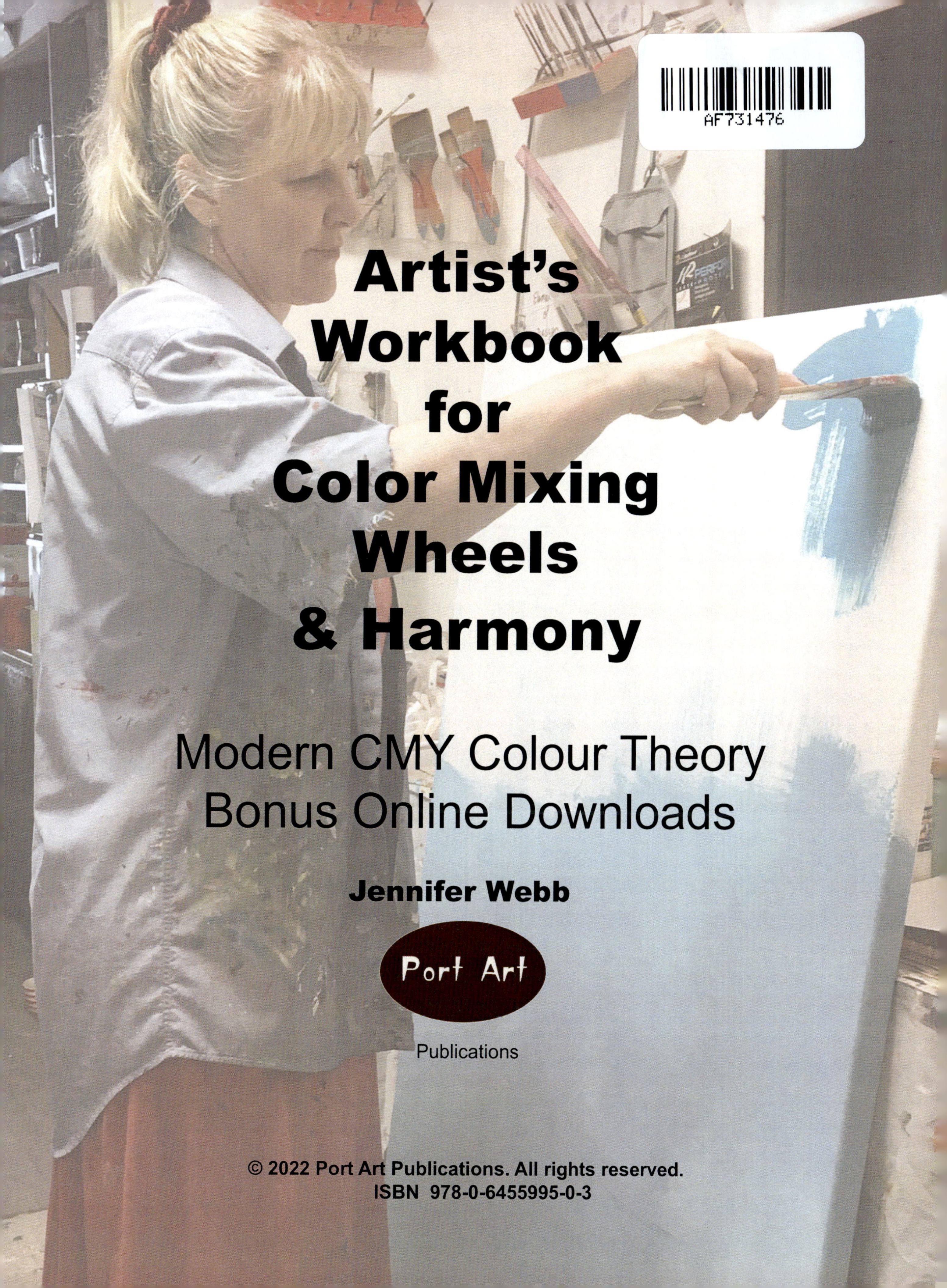

Artist's Workbook for Color Mixing Wheels & Harmony

Modern CMY Colour Theory
Bonus Online Downloads

Jennifer Webb

Port Art
Publications

ISBN 978-0-6455995-0-3

Hey there color loving creatives! Welcome to my studio!

- I am an Australian artist (since childhood) and art educator for 20 years. Wherever you are at in your creative journey, I have been there and I want to show you some very practical DIY exercises to get you confident quickly in mixing exactly the colors and combos you want for any project, any time, any medium.
- This workbook is not about painting techniques with any specific medium (that is covered in another few Modules entirely). This workbook is wholly and solely about thoroughly nailing the goal of mixing harmonious color relationships for your artworks.
- Acrylics are mentioned more in pigment suggestions due to their suitability for use in the paper of this workbook. Feel free to learn how to harmonize, using all 12 hue groups in any medium. (the same principles of color harmony apply, even though all pigment preparations vary.) Just choose medium specific papers to make your individual Color Bible(s) .
- The background theory section is on white and the practical workbook pages are on a black background, so you can flip to your workbook easily anytime.
- The basics of color theory and science are included because it is fascinating and helps to explain some of the fun and freaky phenomena that you will encounter while mixing pigments. There is helpful advice on reaching your goals starting with the bare minimum of 6 specific tubes or pots, so you get complete control and later you can buy more ready-made favorites and 'convenience colors' with the full appreciation of how to fit them into your own personalised harmonious schemes. There are a few general directions on mixing some popular convenience colors, but the main goal is to give all readers the knowledge and practical skills to mix any hue, value and saturation independently (and their mixing partners) while finding your own color and harmony preferences. Have fun!
- PS. I'm in a collaborative studio setting, hence both pronouns, are used, We and I . Please note colors vary a bit from ebook in RGB to printed workbook in CMYK, , out of our control.

TABLE OF CONTENTS

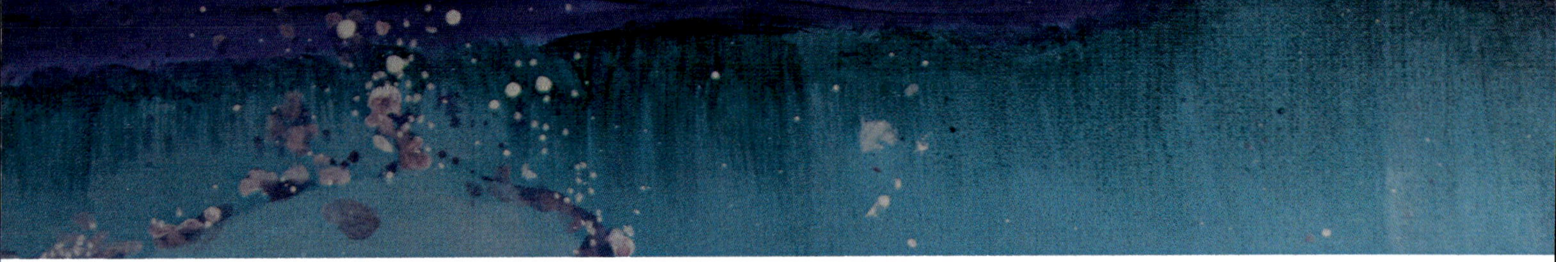

TABLE OF CONTENTS

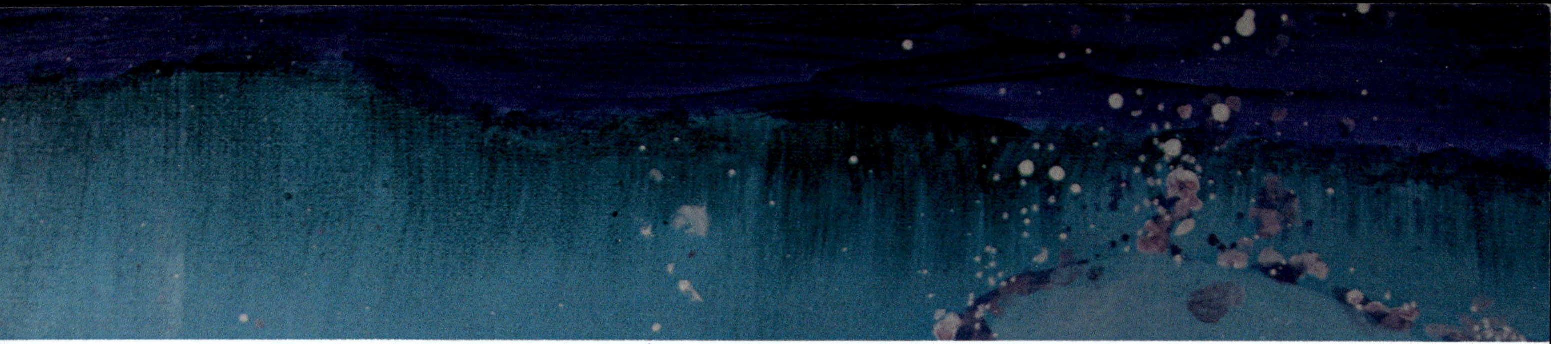

YOUR FREE GIFTS

Welcome to our creativec community. This workbook can be used as a resource while you start (or continue) to discover all about modern color theory, mixing and harmonious relationships. It has been adapted from our online course color module and we would like to give you a free bonus gift as you join our insiders and First Readers list (use this QR code to head to melbourneart-classes.com.au). On this list, you will have an offer of a free reviewers ecopy of future art books as well. We would love to receive a great review from all of our readers who found this guide help-ful. You can never understimate the importance that other potential readers place on the positive experiences of fellow creatives. *****

Your first free gift is '10 Absolutely vital tips for Strong Composition and Design' and will be delivered with your welcome email.

Once you get to the practical workbook pages , you will discov-er a second free bonus . Use the 2ND QR code inside the rear cover to receive your login for these bonus materials.

This will give you the added benefit of videos and downloadable templates for strings and color wheels to use with the work-book, reinforcing the methodologies of paint mixing outlined here in your workbook. Create a wheel (or two) for every medium you want to work in.

INTRODUCTION

COLOR - WHY, WHAT, HOW

After decades of observation and research, it appears that many learners/readers in the area of Color Theory and Color mixing are far more interested in the What and the How of color (mixing) over and above the Why. (Why does color behave or appear as it does?)

A basic introduction to how Color Science and the studies on Psychology of Color are included in the sections to follow. Note, however, that the practical exercises that cover the WHAT and the HOW, make up the most vital messages of this workbook. Like Nike says... 'Just Do it!" This book is for those who have started or are about to start playing with pigments and want some guidance as they already recognize that knowledge is power with color!!

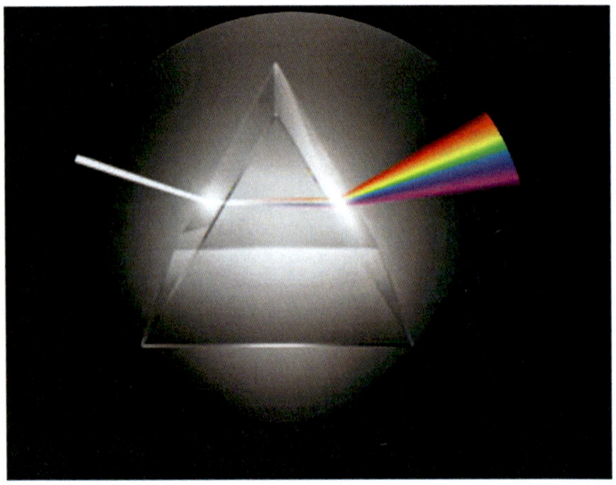

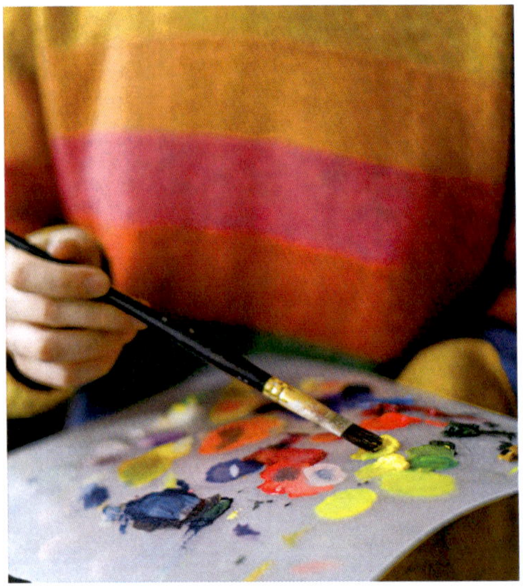

It will also help those who have been confounded and confused by conflicting explanations in their past efforts. Your workbook has practice pages further on, precisely so you can add the color yourself as you learn and practice mixing hues (or you can use medium-specific paper for Watercolor or Oils to carry out your color practice then collage them into your workbook once dry.) You can also create a separate art journal for your color practical studies which you can refer to constantly going forward.

WHAT DO WE MEAN BY "FEEL THE COLOR?"

Ok, so...NO... we don't mean it is all intuitive and you need to wear it and roll in it, meditate first, then use a Ouija board to determine the best colors for your painting!

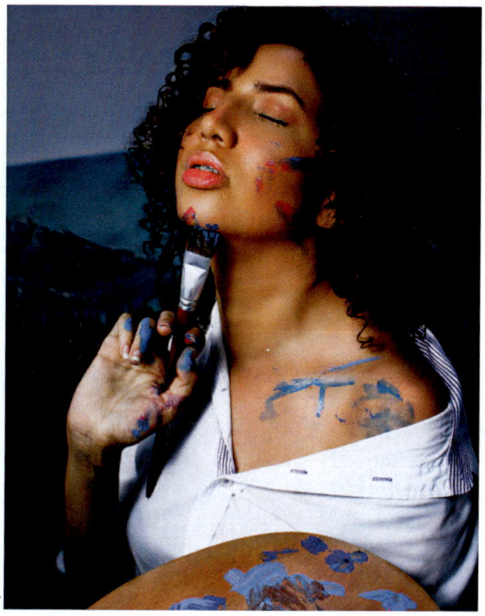

You will find out in practice how to mix any hue and also how to cleverly arrange them in harmonious ways. By practising all of this with your own materials you can use your final color wheels that you have made yourself, to guide you in your color planning. Use the primaries you knowingly chose yourself and gain an understanding of how they all fit together. This is something you will actually 'feel', first with your eyes but mostly with your brain. Before undertaking the practical mixing exercises and making wheels, read the Glossary of Terms and the FAQs section (rear of the book) because you might be new to this subject, but several color seekers have been here before and you'll get the benefit of their questions too. Many have the same questions when starting out with color mixing and harmonization.

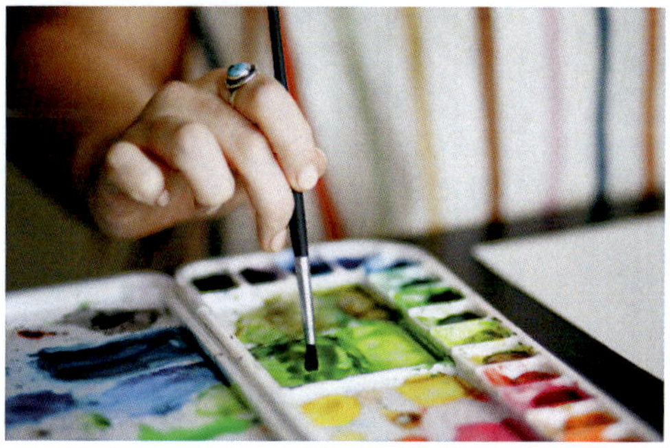

ANY PAINTING MEDIUM CAN BE USED TO PRACTICE HOW TO HARMONIZE COLORS

Regardless of your painting medium of choice, the hues you will be aiming to mix for around the triadic color wheel are generally the same. The pigments however may present somewhat differently in some cases, giving different hue positions, values and levels of saturation (hence different colors). They differ from one manufacturer to another as well as from medium to medium. You will discover what to look for in pigments (whether just the basic 6 or an ongoing endless list).

Due to the nature of the paper in this book, undiluted acrylics are the most suited for carrying out the color mixing exercises outlined, if done directly on the workbook pages (or even colored pencils).

As mentioned already, those working in watercolors or oils (and all who order the ebook) can use their medium specific papers and either collage them into this workbook or create an alternative color journaling folder for future reference. You may find your own color preferences and leanings emerging in sophisticated and personally expressive ways not possible before. Keep all of your studies and exercises going forward to give your creative voice 'wings'. Color mixing and color relationships are subjects we can return to again and again and continue to learn and develop. (Included in this book are some other fascinating things which don't directly help an artist mix pigment, but are fun to know and add some perspective to the quirky stuff like simultaneous contrast and other color conundrums eg. No specific wavelength exists for Magenta (and yet our brain tells us we see it!!)□

If you are tired of mixing dull brownish hues accidentally or if you know zero about clever color relationships and color mixing, you have found the most practical resource. There are multiple textbooks on Color Theory(s) and the science of color (and other books which go on to promote 6 primaries not 3), but in our extensive experience, art students and artists can get more control over their color mixing and harmonizing in paintings with practical exercises that show them what to do (including what to do when your pigment mixture doesn't look like you thought it should) . It all comes down to choosing the best 'primary hues' and their best mixing partners.

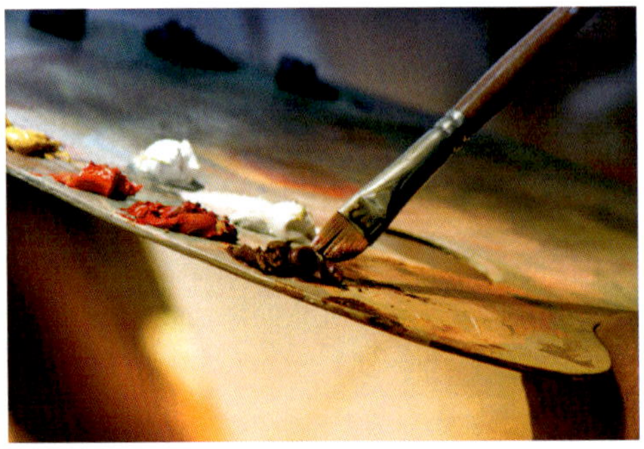

When buying a primary red (aka Magenta) pigment we need to 'see' the amount of bias towards orange or violet and then work around this as we mix and marry complementary partners. This 'seeing' will be covered in more detail as we go on.

https://arstechnica.com/science/2009/02/yes-virgina-there-is-a-magenta/

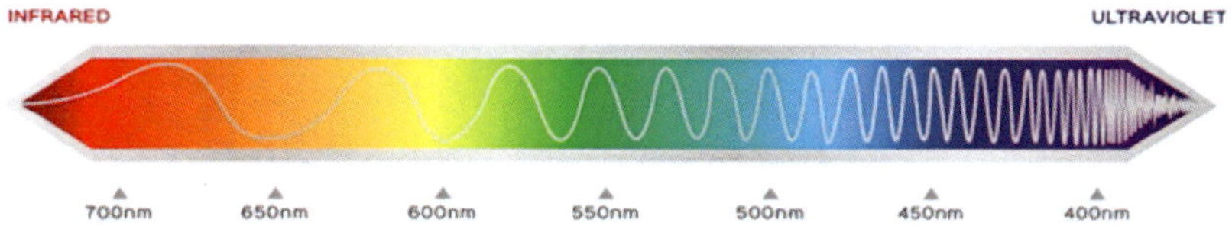

Multiple articles exist about color and light. Read more if you are interested (it is all very fascinating, however it won't change how we show you to mix paint). Pigments are not actually wavelengths of light, let's remember that above all. **(They reflect light in varying combinations and rarely, if ever, fit exactly into the middle of a 12 point wheel hue sector.)**

First you need to learn how to choose your primary pigments, then you'll need to learn to find them their harmonious partners, by making them yourself.

In the world of pigments, some made from natural ingredients and some made in the laboratory, there are those that can best fit the 'Primary' definition (cannot be made with others). As you have fun mixing the hues for your wheel, if your red is a bit orange -biased or violet-biased, there are ways to create/adjust your wheel around them, you will soon see. It is truly in the 'doing' that you will understand about color mixing and relationships. Let's get into it! You choose whether you work through the summarized history of color science and theory or jump straight into the practical advice about choosing and using pigments.

"I found I could say things with color and shapes that I couldn't say any other way - things I had no words for." Georgia O'Keeffe

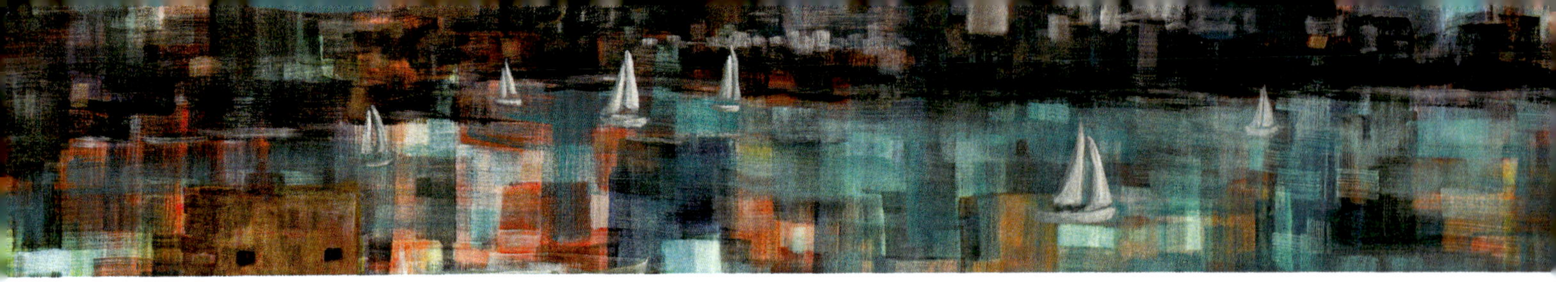

WHAT IS COLOR ANYWAY ?

Color is often called a property of light (Newton went to a great deal of trouble to shine a light through a glass prism and show the spectrum of colors (Red, Orange, Yellow, Green, Blue, Indigo, Violet - As kids we recited from the mnemonic 'Roy's golf bag is violet' to remember the order of hues.) Like many things we experience, color is more a creation or property of our brain actually, which interprets it via the rods and cones (specialized cells of the retina in the eye). Humans have 3 types of cones , sensitive to different wavelengths of color. The rods are most sensitive to light and dark changes. More in-depth information if you'd like on the resources links. Our experience of colors is not just dependent on the wavelength of the light rays that land on our retina, but also other things such as background colors, lighting and even cultural influences. You can do some fun exercises later and see some super interesting color phenomena for yourself.

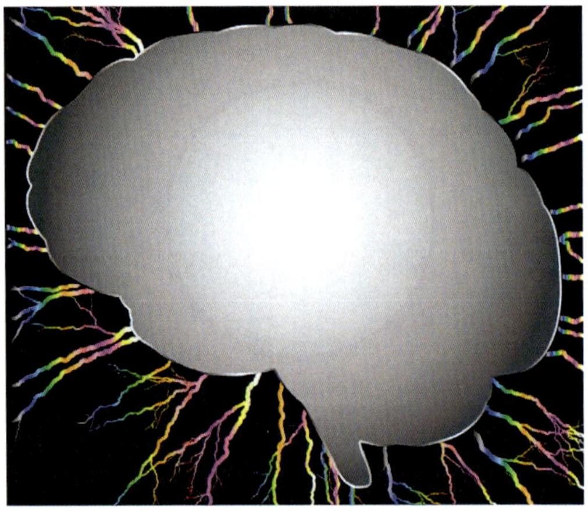

It is also important to understand that Hue , Chroma (Saturation) and Brightness (Value) are all attributes of color. There can be many colors within one hue definition. Regardless of the medium you choose, it is not really essential to have the most expensive materials when you are learning. By the same token, there are always headaches with the cheapest pigments, due to poor pigment concentration or random, misleading names, and so inferior outcomes can often follow.

Concentrate on getting the bare minimum of primaries plus a few extras in as good a quality that you can afford (rather than a tube of every single color of cheap stuff).

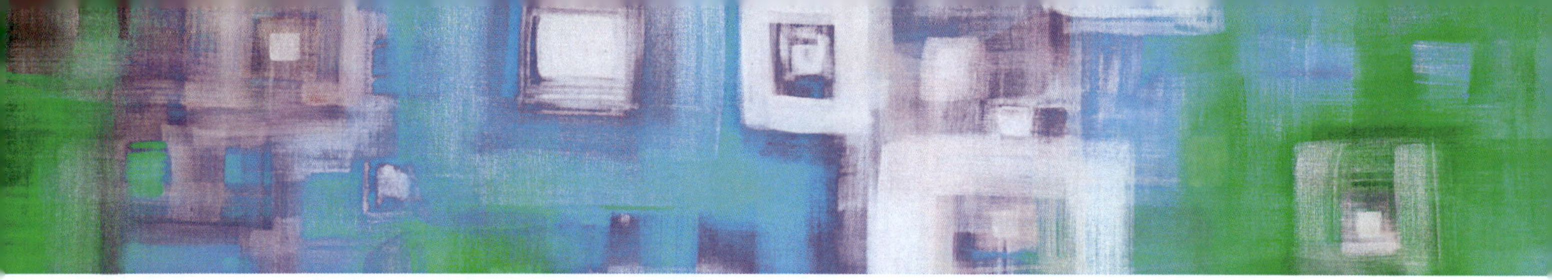

WHAT IS COLOR vs HUE ?

You may have learned in science at school that the human eye can see around 1,000,000+ different colors. If you think that is amazing, would it interest you to know that the Mantis Shrimp has 6 times the number of cones in their eyes, so they can see many times the number of colors!!

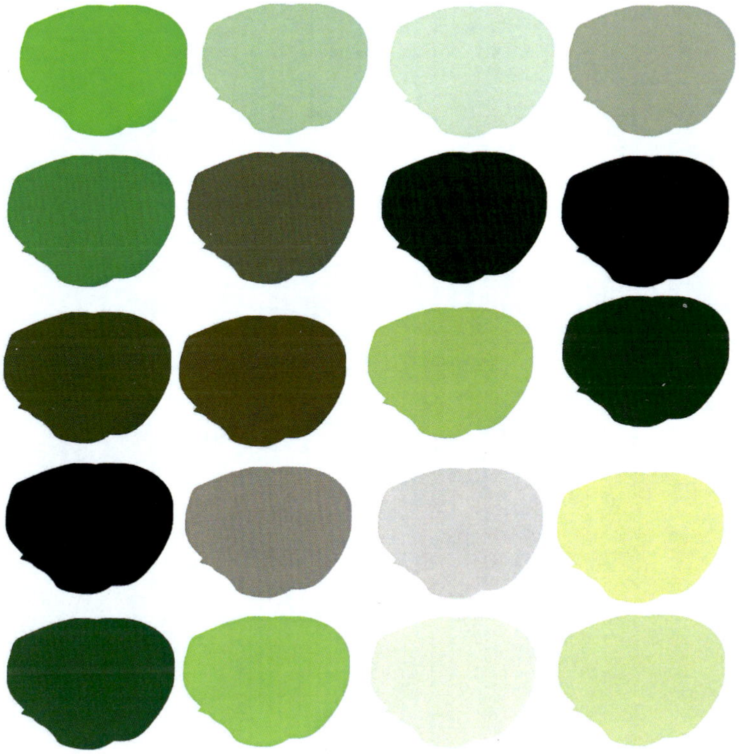

If you refer to the 12 sector color wheel based around the triad of Magenta, Yellow and Cyan , there are just 12 general hue ranges (but 1 million-ish color variations that can fit into this range of hues.) Some people choose to add 6 more tertiary positions to make an 18 sector wheel.

eg. These 20 colors shown in the image here are variations of saturated, de-saturated, tinted and rich grays of the tertiary hue yellow-green. There are so many more possibilities in terms of variations in all dimensions of color of the hue yellow-green (as with all hues).

Our FIRST CHALLENGE is finding and purchasing magenta, yellow and blue (cyan) pigments in your medium(s) that have a minimal bias of either neighbors. Read more about color bias after pigment labelling information.

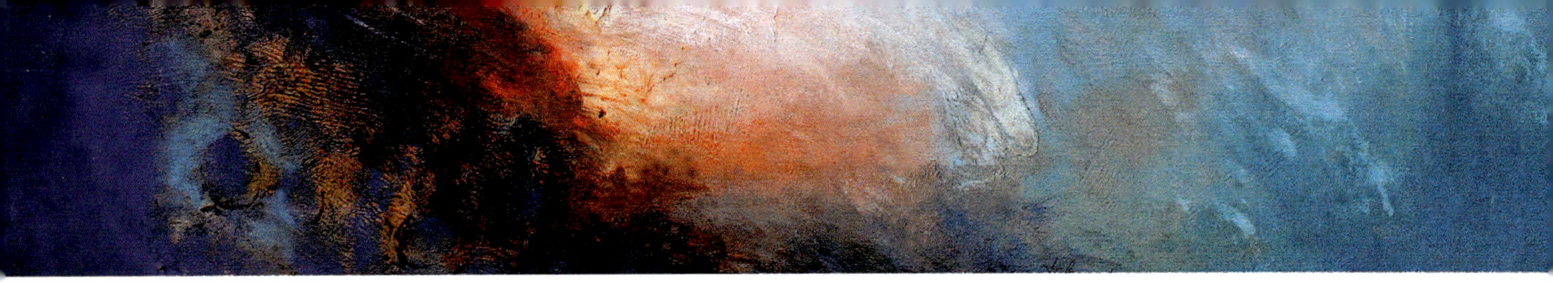

SATURATION AND VALUE

The three fundamental dimensions to be aware of when studying, mixing and mastering color are Hue, Saturation and Value. We have already clarified the term Hue.

SATURATION

Saturation is the "colorfulness of an area judged in proportion to its brightness". There are areas of great saturation in the banner image colors above and also some de-saturated areas. We may refer to an area as having a high chroma, other synonyms might be vibrance, intensity, chromaticity.

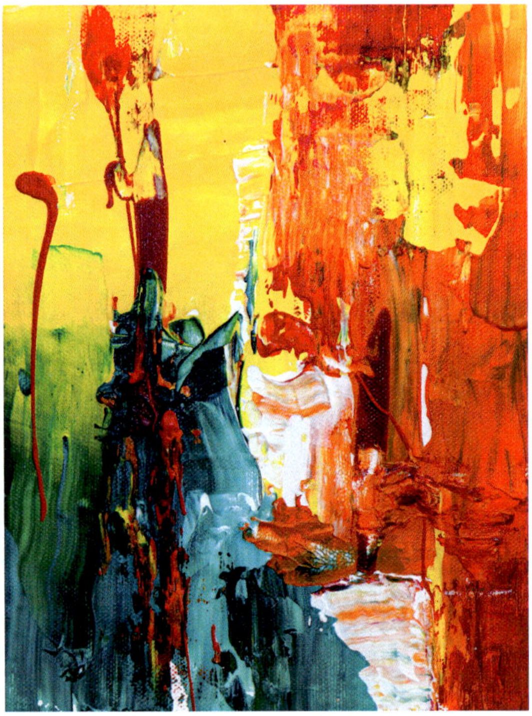

The yellow in this close-up detail of abstract paint marks (right) has the same saturation throughout, whereas the blue-green, yellow-green and the red-orange areas all have varying levels of value and saturation.

VALUE (High key = High value)

The de-saturated reds, greens and blues there also have a lower numerical measure of value. This refers to the darkness or lightness (brightness means a higher value, with 10 being the highest in white, on a 0 - 10 value scale).

TONE is also used to measure how dark or light an area might be, but 0 is measured as white and as tone increases, so does the number. These two terms create a lot of confusion amongst artists and students. Just remember, as you draw in graphite or charcoal the relative tone goes up as you are adding darkness (like with a high tone of voice ie. more=higher).

The value (and key) in reverse, are relatively higher (brighter) as they approach white.

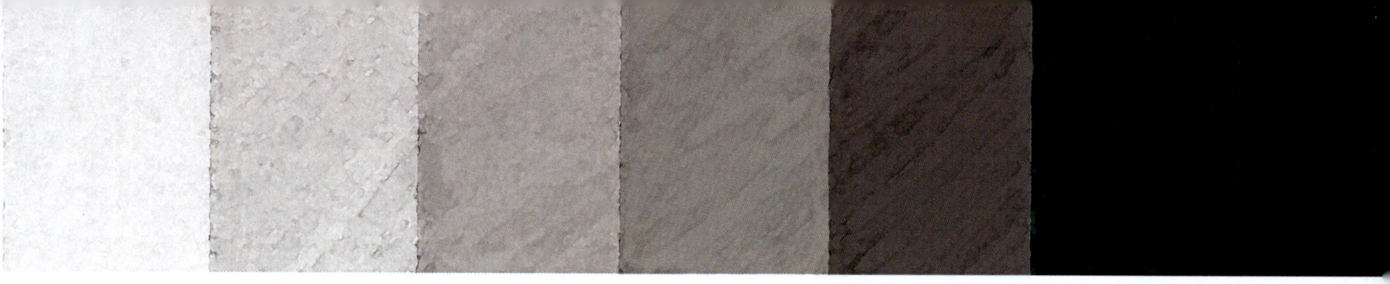

HELPFUL HINTS WHEN USING THE ELEMENT OF VALUE

There is an entire module on our online studio dedicated to the element of Value, it is worth the effort of delving deeply into the study of Value, Contrast, Light and Shade.

www.melbourneartclasses.com.au

- Beginners tend to under-value this (pun intended) and its power to attract and lead the eye. It is as powerful if not more so than color harmony.

- SQUINTING at your work to minimize detail and see the gestalt (the overall) patterns of tonal value helps. What gives away a beginner's work is often a lack of consideration for value, so always make value studies, as a part of your compositional planning. A value pattern is also called a 'Notan'.

- A tonal value scale or grey scale (eg. 0 – 8) helps to assess or measure tone (you could make little holes in each value space on the card that you paint or shade your scale on) until you 'get your eye in' for tone.

- One of the reasons (traditionally) for focusing first on drawing in monochromatic media (before moving onto painting) was to hone not just the observation and drawing skills but also to get a strong feel for tonal values, shading and value contrast.

- Save the highest value contrast for your FOCAL POINTS.

- Lessen the value contrast in the distance, increase it in the foreground.

- Design your dark values in a pattern that leads the eye well though-out a composition.

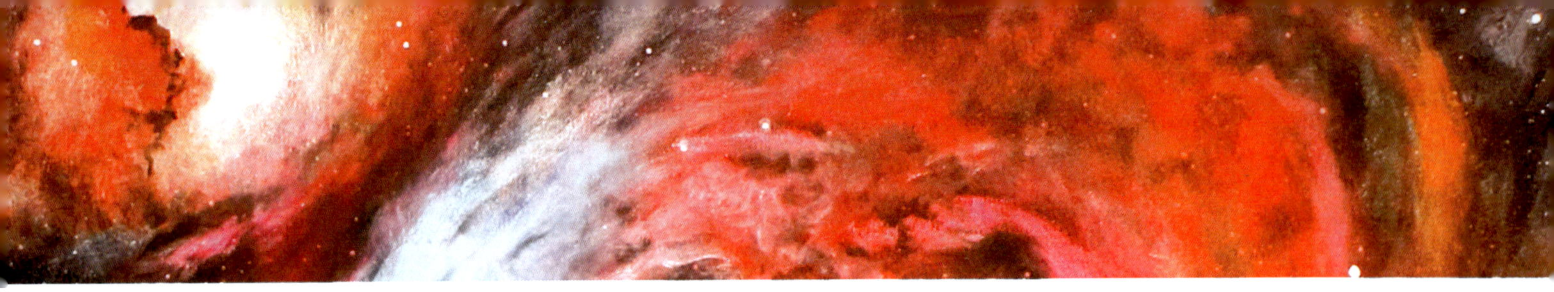

DOT POINTS - HISTORY OF COLOR THEORIES

*~300 BC – Aristotle – had a crack: talked about color and related it to the elements

*~1200AD - Grosseteste (Oxford) - translated Aristotle's writings on black and white and also mentioned that there might also be a violet

*~Mid 1400s - Leone Battista Alberti - Suggested 'four true colors', (not black and white)

*~late 1400s - Leonardo Da Vinci- 'Nope' he said, there are just 3 primary colors and they make all the other colors (they didn't call him a genius for nothing)

*~1704 - Sir Isaac Newton - revealed the spectrum of light by shining a light through a prism, and bent it around into the first wheel. (also thought that music was related to color)

*~1810 - Johann Wolfgang Goethe - studied the sensory and psychological effects of color,disputed some of Newtons findings and began investigating whether one could ascertain rules to govern the artistic use of color. He claimed that blue and yellow were the only pure hues and theorized on the human eye's experience of color

*~1839 - Michel Eugène Chevreul - known for his 'Law of Simultaneous Contrast', applied it to light and pigments. He opened up new areas of interest ie. behaviors of hues. His wheel showed gradations from one hue to the next (12 hues)

*~1879 - Ogden Nicholas Rood - divided color into three constants: purity, luminosity, and hue - equivalent to James Clerk Maxwell's tint, shade, and hue

*~late 1800s - Willhem Wundt - helped establish experimental psychology

*~late 1800s - Albert Munsell - created a system of notations he called dimensions: Hue, Value, and Chroma, plus a solid system with 10 hues - 5 principal/5 intermediate

*-1920 Johannes Itten - expands on color harmony studies, creates his own color circle and color star and teaches at the famous Bauhaus School

* 1963 Josef Albers - Published 'Interaction of Color', working over years, expanding on Rood and Chevreul's 'Law of Simultaneous Contrast' and the practical applications of color behaviors.

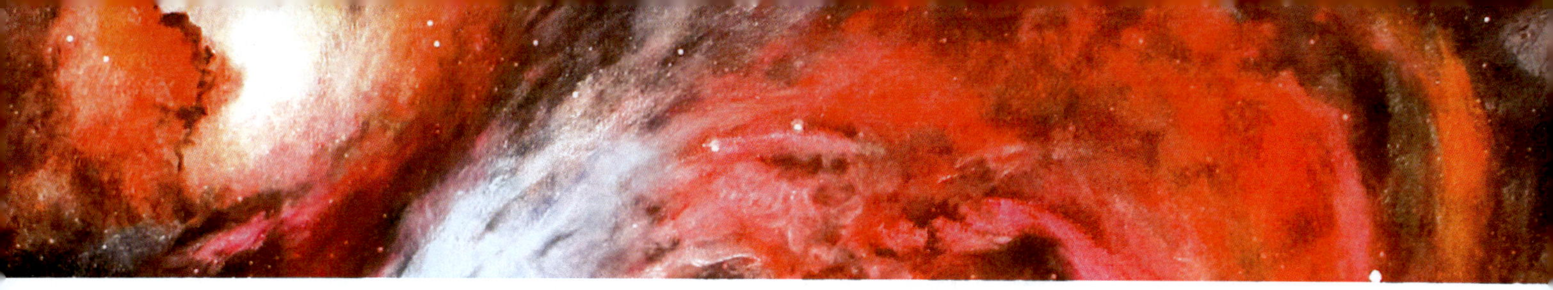

A SUMMARIZED HISTORY OF COLOR THEORIES

HOW MANY COLOR THEORIES HAVE THERE BEEN?

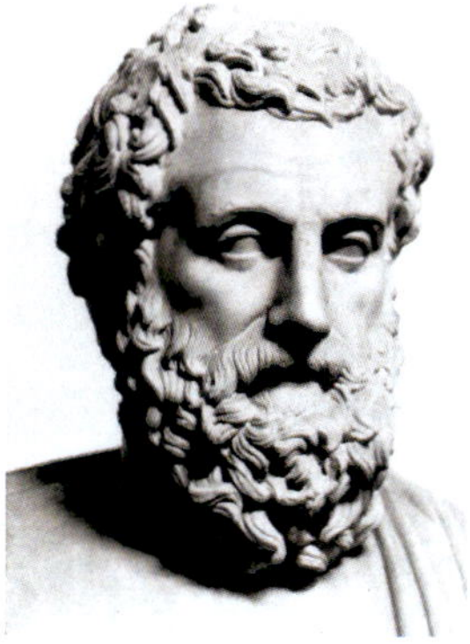

Aristotle (384-322 B.C.) - He proposed that the two principal "colors" were white and black - light and absence of light, and that all colors came from one of the four elements: air, water, earth and fire. He also believed that the true primary colors after white and black were yellow and blue: because we all "see" the sun's bright white light as yellow, and the blackness of space as our blue sky.

Robert Grosseteste - 1168-1253 - First chancellor of Oxford University. He translated Aristotle's writings on color (wrote mainly on light, black, white and violet made an appearance too. He was not so exciting to read about for me; the real fun (and confusion) came after Goethe's challenge of Newton.

Leone Battista Alberti in 1435.-A polymath and priest, he suggested: "Through the mixing of colors, infinite other hues are born, but there are only four true colors from which more and more other kinds of colors may be thus created. Red is the color of fire, blue of the air, green of the water, and gray of the earth... white and black are not true colors but are alterations of other colors."

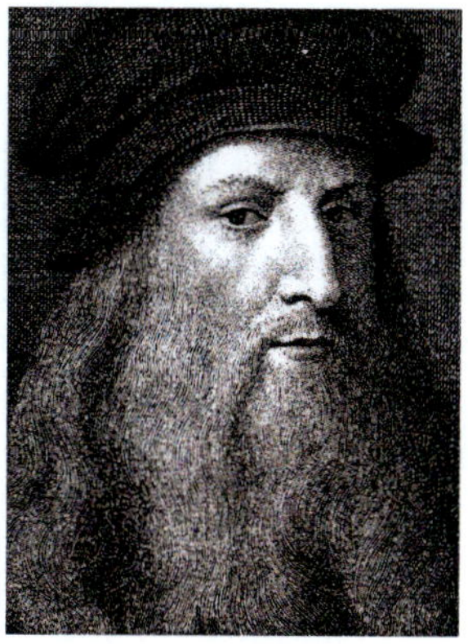

Leonardo da Vinci -1452-1519 - references color theory in his journals in the late 1400s. (The idea that there are three primary colors—i.e., red, blue, and yellow—and that these three colors, when mixed together in specific ways, create all other colors.). He wrote: "To any white body receiving the light from the sun, or the air, the shadows will be of a bluish cast. For those colors which you wish to be beautiful, always first prepare a pure white ground. Black is like a broken vessel, which is deprived of the capacity to contain anything." He also said - "A gray day provides the best light."

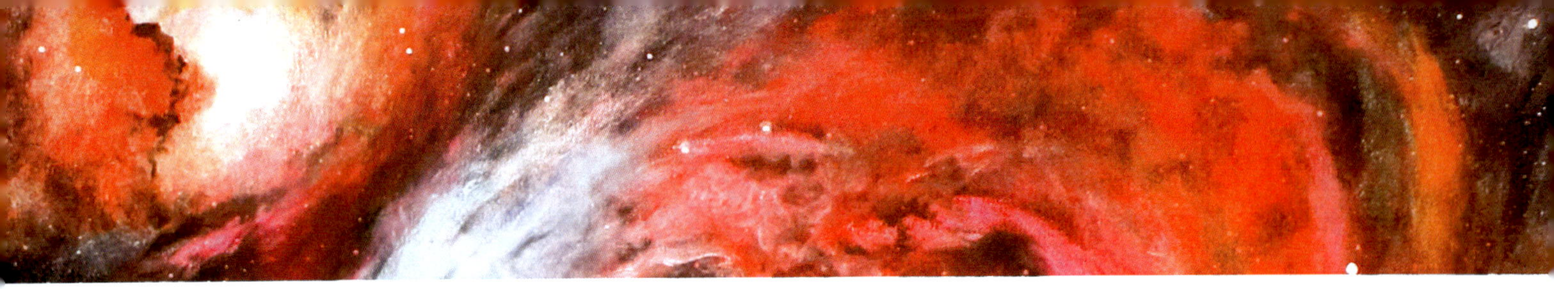

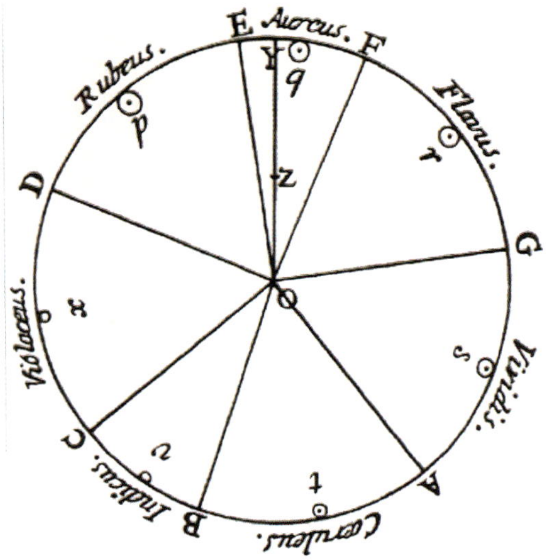

Sir Isaac Newton - Innovated in his 1704 work, 'Opticks'.: 'Color is from light' he said. He passed light through a prism and created a spectrum of colors ranging from red to violet. He then created a closed system or wheel that contained the colors red, orange, yellow, green, blue, indigo, and violet.

Claude Boutet: 1708- made wheels, right, first recorded printed wheels.

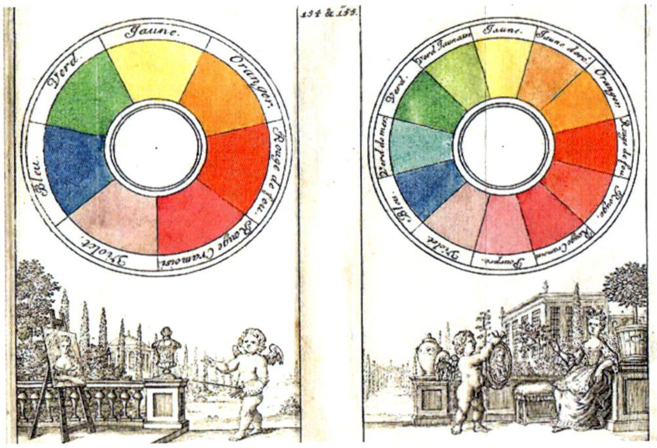

Tobias Mayer - created a color triangle for his book 'The Affinity of Color Commentary', published posthumously in 1775 (he had also tried to define the number of individual colors the human eye can see.)

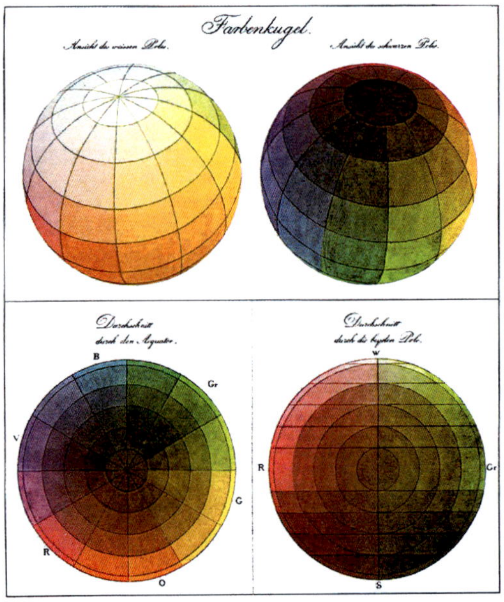

Philipp Otto Runge 1810 - The first color model to adopt the three dimensional form that has become standard in color science was by this German romantic painter. The sphere has the white to black value scale as its polar axis, and Newton's complete hue circle at the equator. Runge's hue circle is also one of the first to divide the hue circle into "primary", secondary and tertiary hues. Munsell worked on the maths aspect later to form his model.

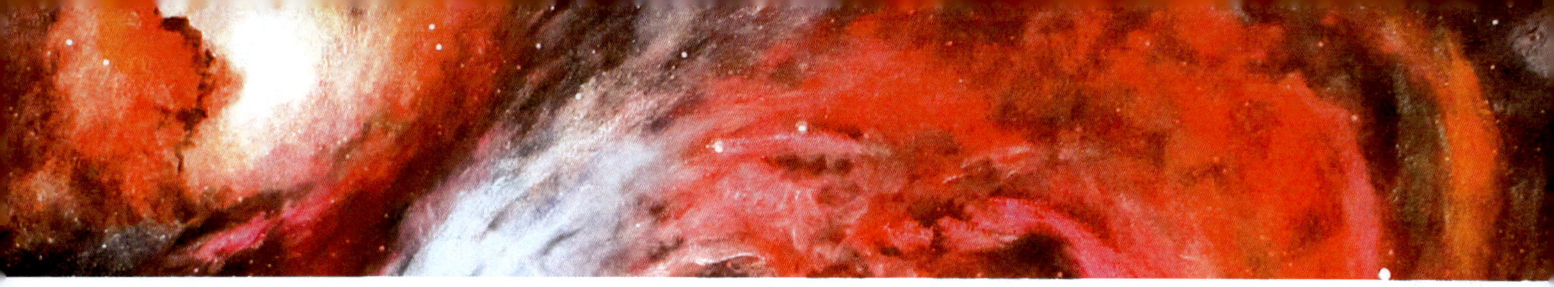

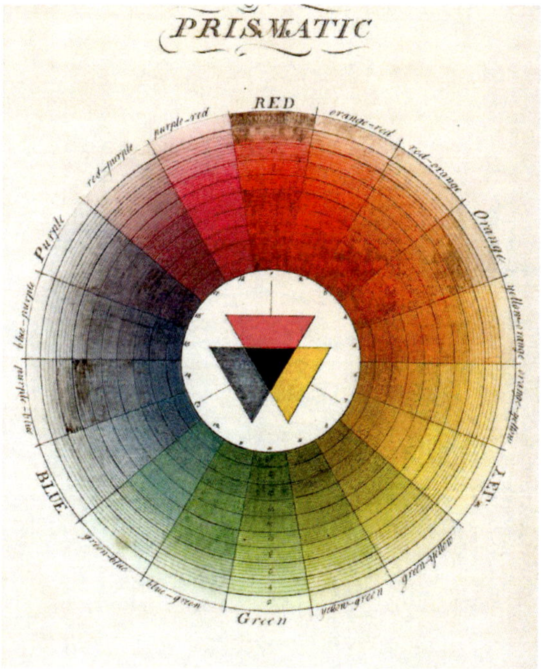

Michel Eugène Chevreul (1839) - His Law of Simultaneous Color Contrast concurred that the three primary colors were red, yellow, and blue (RYB); and that all other colors could be created through various mixtures of these primary colors, and that this theory of color mixing applied equally to the behavior of colors from beams of light added together (additive mixing), as it does to colored pigments added together (subtractive mixing).
R) **Ignaz Schiffermüller** Wheel 1772. (first to show 72 gradations around the wheel).
I see a transition through Mageta opposite secondary green, do you?)

Wolfgang Goethe (1810) - developed a color wheel that described the sensory and psychological effects of each color. eg. Blues give a feeling of coolness, while yellows create a feeling of warmth (he did not consider red as pure). His circle had a magenta. He challenged Newton's scientific methods. He studied after-images and optical illusions as well.
He, Newton and all others to follow inspired many ongoing studies which continue until today.. He published a book, ' Art of Color' and his work on color is also said to be the inspiration for seasonal color analysis.

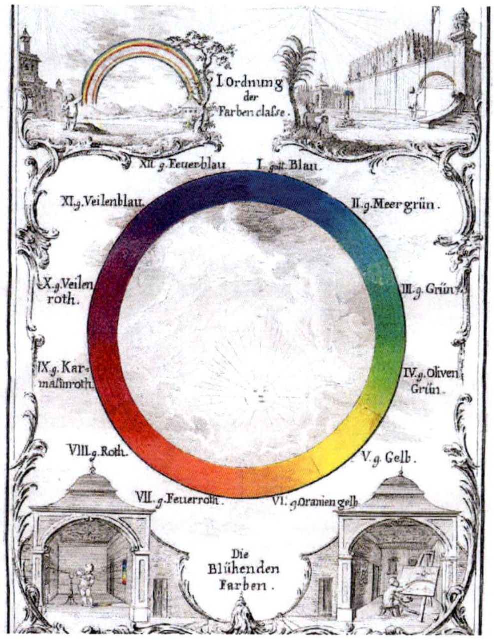

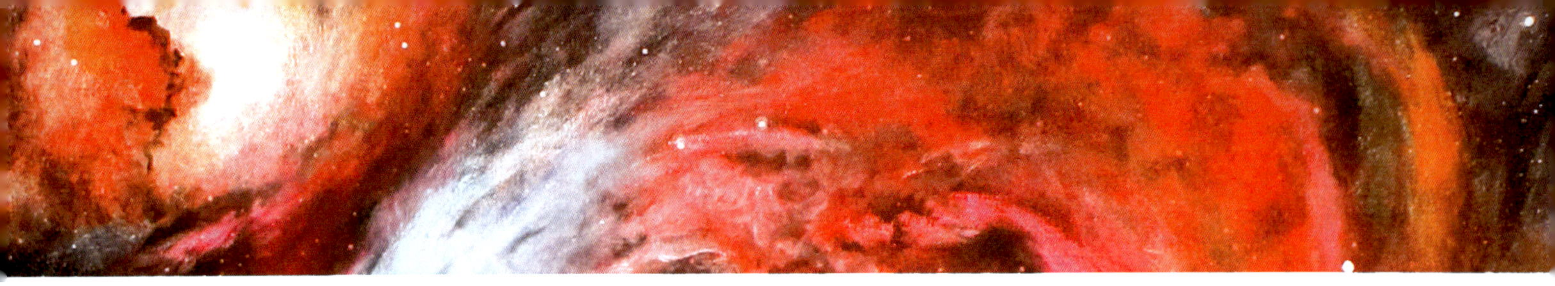

Ogden Nicholas Rood (1831 - 1902) - This American physicist (also a painter in oils and watercolors) wrote 'Modern Chromatics', with Applications to both Art and Industry, published in 1879, with German and French translations appearing in 1880 and 1881. He was a huge influence on the Pointillists like Georges Seurat (who started out as one of the Impressionists and then became a bit more engrossed in the science of color). Rood divided color into three constants: purity, luminosity, and hue - similar to James Clerk Maxwell's tint, shade, and hue. Rood revealed that small dots or marks of different colors, when viewed from a distance, would blend into a new color optically. He stated that the complementary colors, when applied in pairs by the artist, could enhance the presence of a painting: "... paintings, created almost completely of tints that by themselves seem modest and far from brilliant, often strike us as being rich and gorgeous in color, while, on the other hand, the most gaudy colors can easily be arranged so as to produce a depressing effect on the beholder."

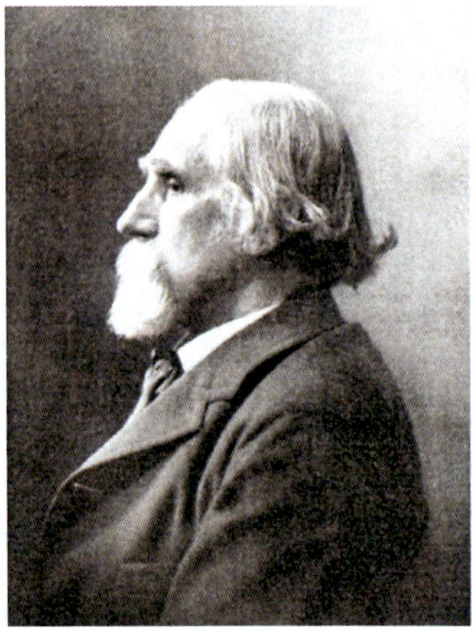

Wilhelm Wundt - (1832-1920)

Psychology emerged as a new division of science towards the latter part of the 19th century. One of it's early pioneers, Wendt, helped to create the experimental branch of psychology and even establish it as an empirical science.

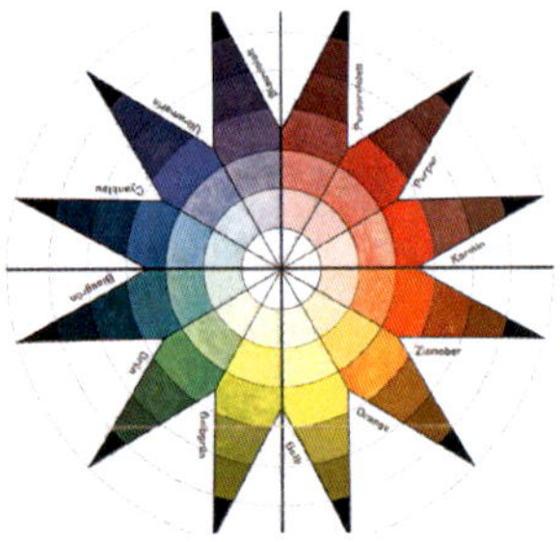

Johannes Itten - (1888 - 1967) lectured at the famous Bauhaus School from 1920, collating all of the classic color theories and coming up with some that resound through to today eg. the 12 color circle, his color star. The most famous of his work revolves around color harmony (tetrads, triads etc already proposed by Chevreul). He created a personal studio in the gothic style Knights Templar building in a park in Weimar (actually designed by Goethe!).

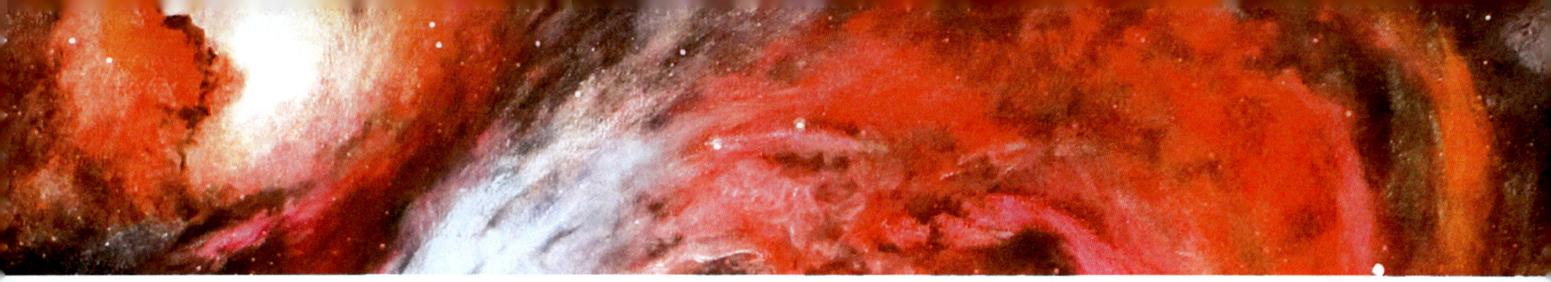

Wilhelm Ostwald (1853-1932) - After he retired from scientific academia he published 'The Color Primer' and also 'The Color Atlas'.

Albert Munsell (1858-1918) - During his study of color, Munsell strived for a much more organized way of defining colors. He created a system that had comprehensive notations of color (he called these dimensions: Hue, Value, and Chroma) rather than just color names that he found were often "foolish" and "misleading". His system has 5 primaries and 5 intermediates.

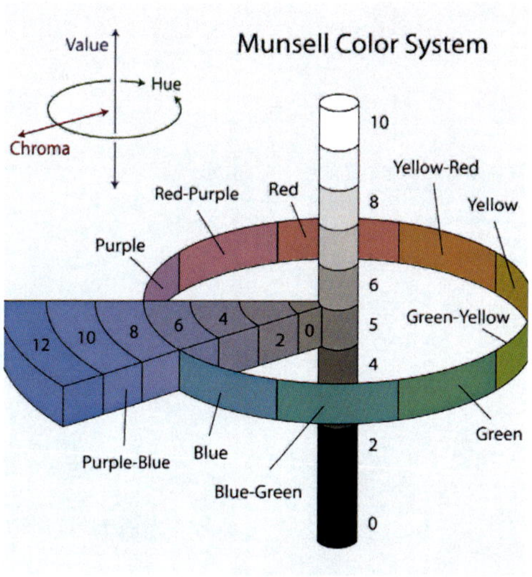

Wassily Kandinsky (1866 – 1944) His understanding of color theory was of colors as having a spiritual effect on the viewer or an effect on the viewer's eyes. He re-iterated the notion that colors have a 'feel' to them. "Color is a power which directly influences the soul." (he also believed that music and color were inter-related as had Newton.) Kandinsky was a life-long friend of Joseph Albers.

Joseph Albers (1888 - 1976) Albers published a book called 'Interaction of Color', 1963. He was at the Bauhaus (with Kandinsky) as a student of Johannes Itten and then as a teacher. He emigrated to the U.S. (early 1930s) and passed on his own teachings (including at Yale), influencing many designers, architects and contemporary abstract artists of today. I am not surprised that his color triangle had spectrum red as a primary red color. None of the Bauhaus school had access to the Quinacridones yet (this happened by the 1950s), so that bright orange-red was still accepted as the primary red all along. The science of color and light played a big role in this from Newton's time right through because there is no wavelength for a Magenta red (but our brain says we see it) so I, for one, need to have it on my wheel. The other reason is because secondary green needs Magenta to mix rich chromatic grays.

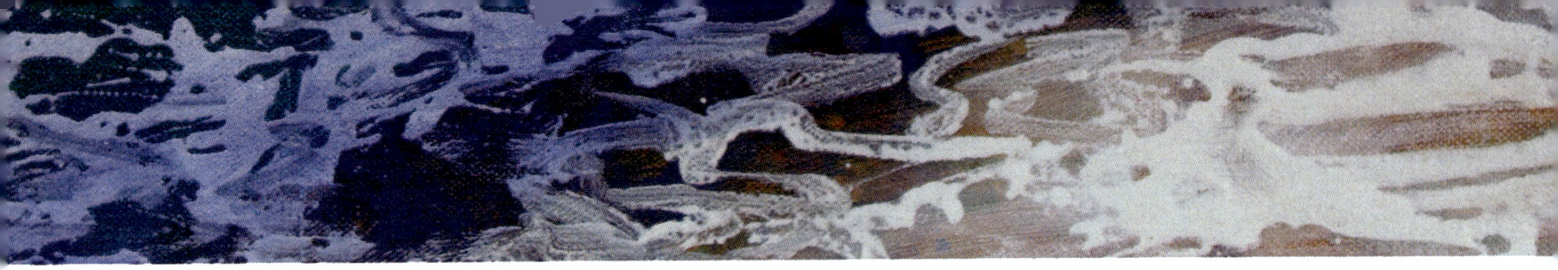

COMPARISON OF SOME CURRENT COLOR WHEEL MODELS

Over the last century+, many other color theorists explored, expanded and challenged color theory(s) to include more about color as it relates to pigments, inks, dyes and paints, rather than light. There are so many more variants when dealing with pigments because they can vary in hue, value, and chroma. (previously referred to as purity, luminosity, and hue or tint, shade and hue.)

Many debates and contradictions rage on to this day (in particular about which red is truly the primary red) but if you stick to the general principles outlined here for color mixing and harmonization plus practice mixing strings of tints and shades, you will find color mixing and relationships will come together for you in your practice . If you undertake the simple simultaneous contrast experiments, you will start to see fun, surprising optical phenomena resulting from juxtaposing one color with different options.

WHEEL 1 - Students walk into our studios with one of those commercially made wheels (which are very snappy in their physical design). The **problem** is that the printed ink colors are hue estimates, never matching your paint (pigment) hues, so students trying to partner their own hues with what is printed as opposites on the wheel sadly end up with mud. The red opposite secondary green on these wheels is usually not Magenta either. You really do much better when creating your own wheels with your own primary pigments, and secondaries and tertiaries made from them. Know your own pigments thoroughly.

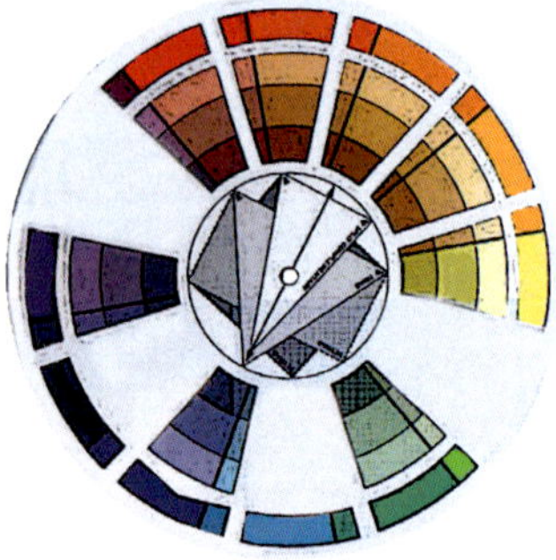

We are 100% committed to the massive benefit of every student making and having on hand their own wheel for every medium they use. It is integral in learning about your own hues, mixing and harmonization. Important information for carefully selecting your first pigments is on p.43-50. Use your second QR login to print as many templates as you need for practising tint/shade strings and color wheels.

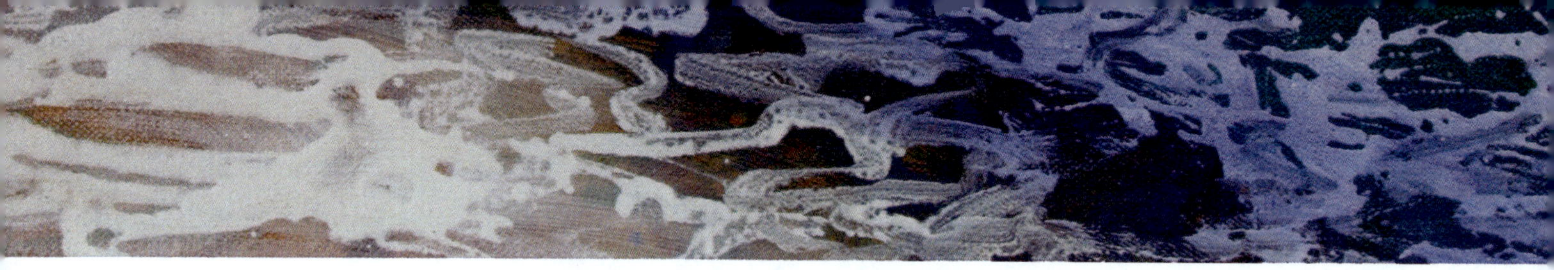

WHEEL 2 - In 1988 Michael Wilcox put out his own 6 split primary color model. Avoiding the confusion of selecting your primaries by calling all of these 6 hues 'primary' was one attempted work around for pigment selection, (to avoid muddy mixes). I support the fact that no pigment sits exactly bang in the middle of a theoretical hue sector but I feel like he threw out the baby with the bath water! The standard 12 hue sector triadic wheel with 3 primaries shows much more information and is great for learners as long as they learn **how to select and partner those primaries.** Google <Wilcox Handprint> for a comprehensive critique of the Wilcox claims. (some of which have been refuted.) - Like most wheels before, this wheel gave in one hand and took away in the other. We just have to decide on three primaries to give us our secondaries and tertiaries. For us, that is why the others sit in the tertiary sector on the wheel. (you will ultimately see this in practice as you make your own wheels), plus great ways to arrange your schemes beautifully. Another reason to DIY your own wheels. Any color bias (there is usually at least a little of this) can be balanced as you are mixing chromatc grays for your wheels.

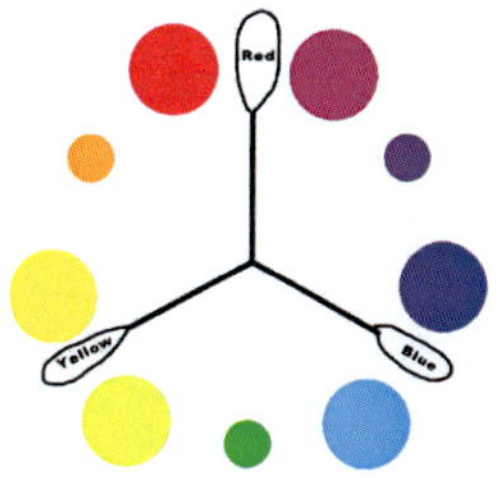

WHEEL 3 - An American artist, Stephen Quiller, went to the effort of actually placing the pigments (names) in hue spots around his version of the color wheel and publishing it for sale. Once again, great business idea ! (We have always done this pigment mapping at the studios, albeit not officially or commercially.) It helps all students of color to understand the 244+ tubes of color they had randomly bought or collected without knowing how to knowledgeably partner them, mix them and relate them well within their compositions. Download one of our wheel templates with a pigment mapping section (I suggest writing pigment numbers and brands as well). You don't need to buy this circular list of pigment names, as you can keep your own individual records on your own individually made wheels.

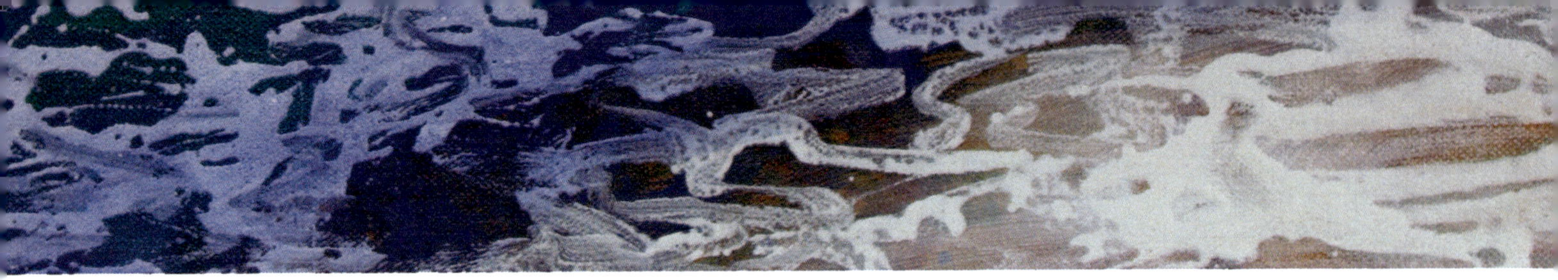

My beliefs and practical applications in pigment use are founded in my own observations over decades (since age 11yrs). Although a few thousand years of others pondering color, studying light and proposing models is quite interesting, nah, ...bloody fascinating. If you are like me, the practical mixing of hues and the creative expression empowered by first-hand knowledge of their interactions IS THE BOMB! This is the 'what' and the 'how' of mixing pigment colors. After the pages on pigment selection, you can make a few different models of color wheels and decide for yourself which is going to be best for you as you create.

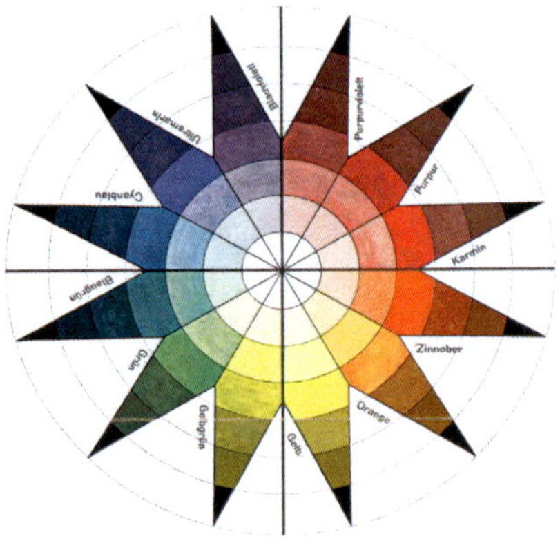

WHEEL 4

You could make a Johannes Itten star-style wheel, but using your new knowledge of modern pigments, the CMY hues of todays printing systems which clearly acknowledge Magenta would better guide you for the saturated hues. We have a few different DIY color wheel options for you later on and they are so super-informative to make for yourself.

WHEEL 5

A good clean magenta pigment is easier to find now, so the 12 or 18 part triadic wheel can be accurate in a way not so easy in previous times. eg. PR 122 is commonly used in magenta ink and also in some artist pigments (it has minimal bias unlike most red pigments). It is also ideal as a mixing partner for secondary green.

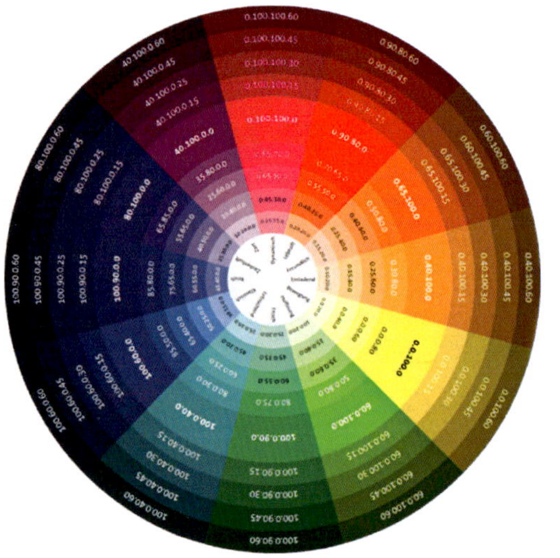

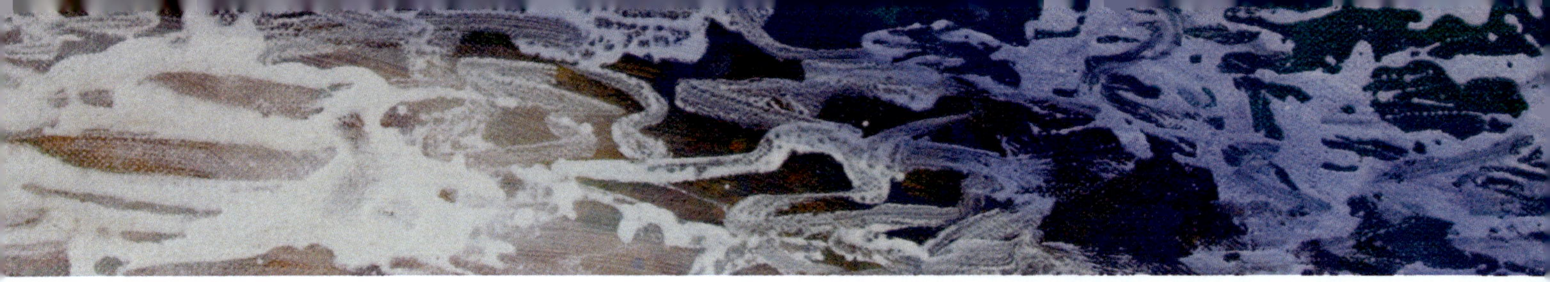

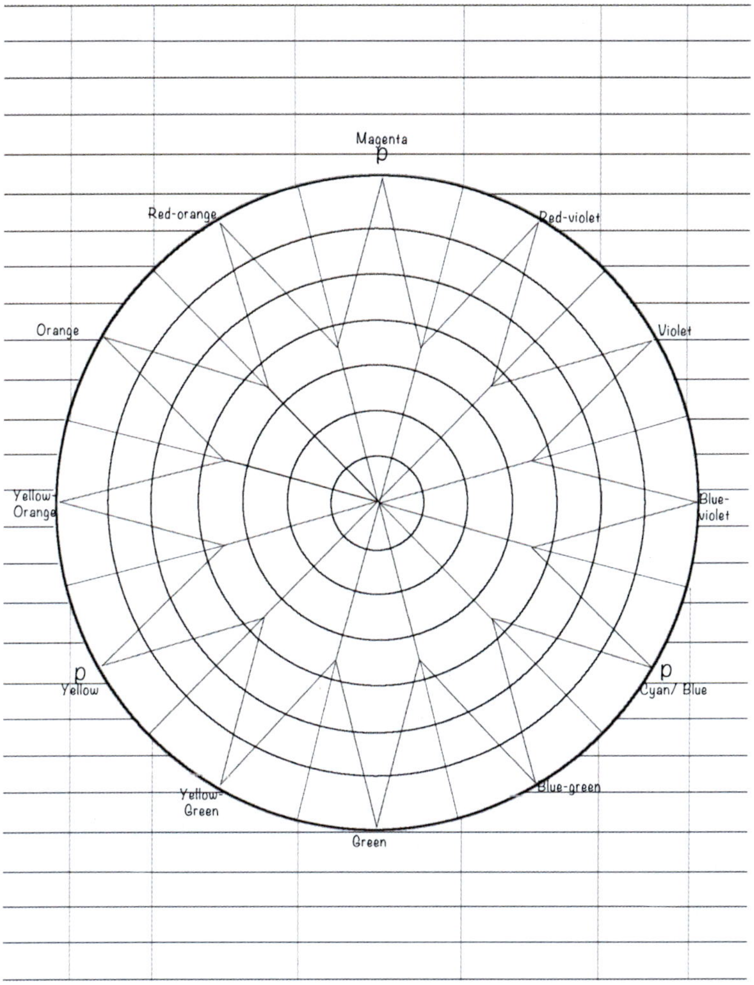

You can download a few different styles of color wheel using the QR code on P. 177, to create your own with pigment mapping or without (There are simple templates as well. This one is a tribute to Johannes Itten.)

Having a reference for your very own combination of pigments, with mixing partners opposite each other in order to create chromatic grays (not muddy hues) is ideal for all those who are trying to master color mixing and harmony

UNTANGLING THE CONFUSION ABOUT PRIMARY COLORS

Primary red (in our triadic system this is Magenta) can be a most confusing Hue to define and to buy for yourself confidently. This is because some 'Magenta' red pigments sold are often a bit towards the red-violet section of the wheel, (hence tertiary and also sometimes towards red-orange (also tertiary on this wheel). Maybe this is why the author who wrote about 6 primaries in their theory model did so. (a cool and a warm one of each primary color). They were maybe trying to overcome the confusion of "What is primary red, primary yellow and primary blue" in pigments, by announcing that there must be two of each. I see their confusion, as pigments do offer a range of reds, but in the middle, there are some clean magenta reds available to us which can then create a typical "spectrum red" (red-orange) by adding a little yellow and create a red-violet (purple) buy adding a little blue. So why call that

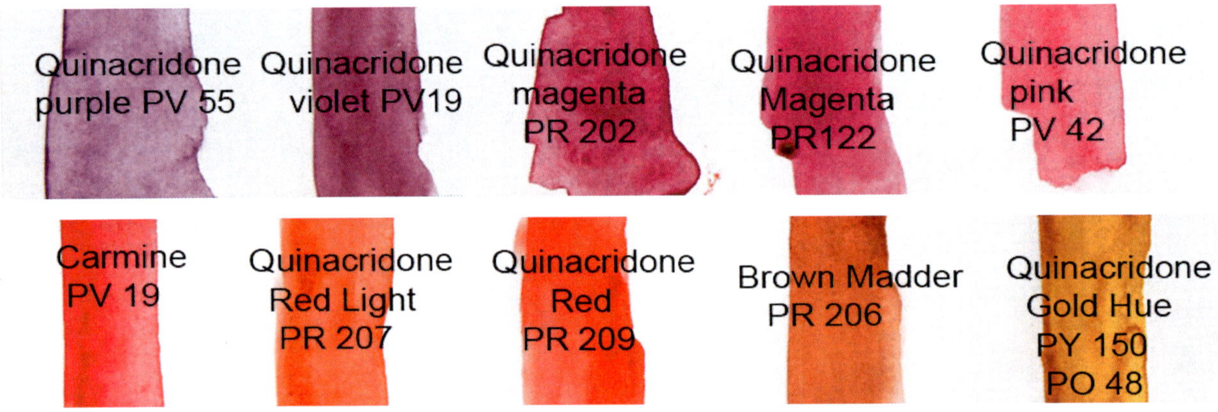

'fire-engine red' your primary if you can make it with two others.? So in our 12 sector triadic wheel, what we place opposite secondary green is this rosiest red (dark pink) hue because that is what gives it the best rich grays in paint mixing.The first Quinacridone compound was discovered in 1896, but it's desirability as a pigment wasn't recognized until 1955. Processes for synthesizing Quinacridone pigment were developed, and in 1958 it came onto the market. Look at PR 122 and PR 42. Not typical 'red' and not red-violet.....Magenta ..ta-da!! (I am not a fan of magenta myself, but it is what belongs opposite secondary green on the triadic color wheel, no denying once you have seen it.

The Quinacridone red range, PR 122, PR 42, PR 202, PV 19 are a good place to look for your primary red, although there are variations. The most confusing part of searching for your primary red is that pigment companies use the same code, name and/or number but often with it comes a somewhat different hue or color range. The Quinacridones range in bias from orange, red-orange, magenta through to red-violets, as seen on the previous page.

To avoid confusion, look at the pigment number, the description and the color sample. The untinted, usually transparent, strong DARKER ROSY color is what you can safely use to make the other two tertiary reds yourself (red-orange hue and red-violet hue) by adding yellow, or blue, respectively. The image shows some swatches of PV19 from different suppliers. The middle column are "rosier", the left column appear to have an orange bias (hence would fit into the tertiary red-orange area of the wheel) and the right column a violet bias, hence would fit into the tertiary red-violet zone on your triadic

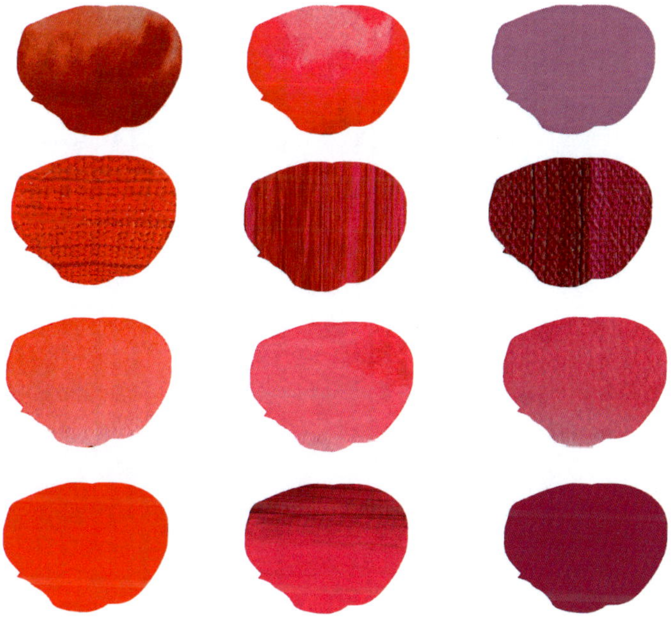

wheel. CHOOSE a pinky red (untinted) as your primary and you can make a version of the red-orange and the red-violet hues easily.(in a range of values if you choose one dark in mass tone.). When you are confident mixing tertiary reds from primaries, you may wish to get an opaque version of vibrant tertiary red eg. Cadmium, Pyrrole & Naphthol families for some orangey reds (eg. PR 9, 101, 108, 160) and for ready made single pigment violets , try Ultramarine violet PV15 (transparent) or Dioxazine 37 (semi-opaque) but many of these hues are easy to mix yourself with your primaries..

The name **MAGENTA** was given after a battle in Europe (previously named Fuscia after a Botanist Fuchs) and all of this was at a time when most available pigments from this dye leaned to the red-violet (purple) side of the hue sectors. Today we are still using the name 'Magenta' (for a range of different hues) but I wish that paint manufacturers might be induced to call the cleaner less biased pigments 'Primary Magenta Red' (in untinted form) and separate it from purple (red-violet), mauve and any pigment color that has a strong violet or orange bias. This would help them sell more tubes of paint and also prevent students from relying on out-dated charts that show orange-biased red as 'primary'.

CASE IN POINT- take a bright fire engine red eg. Cadmium red light, often touted in books and videos as your warm primary red , and try to mix that with **secondary green** or even a yellow green which is often shown as the complementary color of red...MUDDY...MUD for sure. If you mix the cadmium red with a blue-green however, you now have a chance to make a rich and harmonious gray (or shadow color). Also, if you were determined that vibrant orange-biased red was to be your primary (maybe it came in a pre-made gift set or you can't buy a Magenta for now,. all you would need to do is make sure you choose (or make) a blue-biased green (to call your complementary secondary partner, for your chosen 'Primary Red') and to mix this with the red-orange when aiming for the most harmonious neutral gray shadow colors for one or the other). The key is correct partnering of complementary colors. (it is a matter of 'relativity' like many things in art.) Green misses out on a partner if you have no Magenta. Actually the reds I favor (in my own schemes) are more towards tertiary red-orange because it is the complementary partner of my happy color,Turquoise. I rave on a lot about Magenta however because there are still a lot of Magenta deniers out there promoting a color wheel without it, which is causing a lot of frustrations and muddy mixing.

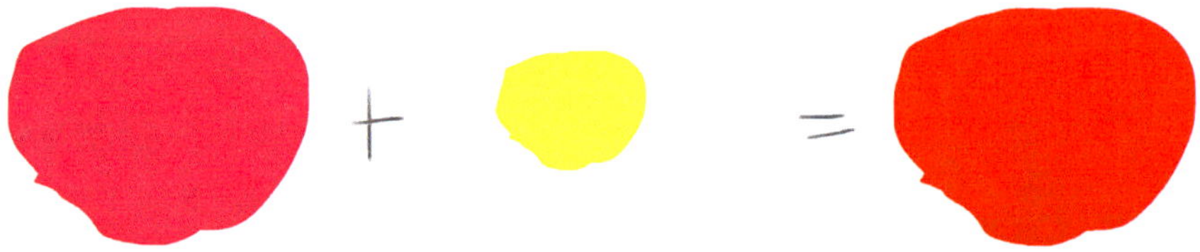

The historical red pigments until recent times have mostly leaned towards spectrum red (made from ochres, carmine, madder, cinnabar, cobalts etc) or quite into the red-violet sector (from manganese and hematite (pre-historic use) Tyrian purple (crushed molluscs), annilines (fuscia color, chemical 1860s). See links in resources on extensive pixgment research. There is no benefit in using the words right or wrong when teaching or learning art, in particular about color. Every color scientist partially debunked a predecessor and was then in turn partially debunked. Contradictions abound even today.

We can, however, ask ourselves reasonable questions such as:

"What bias does this pigment have?" or "how do I balance this bias for a mixing partnership?"

"How do I create that color?" or " Is that the hue I was aiming to mix?"

"Which harmonious scheme relationship(s) am I planning to use?"

"How can I make this color here pop in my composition?"

" Where (around my triadic wheel) does this new tube of pigment I just bought fit in?"

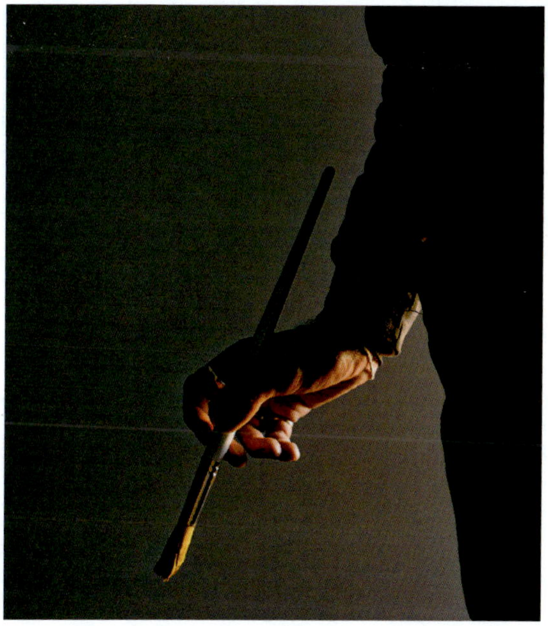

I believe that with color there is truly no absolute WRONG but there is most certainly a good, better and best and a successful Vs unsuccessful if you are keen to harmonize knowledgeably, and achieve the mood, ambience or feeling you were going for in your art work. Make your way through the exercises in this work book and you will be answering all of these questions for yourself and more, to move forward with color mixing and harmonisation, full of confidence.

TIPS AND HACKS FOR USING RED PIGMENTS

When painting with reds in your schemes:

- Keep in mind that warm colors appear to advance toward the viewer and cooler colors recede. Utilize this in your compositional planning regardless of genre.
- Use your knowledge of each red's perfect mixing partner (complementary or opposite on the wheel) and remember that this color placed alongside will actually intensify the red.
- Adding white or tinting tends to reduce the lightfastness of pigments, so use your cheapest reds at full strength (if and when you are going for longevity, avoid them altogether.)
- Try glazing successive coats of a transparent red over a value modeled subject or shape with strong white highlights. Compare these glowing highlights with those achieved by adding white as we do mostly when mixing up tint strings.
- White tends to 'pink up' a red quickly, try a yellow or combination of yellow and a little white for a brighter tint to reds.
- To get a 'shot' look when painting fabric eg. folds, clothing, paint a cooler dark red subject with strong contrast in values (white highlights) and glaze a warm red transparent layer over.
- Remember that a little bit of red goes a long way, so finding options where reds are a part of a balanced color scheme is a good idea when harmony is the goal.
- If you want to create earthy reds utilizing your basic 6 hues (rather than purchase more tubes or pots for rarely or less used colors, visit the 'convenience colors' pages and experiment with making a range of earthy hues which you can store in small airtight screw-jars.
- Consider the symbolism of red colors (read more about that in the section on Biology and Psychology of Color) when you are looking to express certain moods, feelings or interactions within your visual story-telling. Remember the contextual variants in these 'color meanings'.

LET'S TALK ABOUT YELLOWS

To decide from the plethora of yellow pigments available, which is to be your primary, we look again at the color 'bias', ie. does the color appear yellow only, or is it a slightly green-shade yellow or somewhat orange-shade yellow ??? (this will affect your mixtures)

Why is this important?

If you use your 'primary' yellow to make a green with your 'primary blue' and unknowingly you chose an orange biased yellow, the bit of red that gives it that yellow-orange look will neutralize your resulting green. (which you may want sometimes), but other times if you want a really vibrant , saturated secondary green, it won't be possible if your yellow has an orange bias. (like the far right column). Likewise if your yellow has a green bias and you want to mix a vibrant orange with your primary red, that green bias will give you a more neutral brownish orange (you may need to see this happen to really get it. This fun part is coming up soon in the practical Workbook section.)

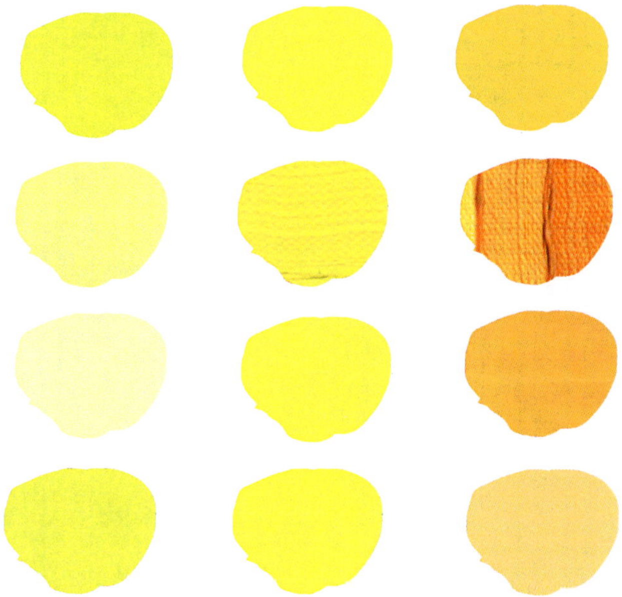

So in our yellow pigment suggestions from a few well known brands in pages to follow, you will see the Cadmium family PY35 appear or 'hues' (Cadmium Yellow Medium Hue PY74+84 is a touch warmer but is more lightfast, in acrylics).

Regardless of the brand you choose, just try to choose the bright yellow with no or minimal green bias, no or minimal orange bias (and preferably, no tinting with white.)

AVOID - PY1 Hansa Yellow, PY17, PY55 and PY83 , PY40, they are among the most fugitive (not very lightfast at all).

LET'S TALK ABOUT THE BLUES (sounds like a song!!)

Cyan is theoretically a blue that has a bias toward green.(on the light spectrum, 490 to 520 nm . Blue sits at 450-495 nm.

To decide on your Primary Blue, one would think that the paint manufacturers would give the best suggestion, but unfortunately, they often suggest their own tinted mixture of Phthalo blue mixed with PW6 white (in acrylics). That results in our inability to mix dark blues, greens, violets with it because of the white already mixed in.

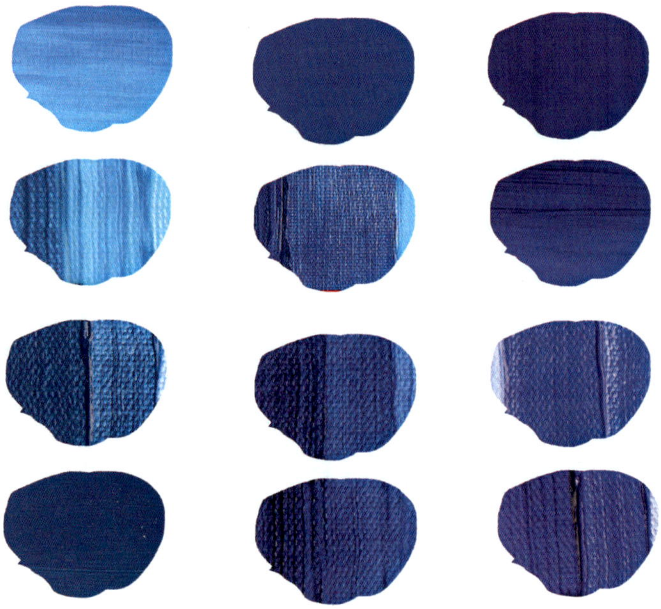

Phthalocyanine pigments range widely from a yellow-green hue, green-blue, blue-green, (PB15:3 and then red shade blue (PB15). So even though phthalo blue is often chosen as a primary (it even has cyan within it's name), this punchy pigment can overwhelm other hues when mixing. Even so, you can always warm up your green shade Phthalo blue by adding some Ultramarine Blue (and call that mixture your primary, and these two blues on their own are great base blues for blue-green and blue-violet ranges. Once we understand their relative bias we can adjust our complementary opposite mixes accordingly. The blues in the left column have a relatively green bias, the blues in the right column have a violet bias, so you need to be aiming to mix the middle column type blues. Phthalo 15, 15:1 , 15.6 are your mid-range or red bias blues and Phthalo Blue 15:3 is green shade blue. For most students (spending wisely to start) this is why we recommend a green shade Phthalo blue 15:3 plus an Ultramarine PB29 (a warm and a cool blue) as **this combo offers more versatility in all hues and values of secondary and tertiary mixing. You can always get many more blues later once you are the boss of the ones you have!**

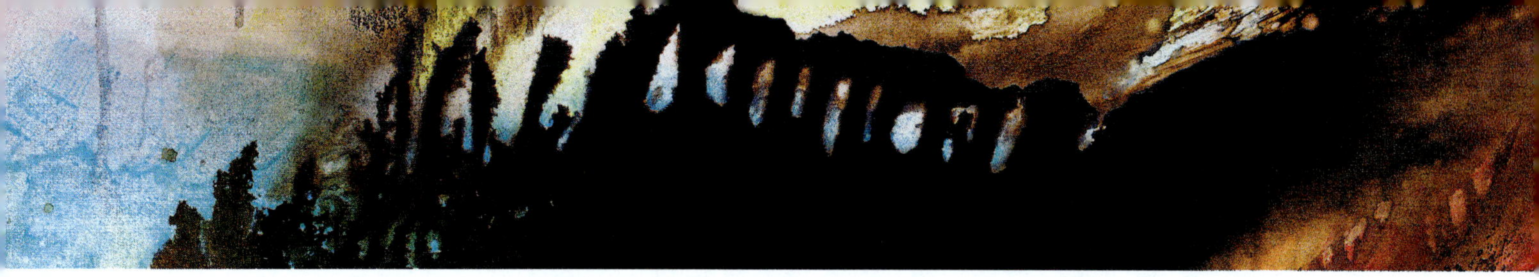

A WORD ABOUT THE WORDS: SECONDARY AND TERTIARY

The same kinds of confusing and conflicting statements, claims and descriptions that surround the definition of a 'Primary' color also surround the term 'Secondary' and 'Tertiary'. Everybody thinks they are right, funny arguments break out in art forums, but mostly on this subject I believe it to be a question of misunderstanding the triadic wheel relationships.

There are many elements in art that need to be measured **relatively, not absolutely ,** and in the end, it is about the color relationships not the name for the position on the wheel, although having names allocated that you 'get' is most helpful, its why we have a wheel after all.

We could just as easily call Secondaries a 'middle intermediate color' and call Tertiaries a ' Secondary intermediate', but we simply don't need to. The good old triadic system works if you know the pigment allocation secrets!!

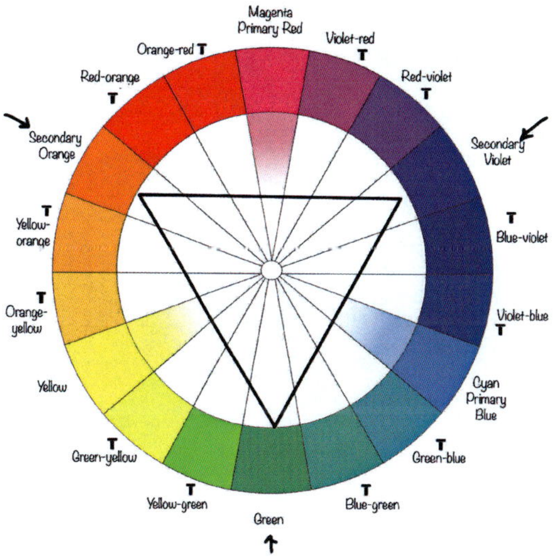

SECONDARY - Most agree this is made by mixing two primaries. Some try and say 'add a little yellow to magenta it is a secondary, add more it is a tertiary'.(ie. like education, primary is first, secondary then tertiary... but no, it is a bit different here). Most agree that a tertiary is on either side of a secondary and next to the primary. This is the triadic color wheel model (the split primary model calls the tertiaries 'warm and cool primaries', I don't subscribe to this at all, not since fairly minimally unbiased 'Magenta' type hues are readily available, the same with yellows, and blues can be averaged or balanced out and mixing partners found according to that which makes a nice clean chromatic grey. You will discover it **all in practice in the workbook section.**

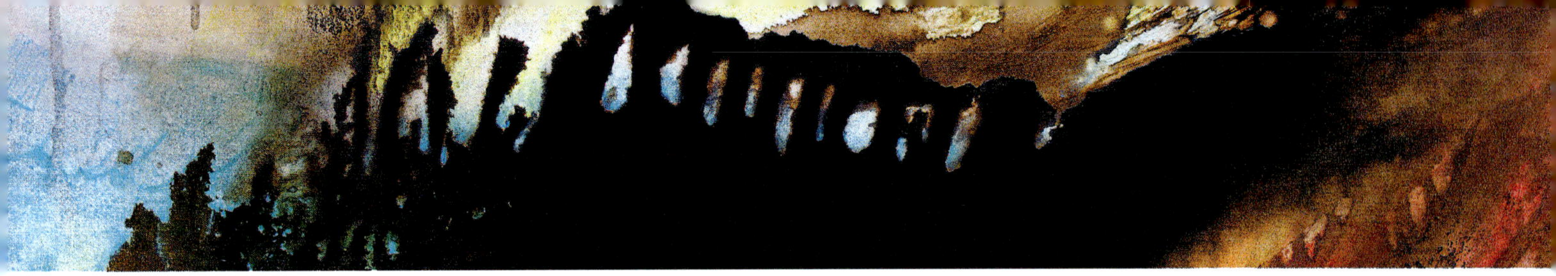

TERTIARY COLORS

Do we use our primary's name or secondary's name as the 'adjective'? eg. Some insist that tertiary red must be called 'Orange-red' not 'Red-orange'. I agree with this in principal (only the principal of the English language!!) and only if I add another 6 tertiary divisions to my 12 sector wheel.
Here is an 18 sector wheel below showing eg. the Red-orange as the Tertiary hue closer to orange ie. a reddish orange and the other Tertiary called an Orange-red. It is all relative!

Since we mostly use a 12 point wheel, we use the Primary's name first for it's tertiary name, but here the top 5 on this 18 point wheel are all of the Red family so we red(dish)-orange for the one closest to orange and orange(ish)-red for the other. Call them what you like BUT neutralize them with the ideal partner opposite (find out how in the practical exercises! This is where the real power is... in the visual relationships).

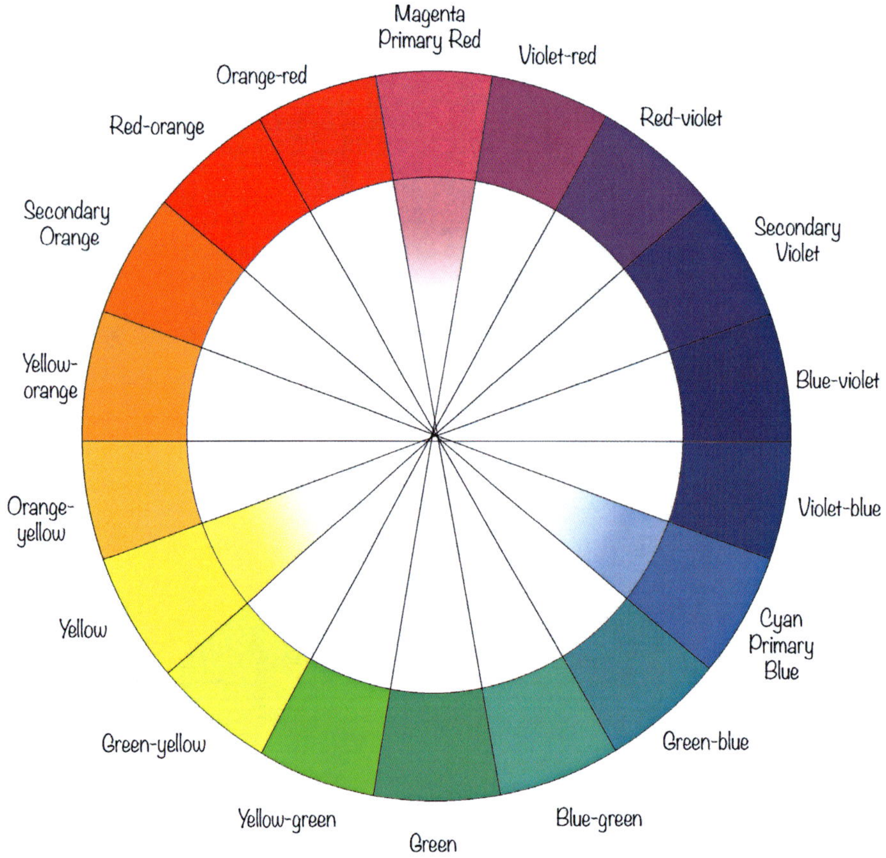

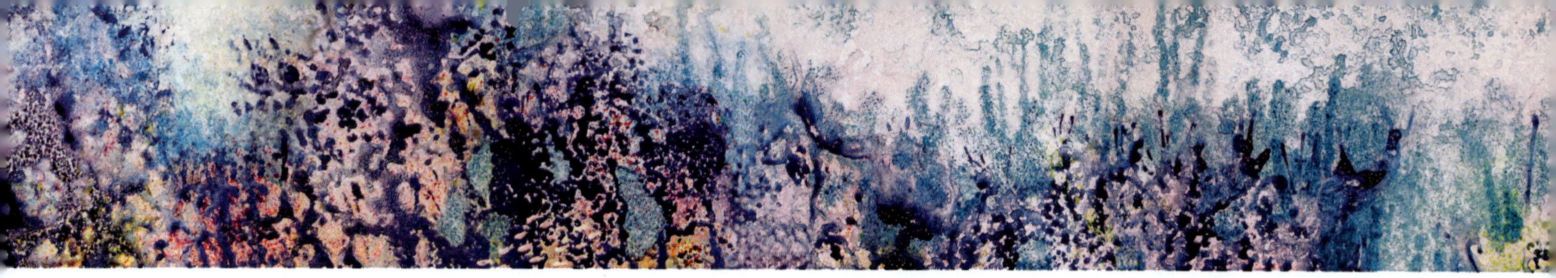

THE RELATIVITY OF 'WARM' AND 'COOL' COLORS

How do we know which colors are cool and which are warm? Most of us learned early in school that violet, blue and green are cool colors and that yellow, orange and red are the warm colors (this debate continues for some folks). After many decades of experience, we find that relativity is definitely a concept which abounds here with color temperature as it does with all other elements .

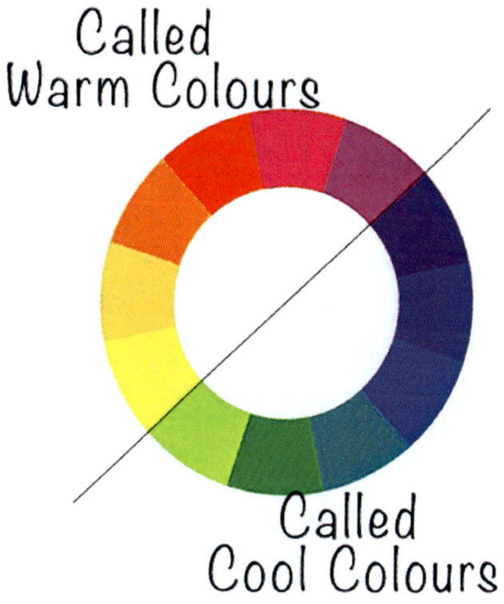

Color Mixing Example - Take your Blue (let's say you choose warm Ultramarine PB 29) and drop in a little clean (reason-ably un-biased either way) Magenta, you can make a Blue-violet (aka Indigo). Then you add some more Magenta and you can make a secondary Violet. You are taking your blue closer to red each time, in effect 'warming the color'. Conversely, take some Yellow, add a little Blue, you can make a Yellow Green, then add some more blue, you can make Secondary Green.... you are cooling it by taking it closer to Primary Blue. (NB. if either hue has a strong bias, the secondary will be somewhat muted / de-saturated.)
Imagine if we divide each twelfth of this triadic wheel again into a total of thirty-six?or Seventy-two or even more? Basically, that is how the spectrum is, a gradual transitional change in wavelengths. There is not a great deal of benefit to us in color mixing by having more than 12 or 18 sectors to work within. As long as you have enough practical experience with mixing and enough practice with teaming colors together harmoniously, every transition along these 12 or 18 sectors can be valid within your color plans and palettes.
Every cool color has a RELATIVELY WARM neighbor. Each warm color has a RELATIVELY COOL neighbor. I would call that a relative fact! A great pro-tip is to always let one temperature dominate in your color compositional planning.

WHY ARE WE SUGGESTING TO START WITH A MINIMUM KIT OF 6 ? ?

We give a basic minimal list of 6 pigments shown further on so you can discover (by doing it yourself) how to make **a version** of all the hues around the wheel, plus a neutral and a gray version of each and some convenience colors too . You can certainly enjoy adding to your paint collection later if you wish, armed with great skills to choose wisely and combine them and team them up knowledgeably.

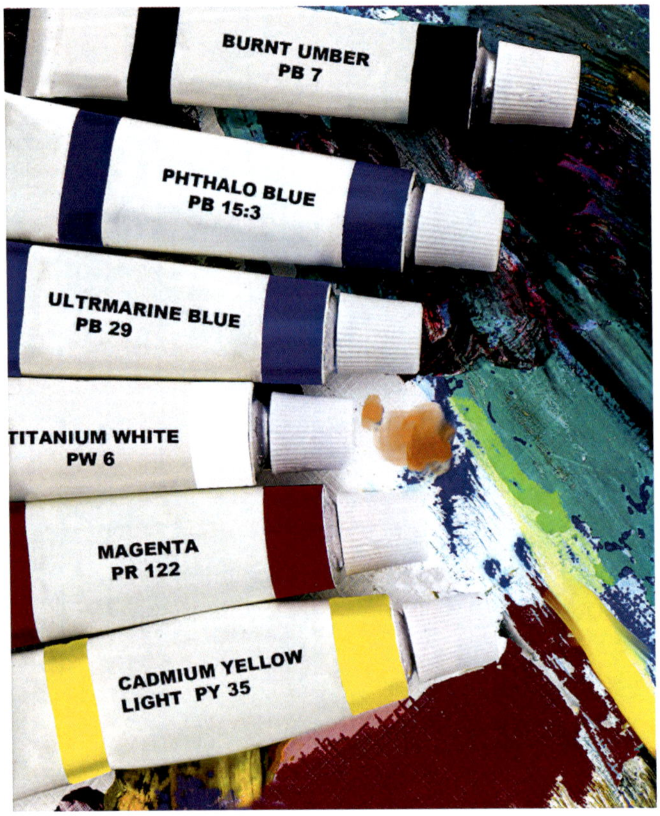

More important than the pigment's name will be it's relative hue sector position and your understanding of how it relates to all of your other hues and how to use it in your harmonious schemes (or your truly discordant ones for that matter, if that is how you want to use your newfound power with color!)

There have been some different systems of Primaries for Photographic, Screen and many other color applications over time but here in your practical workbook we are going to concentrate on pigment mixing (subtractive mixing) with Magenta, Yellow and Blue (aka Cyan) as our basic three Primaries.

PRIMARY by definition in English implies the original, beginning, prime ie. cannot be made with other hues. Because pigments are rarely unbiased (exactly like the theoretical color on the wheel), the pigments you will probably want to buy after the basic 6 are other versions of the 12 hues of our basic wheel, transparent version of yellow, opaque version of red-orange, maybe several options of your favorite hue, only your budget determines the extras you will get.

READ THROUGH FAQS, TROUBLESHOOTING AND GLOSSARY OF TERMS FIRST TO PREPARE YOURSELF FOR CARRYING OUT THE PRACTICAL EXERCISES

The FAQs are compiled from many students over the years, asking similar questions due to common struggles when mixing pigments. The Glossary of Terms (after that) in the back of the workbook is a very helpful resource as you start to comprehend the many specific terms and concepts in this area of artistic practice.

Many a student and artist has commented "I just prefer to use color intuitively". Armed with a practical guide of how to maximize harmony with color relationships, intuition can find it's mark knowledgeably and good art can grow to be better and onward to best. Of course their are other elements to utilize in this goal of getting to your own best and many helpful principles exist to guide us, we cover these in other modules.

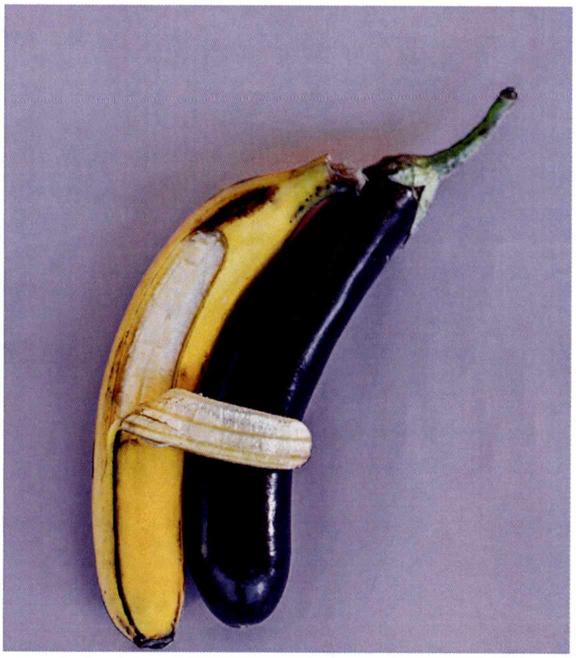

There is also no denying that there is definitely a precise complementary mix for each hue (for example) Secondary Violet, that will successfully give you a harmonious rich gray or shadow color for Primary Yellow. It is not Red-violet (whoops...made brown) and it is not blue-violet...uh-oh...you made Green (because of the Green color bias in the Blue you used in trying to mix your violet). It is precisely Secondary Violet that you will learn how to mix for a rich shadow gray for your Yellow. You will get to practice this and everything else in the color exercises soon. They are the end goal of this book, the DIY mixing exercises.

Harmonizing the color relationships in your composition is a far more flexible situation than mixing two perfect partners into a shadow color. This is evidenced by thousands of well loved pieces from old and modern masters. Any of the reds can harmonize to a degree with combinations of any of the greens and so on, however you will not see in many of those well loved art works (except perhaps some from the Fauve movement) a random cacophony of hues from around the wheel, indiscriminately placed on a whim. Great artists have for centuries been using their understanding of color relationships, together with their individual prowess with drawing, compositional designs, mastery of medium, use of value and contrast etc. to create strong and engaging art works that indeed can evoke a feeling or mood (aided by color harmony of course, or purposeful discord for that matter).

Fig 1 , Vincent Van Gogh has used the less complementary pairings to show tension or discord in his painting. When describing the painting below he commented to his brother Theo:

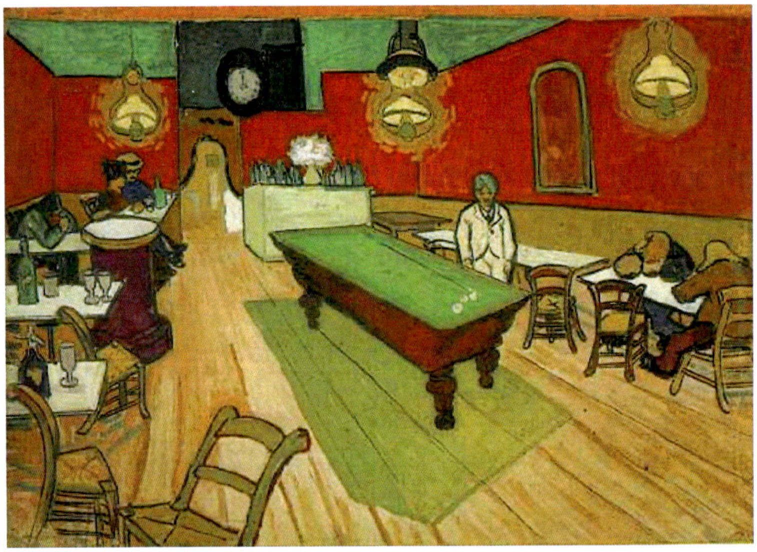

"I have tried to express the terrible passions of humanity by means of red and green. The room is blood red and dark yellow with a green billiard table in the middle; there are four citron yellow lamps with a glow of orange and green. Everywhere there is a clash and contrast of the most disparate reds and greens…."

Follow the color exercises and you are going to be the boss of your colors too and by testing your secondaries and tertiaries as you will be shown, you will be able to mix any hue, neutral, tint, shade (or rich gray) and avoid confusion and unwanted muddy mixes.

Cheap pigment 'kits' offered by some paint manufacturers often have chalky colors full of fillers and very little pigment, named vaguely and not helpful when you are learning about color mixing. They rarely include a clean primary magenta and often add a lot of white and fillers to all of their colors. Even Golden, arguably one of the best known for quality pigments, puts out a professional acrylic called 'primary blue' that is Phthalo tinted with white (what are you supposed to do if you want a dark value of the hue for this primary color??). Not their problem, it is ours to wade through and sort. The aim of the pages to follow is to assist in exactly this goal.

Choosing your primaries carefully is the first and foremost task to enable you to mix a full wheel of saturated hues, neutrals and grays. (and only mix browns when you intend to!) Because no paint company has gone to the trouble of presenting a relatively deep shade of primary red or blue hue to call a 'primary' (while also providing an informative swatch showing the pigment's dark, medium, light, or mass tone and thin glaze of this paint) it is up to us to select as best as we can to maximize our mixing possibilities. Paint manufacturers tend to either refrain from labelling anything 'primary' (who can blame them since the 'experts' are still arguing about what 'primary' is) or they add white to a Phthalo blue and call it 'Primary Blue' and add white to a red in the same way.

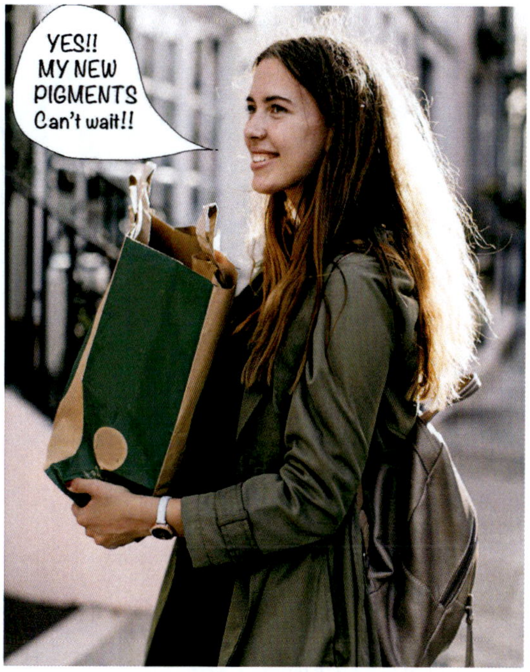

For this reason it is a good move to choose first the single pigment, deeper, untinted, minimally-biased primary pigments preferably transparent in nature (for magenta and blue, transparency is just incidental but offers more versatility in application techniques).

There are just 6 tubes (or pots) required to get started, to enable you to make all hues around the triadic 12 point color wheel and the neutrals and rich chromatic grays across the middle of the wheel, so you will be able to find places and relationships for all future colors that you buy. Once you have made your wheel, you can know exactly where any new pigments fit in.

It is worth getting some small airtight pots to make a decent amount of the secondaries and your own convenience colors as you create them later. Then you will learn how to make harmonious relationships to express a mood or bring an idea to life with a scheme that befits the subject or theme. (there are endless paint colors available out there in all manner of media with custom names, traditional names (but different pigment numbers), colors with multiple pigments added or single pigment colors. It can be very confusing to go into an art store (or order online with no advice) but if you ask for or look for the actual pigment numbers suggested below you will get less confused by staff bias, inaccurate color swatches and random mixtures, convenience colors etc. If you buy in an art store, ask them to thinly streak a little of the dark red or blue and yellow across white paper to show you any undertone or color bias before you settle on it as your primary. Later as you are in control of color mixing you may wish to buy pre-mixed secondaries, plus tertiaries, tints, convenience colors, metallic, transparent, etc, especially as you discover what you like to use a lot of, and how it fits into your favorite harmonious schemes.

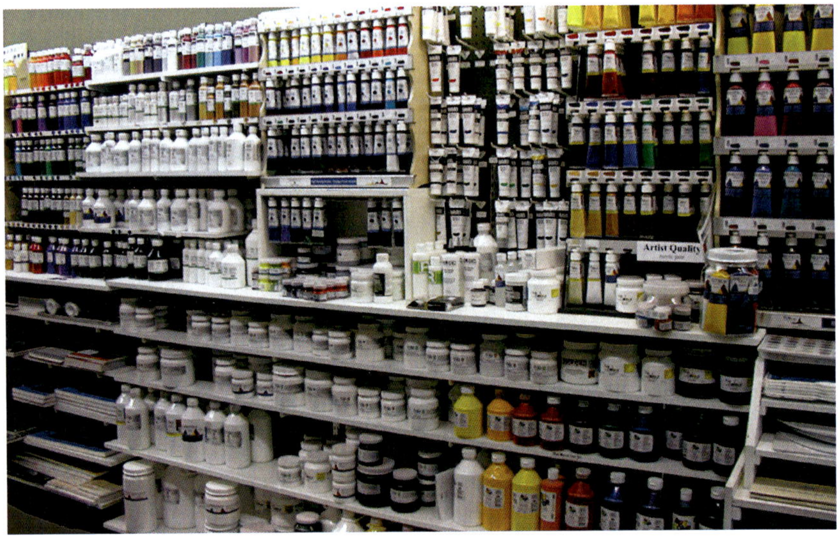

Eventually having each of the primary hues in both an opaque and a transparent version opens up many more opportunities as you develop diverse paint application skills, like transparent glazing. To get started with making your own wheel and learning how to combine and harmonize, it is not at all essential to have all transparents. The two blues and the magenta on our basic list happen to be transparent or semi-transparent, but are also dark in mass tone value, which gives more mixing options from the basic 6 to start out with. Opaque pigments are necessary to get quicker coverage, but not as good for glazing, so because our list of 6 is geared to minimum outlay, maximum possibilities, we suggest transparent options for yellow can come later. If your budget is not restricted, there are some longer lists to guide you on basics then get anything else you love the look of, but take care with Lightfastness ratings if you want your colors to be lasting well. ie. for longevity, and/or for professional sales.

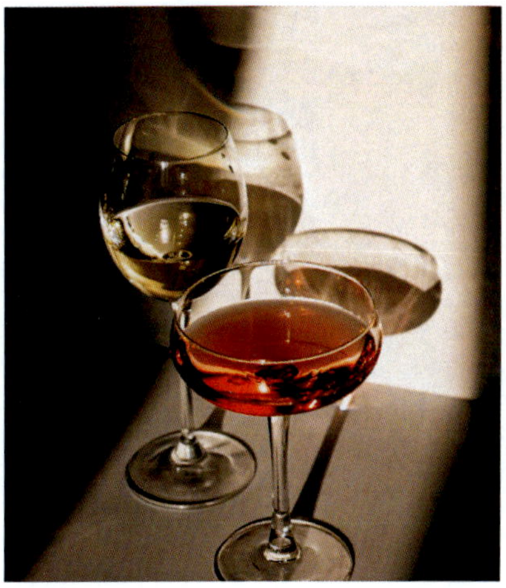

A good aim in the triadic system is to buy your primary paints with these three pigments Magenta - PR122 , PV19 (pick the magenta with the least orange or violet bias) in other words, a dark pink, rose like hue. Yellow PY35, or PY3, or PY74 and Cyan (Phthalo) PB15 OR PB15:3 (which we combine with Ultramarine Blue PB 29 to tweak the PB 15:3 a bit closer to 'Primary' hue position). Red shade Phthalo blue is ok for this too (but Ultramarine has extra charms so it serves two purposes in your minimum basics of 6) . You will see on the basic pigments lists, get double quantity of titanium white - PW 6, plus some Burnt Umber- PB 7 which are helpful as will be shown later on, for tinting or for your own 'convenience colors'.

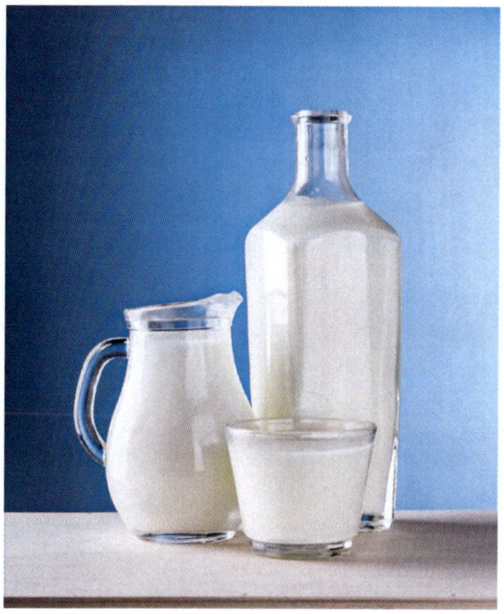

MOST IMPORTANT INFORMATION ON A PIGMENT LABEL

Once you have chosen your primary pigments, the rest of the exercises in this workbook will help you to find the appropriate complementary partners for them and practice making great harmonious schemes that you can utilize in your paintings or designs.

Brand's name for the pigment may be a traditional name based on it's composition or could be a "hue", which means it looks the same eg. Cobalt Hue (not made from Cobalt but looks similar. Paint companies have also been coming up with their own 'convenience names' for centuries. To avoid confusion, look at pigment numbers and/or color descriptions. **Pigment number** -eg. PR (red pigment) + a number eg. PR 122 is Quinacridone Magenta Many brands don't include this info.

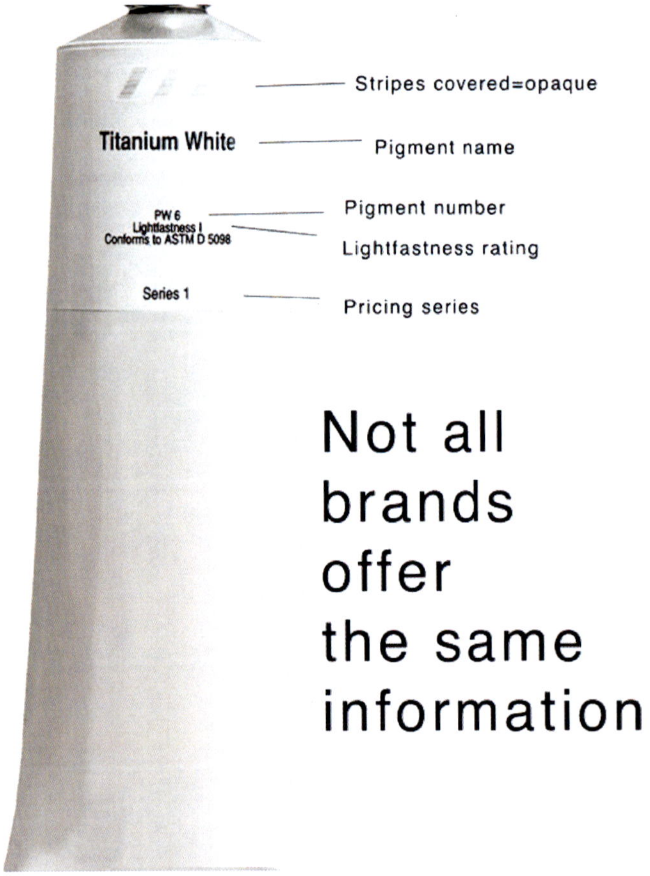

Transparency/ Opacity - some brands use an empty circle, a filled circle or a half filled circle to denote transparent, semi-transparent or opaque. Others have stripes covered (or showing or half-showing). some use star ratings. Some brands do not even mention opacity or transparency at all.

LIGHTFASTNESS

Pigment Loading - The main two differences between an artist standard of pigment and a student standard is the likelihood of cheaper and fugitive pigments in student and lower priced paints and also the lower concentrations of pigment with so many fillers being added. So in effect, you may pay less for a tube of cheap and cheerful color, but you are paying for a lot of filler and minimal pigment. eg. The cheap kit tube of white will have a large amount but the actual white pigment titanium dioxide is in a lower proportion (weak tinting strength).

Lightfastness rating and permanence ratings

ASTM Rating - many artist brands use the ASTM rating system, (American Standards for Testing Materials) . Choose from ASTM 1 (the most lightfast) , ASTM 2 are ok, but III and IV are to be avoided, especially if you are wanting to sell work one day. For students, this is less vital. (The ASTM system uses the Bluewool testing methods) The Bluewool scale (For artists) is more definitive for the upper end of lightfastness but not denoted by very many companies. It has a 1 to 8 scale with 7 & 8 ratings being the best for professional artists.

The Star System - Some companies use a star system (4 or 5 stars ***** is what you would look for), 1 or 2 stars are the most fugitive in this system).

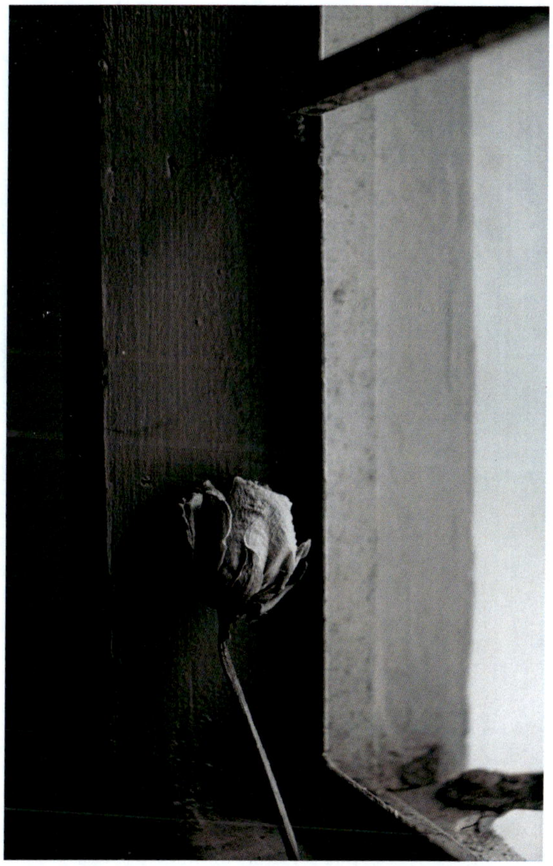

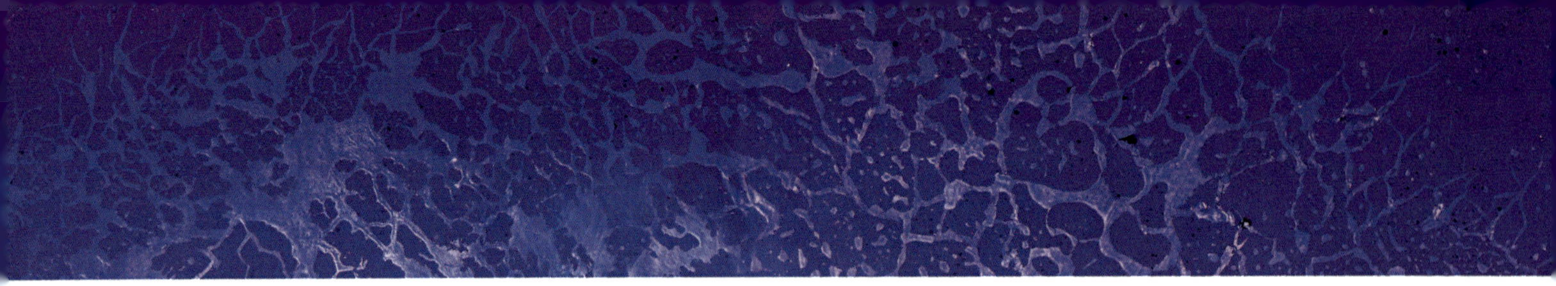

LIGHTFASTNESS CONTINUED

Lightfastness I: Excellent lightfastness.- The materials will exhibit no noticeable color change after being exposed to the appropriate lighting equivalence of 100 years of indoor museum lighting.

Lightfastness II: Very good lightfastness. These materials are suited for indoor exposure, but should not be used for works that will be installed outdoors and receive heavy exposure to ultraviolet light .

Lightfastness III: Marginal permanence. These are "fugitive" materials that are not recommended for permanent works.

Some companies also display a permanence rating eg. AA (best), A, B ,C(fugitive). This indicates other factors like chemical reactions(to heat or humidity) other than or as well as fading under UV. (eg. Winsor & Newton use this.)

The more common hues to show fugitive behaviors upon testing are some of the reds and yellows, although false claims are a subject of contention in the art world. Some say false information is on many labels (or very old data is used by paint companies to self-rate their own pigments.) GOLDEN, known world wide as the 'best' acrylic pigments, are known as truly fastidious and diligent with their lightfastness testing , hence their products are at the top of the price range.

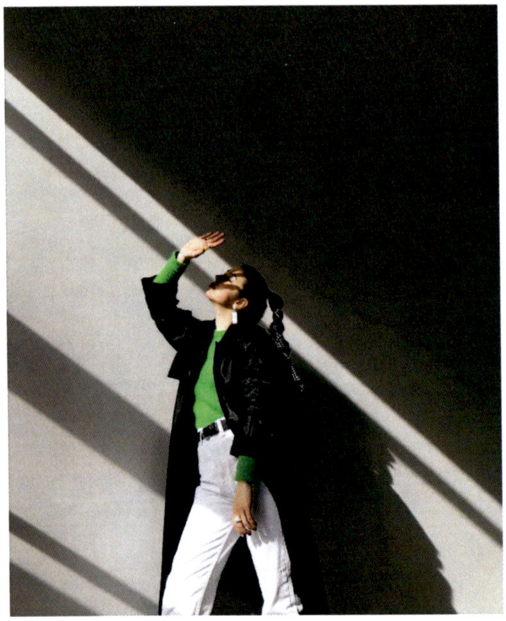

It is important to note that the lightfastness of a particular pigment can differ with the vehicle used. For example, Vermillion has a lightfastness rating of I (excellent) when mixed in oils and acrylics. However, in a watercolor mixture, it has a rating of III (fair). For this reason, we should always check the lightfastness rating for both the specific manufacturer and also the particular medium.

*** Reliable Data on Pigment Lightfastness Testing is found on the Resources page.**

GETTIING READY TO CHOOSE YOUR FIRST BASIC 6 PIGMENTS

See the 6 basic suggestions from a few universally available brands on the next pages. We suggest to always get the darkest (often transparent or semi-transparent hues) in blues and reds to start as you can always tint and opacify them yourself with white. You can't make a light pigment deeper without changing the hue or de-saturating (and please.... you would not want to be adding black always to darken a hue, although it is a sad old cheat commonly used and even taught first up by those who don't know a chromatic way.) In your workbook here you will make rich grays and natural black without a tube of Mars or Carbon black. Later, if contemporary approaches are your leaning , sure, grab a pot/tube of black , because you will eventually form favorites in some secondaries and tertiaries and convenience mixes too, and naturally you would add more paints to your kit, but we suggest not to buy more tubes/pots until you are very familiar with making a version of all hues from 3 primaries and discovering their harmonious partners and various relationships. This is the real fun!!

Depending on your budget, you may need to buy the cheaper student ranges and that is still ok for learning. Just try to choose the darker rosiest red as your primary (not too much violet or orange bias)- read in the Glossary of terms all about color bias. Get the yellow that has minimal orange bias or green bias and for blue, an untinted Phthalo (PB15). Companies sometimes suggest 'primary colors' in labelling, but they are often tinted with white. Avoid that if you are trying to start with the most mixing options from only 6 tubes/ pots. Avoid pre-made "starter kits" of pigments .if you can.

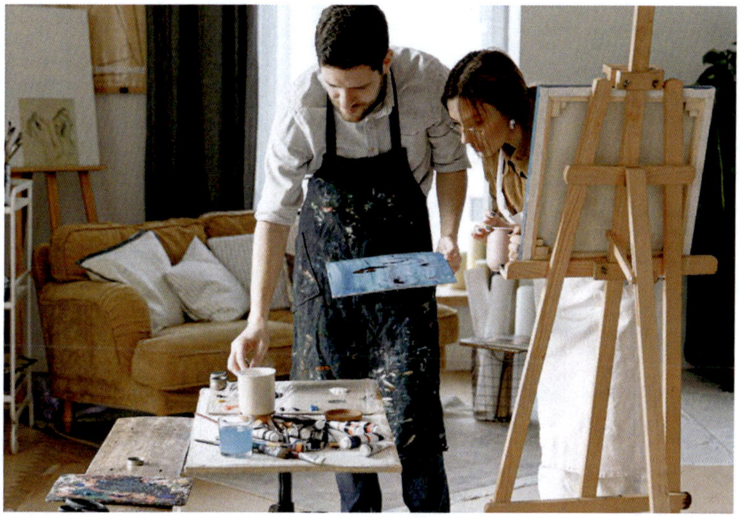

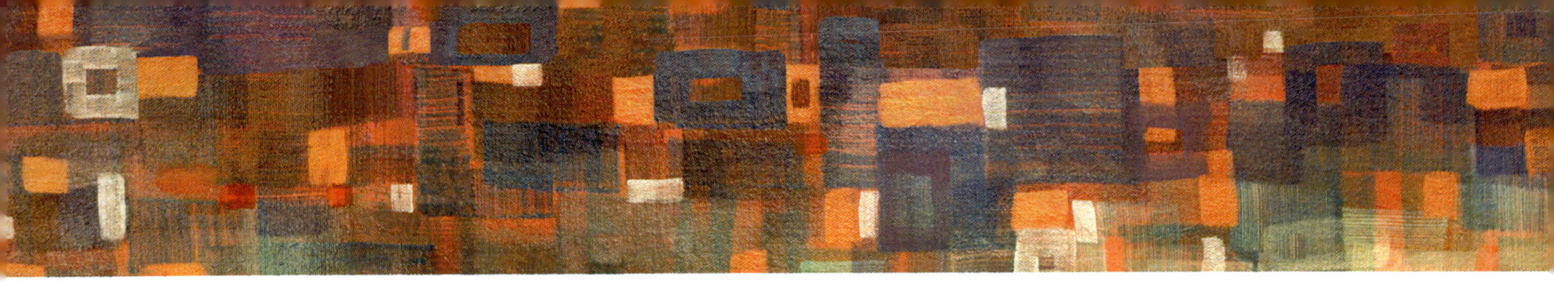

Why do we include Burnt Umber in our beginning pigment list of 6 ??

This is because: You can make a dark "Natural Black" (like Paynes Gray but more neutral) with Burnt Umber and Ultramarine Blue (unless you buy a cheap paler Burnt Umber which is not nice and dark, then you will have a darkish gray, but no natural black.The cheaper the pigment the less 'burnt' is the Umber we find.

Making the rich chromatic grays across the wheel often results in greenish, violetish or brownish mixes until you get the partner balance right. Adding more blue where it belongs to 'gray off' any brownish mix comes naturally once you have already made black with dark brown and dark blue.

CHOOSING WATERCOLOR PIGMENTS- If you are on a reasonably tight budget, it may be best to learn in acrylics first. They're generally cheaper and can give some watercolor-like effects and some oil-like effects. Watercolors are the most unforgiving pigments, not the cheapest and not the easiest as some may believe (really worth it, we love watercolors), but you must learn exactly about how to use them as even though they are a water based medium, the behaviors and the techniques and substrates vary enormously.

If you are determined to make watercolor your first medium, or if you have already started down this track, these would be our budget suggestions (don't buy readymade "kits".) If someone gifted you a box of watercolor pans or tubes, check what hues are included and add a tube of what is missing from the basic first 6 we suggest. - **BLICK** - Cadmium Yellow Light PY 35 , Alizarin Rose PV 19, French Ultramarine Blue PB 29, Prussian Blue PB 27, Burnt Umber PBr 7

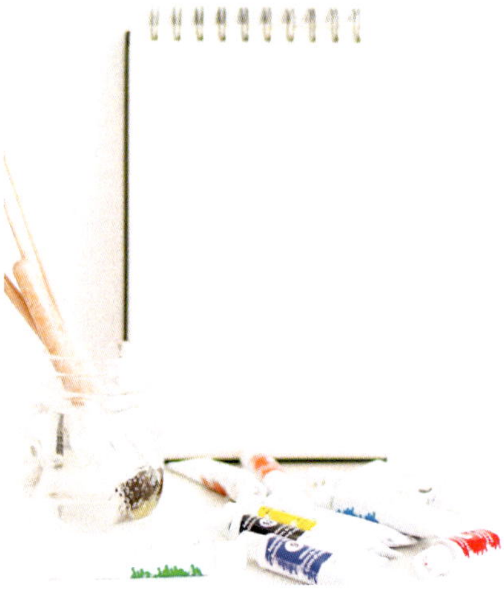

Many teachers would be giving you a long list of 'landscape colors', 'portrait painting colors to choose' etc. 'Indian red', 'yellow ochre' , these are all convenience colors which you could buy if you have a great flexible budget. There are some amazing pigments to explore if you have the budget for it. In our section on convenience colors, some of the most common ones are shown (how to mix a version yourself from your basic 6).

Great comprehensive resources for learning about and choosing watercolor pigments are:

https://www.handprint.com/HP/WCL/palette1.html#bluegreen

https://www.kimcrick.com/

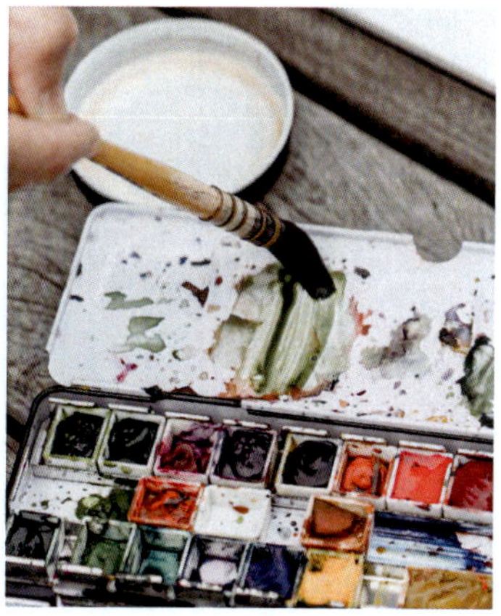

We always recommend buying watercolor tubes over pans. Firstly, pans are mainly good for working quite small. To make a good 'puddle' of paint (when you want to go larger) is a little harder with a small dry pan of pigment.

If you grab an ice cube tray you can mix your own 'pans' of secondaries, tertiaries, convenience colors with your basic 5 or 6. We don't add white to that list as when learning in watercolor, you will find out how to preserve the white of the paper, then later you may wish to have white as an option.

ESSENTIAL BASIC 6 WATERCOLOR TUBES

Winsor and Newton Professional

Cadmium-Free Yellow Pale PY 35

Quinacridone Magenta PR 122

Ultramarine Blue PB 29

Phthalo Green PG 7

Phthalo Turquoise PB 16

Sepia PBk6 · PR101 (instead of Burnt Umber)

Cotman (Student Range)

Cadmium Yellow Pale HUE PY175 · PY65

Permanent Rose PV 19

Cadmium Red

Ultramarine Blue PB 29

Intense Blue (Phthalo) PB 15

Sepia PBk7 · PBr7

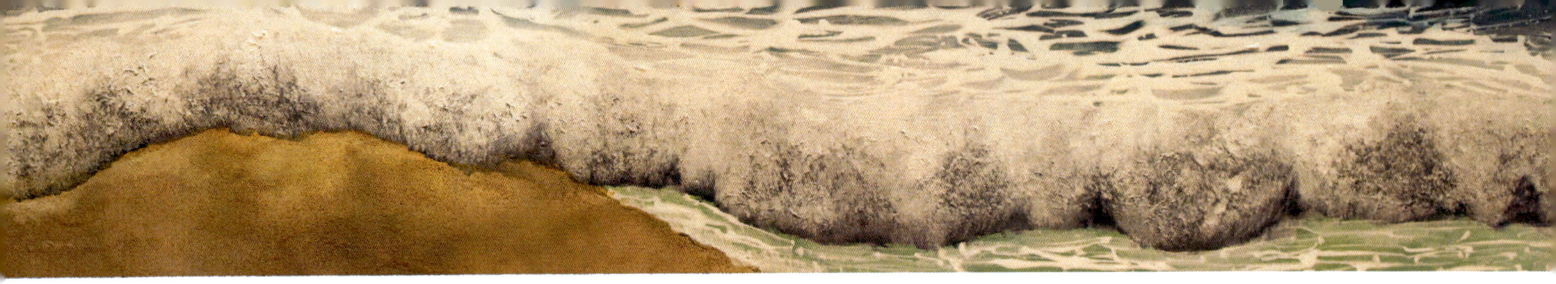

ACRYLICS - PRIMARIES : FIRST 6 FOR COMMON BRANDS

WINSOR & NEWTON

Professional Heavy Body Acrylics. ?what to buy first

Essentials 6

Primary Magenta

PV 19 Permanent Rose - (transparent) or Perm. Alizarin Crimson hue PR177 + PV23 -transparent (NB. this is not the old fugitive PR83 Alizarin Crimson)

Primary Yellow PY 35 - Cadmium Yellow Light or PY73+83 (Cad Yellow Medium)- (both opaque)

Primary Blue PB 15:3 - Phthalo Blue (Green shade) - transparent and Ultramarine Blue - PB 29 semi-transparent

Titanium White - PW 6 opaque -double quantity

Burnt Umber - Pbr 7 semi-opaque

Handy Extras (not totally essential to start)

Tertiary Red - By adding a little yellow to Magenta , you can get a red-orange hue, but it will be semi-transparent and made lighter by the Cadmium yellow, so if you love strong opaque red, get a PR 108 Cadmium Red Dark (or light) or Pyrrole Red PR 254

Tertiary Blue-green- a beautiful pale turquoise, PG50 (Cobalt Turquoise light or PB36 Cobalt turquoise (you could make a deep turquoise with phthalo blue and some transparent yellow, PY150 or Nickel Azo Yellow - PS. if you have all 3 primaries in transparent form, you can make all 12 hues in transparent form for glazing (if you plan on learning about that.)

A really cool thing about Winsor and Newton acrylics is their unique transparent emulsion which means no darkening or subtle shifting of the colors as they dry (unique feature in acrylic paints)

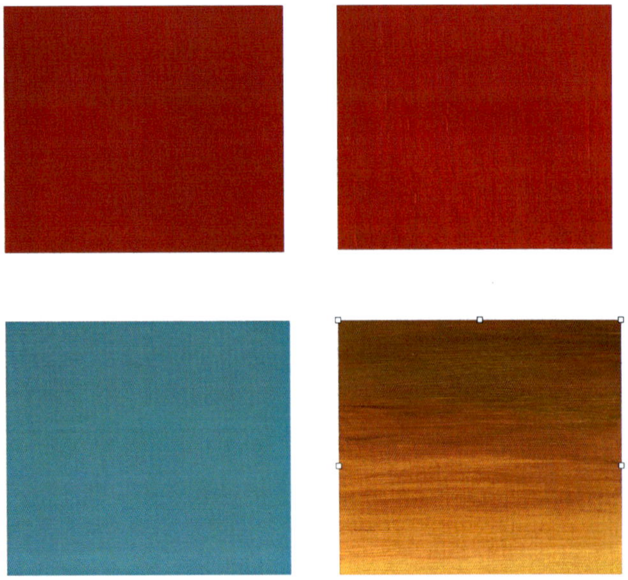

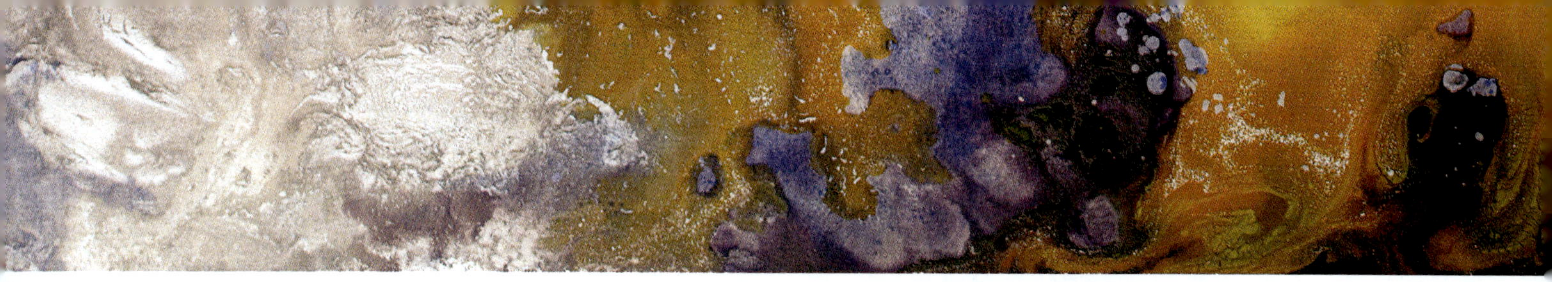

GOLDEN

Pricier but thought of as the best range and quality - better value per ml in general terms of pigment loading and accurate lightfastness ratings.

Essentials 6

Primary Red/Magenta - PR 122 Quinacridone Magenta or Magenta'Primary' - PV 19 (a little more violet biased)

Primary Yellow PY 35 - Cadmium Yellow Light

Primary Blue PB 15:3 - Phthalo Blue (their tube called 'Primary Blue' is Phthalo plus white, just get Phthalo Blue & tint it when needed) add Ultramarine Blue - PB 29 for Primary blue

Titanium White - PW 6 -double quantity

Burnt Umber - Pbr 7

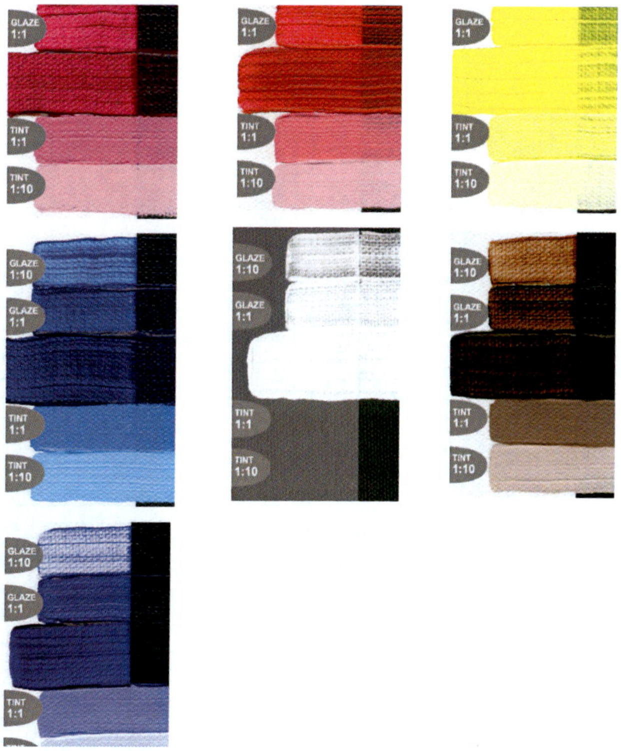

Handy Extras- not essential to start

Tertiary Red - mix your own or for a bright opaque red, get a PR 108 Cadmium Red Medium (or Cadmium Red light) or PrR5 - Naphthol Red medium

Tertiary Blue-green- a beautiful pale turquoise, PG50 or PG26 (you can make a deep turquoise with phthalo blue and a little Transparent yellow- PY150 Azo or PY42 Transparent Yellow Iron Oxide

If you have all 3 primaries in transparent form, you can make all 12 hues for transparent glazing (get your color exercises nailed first.)

Transparent Burnt Sienna PR 101

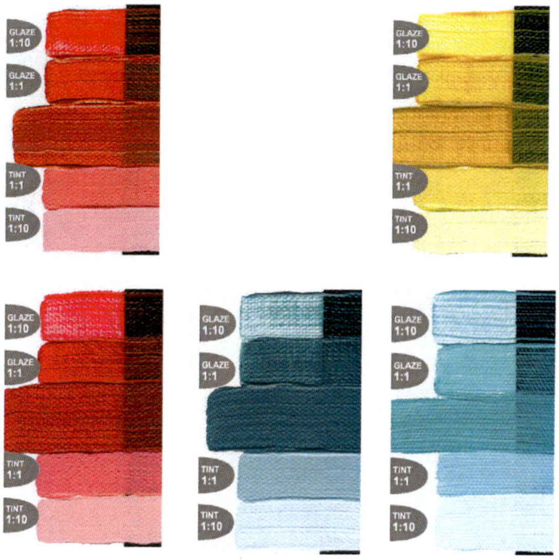

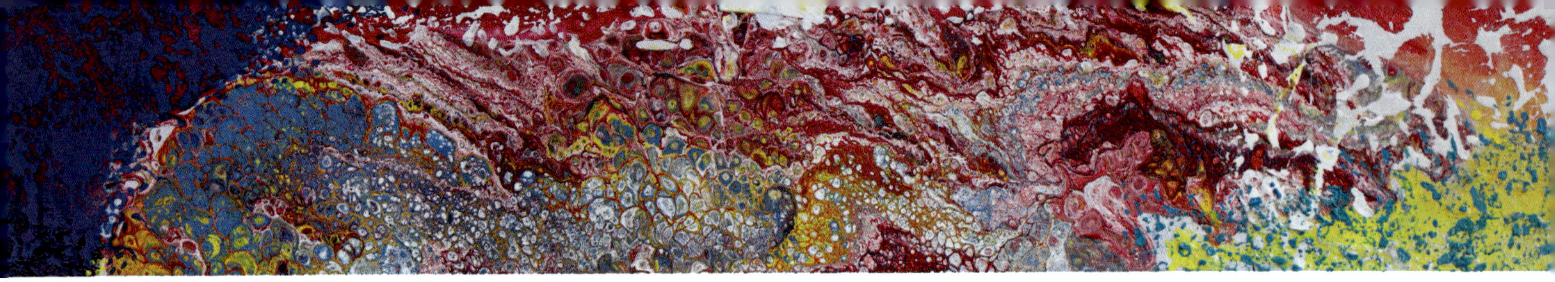

ATELIER FREE FLOW

BY CHROMA (shop around for best prices) These are the choice of many of our students with a higher budget (they can add a gel medium if they want it to be heavy body). They use it diluted for watercolor-like effects too. It is a professional, lightfast range and usually not quite as pricey as Golden (although Golden have larger ranges of mediums etc.) Get some little squeeze bottles and you can make your own versions of Secondaries, Tertiaries and convenience colors **with this list of 8 here.** Our full start-out list for students who have a good budget and plan to get imore at the beginning.

Magenta PR122

(or Permanent Alizarine PR 122+PR175)

Cadmium Yellow Light Hue PY35

Ultramarine Blue PB 29

Phthalo Blue (green shade)PB 15:3

Burnt Umber PBr 7

Titanium White PW 6 - double quantity

Transparent Raw Sienna PY42

Transparent Burnt Sienna

PR 101

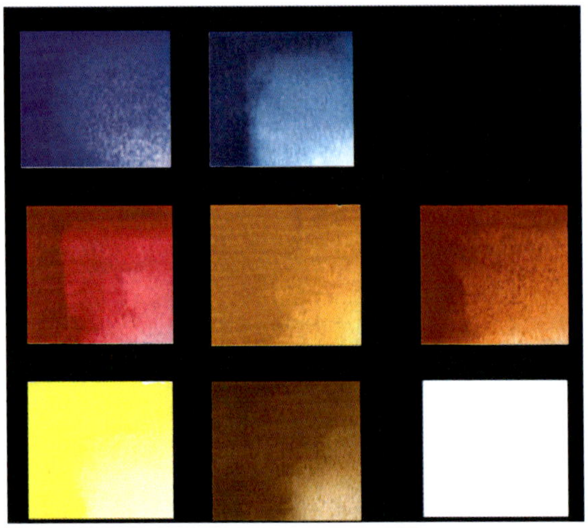

There are two other transparent pigments added to this list, giving many more glazing opportunities. (they are the first 2- if you can, there are numerous lovely colors to buy later, mainly for convenience or personal preferences.). All of these pigments listed are labelled as super lightfast - 8/8 BWS with very high pigment loading.

They come in little 60ml bottles but the economical value increases plenty with the 250ml bottles and then you have more volume to make all of your secondaries, tertiaries, your special convenience colors (storing in those little bottles is a great way to turn 8 colors into 40+ of YOUR OWN SPECIAL MIXES. We get multiple advantages out of each hue in the list of 8 eg. Ultramarine Blue added to Phthalo Blue in a new bottle becomes your 'Primary', while adding Ultramarine to Magenta gives a bright violet, phthalo blue is green shade blue so gives a bright turquoise with a little yellow. In addition they are both dark in mass tone giving a larger range of values compared to other blues eg. cerulean(cool) or cobalt(warm), lovely but lighter in masstone, less options for values.

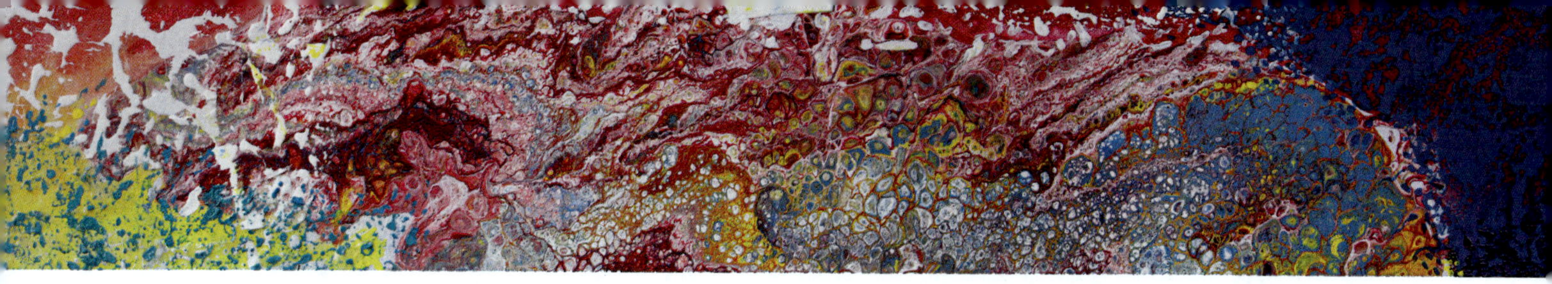

LIQUITEX - **their swatches are not the most informative- they don't show the variations from mass tone to tint or dilution in their website swatches but there are options of both student and professional ranges.**

Essentials - professional heavy body

Primary -Quinacridone magenta PR 122 or PV19

Quinacridone crimson

Primary - Cadmium yellow light PY35

Primary - PB 15:3 - (dark in mass tone, vibrant thinned and tinted, their swatch does not show this, also is not showing transparency as in Golden and W&N)

Ultramarine Blue - PB 29

Titanium White - PW 6 -double quantity

Burnt Umber - Pbr 7

Extras- not essential to start a wheel

Tertiary Red - Add a little yellow to Magenta , you can get a red-orange hue, but it will be semi-transparent and made lighter by the Cadmium yellow, so if you love strong opaque red (tertia-ry), get a PR 254 Pyrrole Red

Tertiary Blue-green - They have a color called Brilliant blue, (PB15:3, PG7+white), but you can make a light turquoise by adding white yourself to Phthalo !5:3 plus a deep turquoise with Phthalo blue and a little Transparent yellow-PY3 Hansa - Light (A Transparent yellow.) For a mid-range pricing, they seem ok.

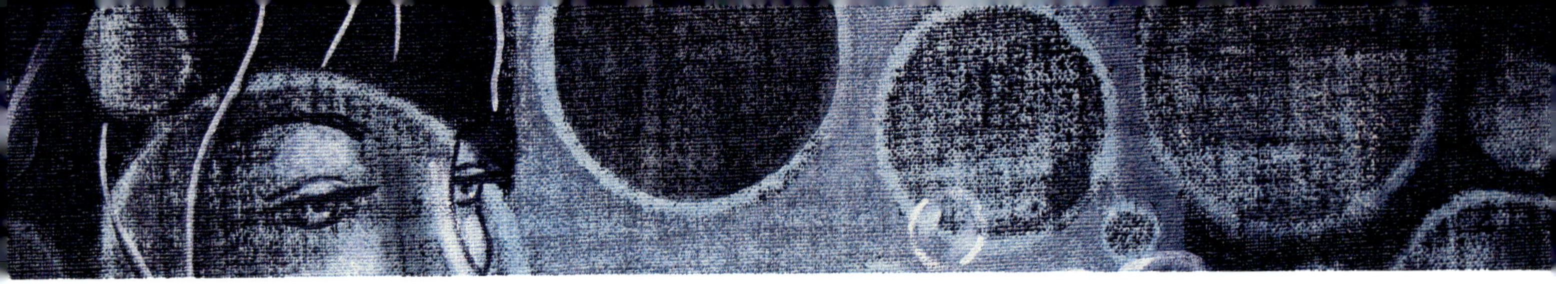

BLICK - a low budget option (compare also from Blick- Chroma A2, (page 48) quite good as student choice, better lightfastness, darker burnt umber). Many of our students start with this.

Essentials

Primary Red/Magenta

You could use PR 122 Quinacridone Magenta or 'Alizarin Crimson' PR 202 + PR206 (we favor PR122).

Their so-named 'Primary red' is actually a tertiary red orange , you can make that by adding some yellow to 'Alizarin Crimson' or Magenta >>>>

Primary Yellow Cadmium Yellow Light 'Hue' PY3 + white

Primary Blue PB 15 - Phthalo Blue (15.3 is more 'cyan' but PB15 can be your primary blue too, mix PB15:3 and Ultramarine Blue - PB 29 (for primary position.)

Titanium White - PW 6

Burnt Umber - a convenience color made with 4 pigments by them (not the greatest for making a natural black). Buy a black as well for darker shades.

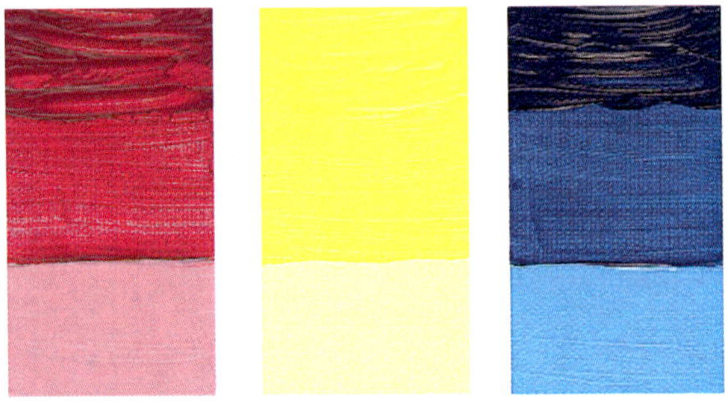

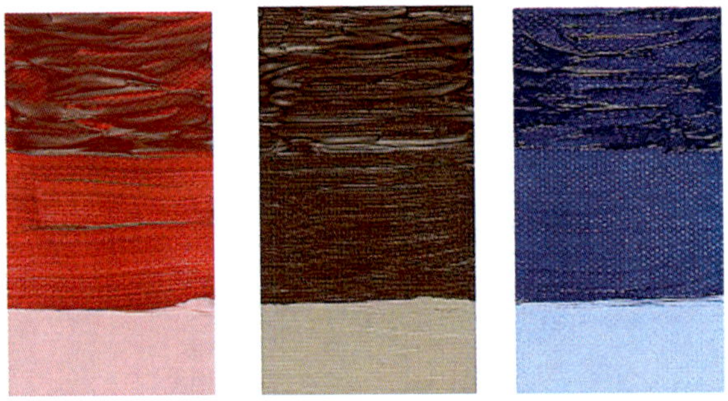

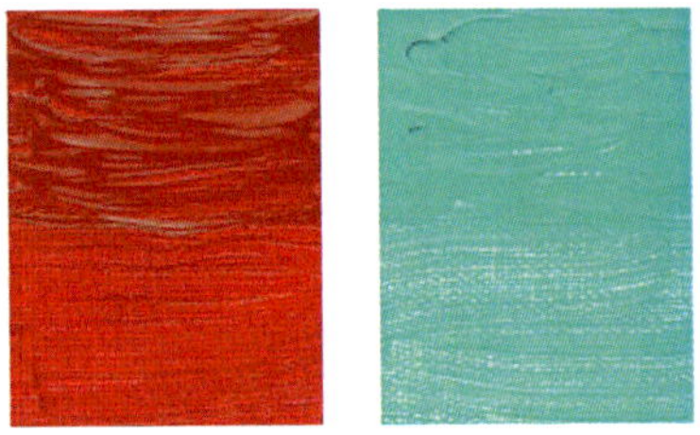

Extras - not really necessary to start making all 12 hues around the wheel - since they are a few dollars you could get a tertiary red-orange(opaque), a black , and buy 2 white tubes.

Tertiary Red - For an opaque bright red, try a PR 108 Cadmium Red Dark (or Cadmium Red light)

Tertiary Blue-green- for a pale aqua PG15+PG7+PW6 or PG26 (you can make a similar color with phthalo blue, yellow and white.) You can also make all violets, oranges and greens with your basic 6 tubes, the rest of Blick's convenience colors seem tinted and full of fillers.

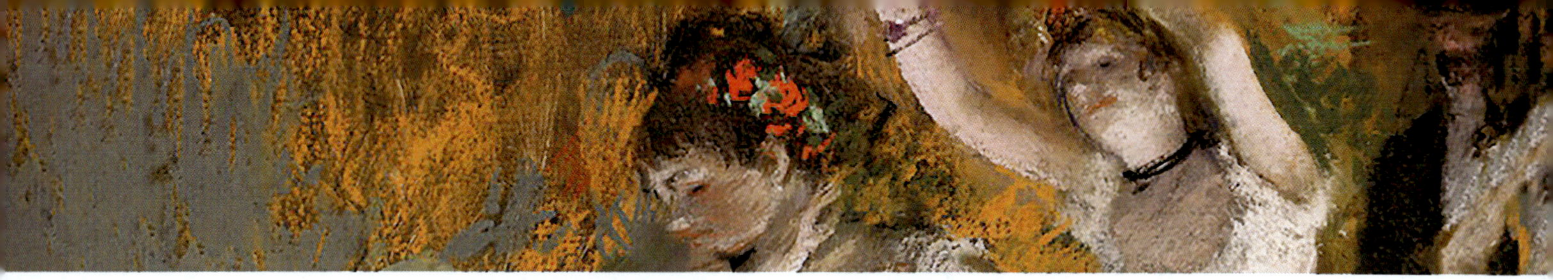

WORKING WITH COLOR IN DRY MEDIA

The main difference in applying color theory when working in dry media compared to mixing paint is the different ways of working with tone and saturation. Some artists also use optical blending with dry media instead of physical pigment blending (as it was with the Pointillists, who broke away from the Impressionists and became quite deeply committed to the practical application of color theory (including with use of optical blending.)

COLORED PENCILS - Kits of pencils vary in quality, number and available hues and value ranges achievable. This workbook will be of great value in the practical color exercises for those who have already learned the basic techniques for blending colored pencils. Visit this link for color pencil blending introduction.

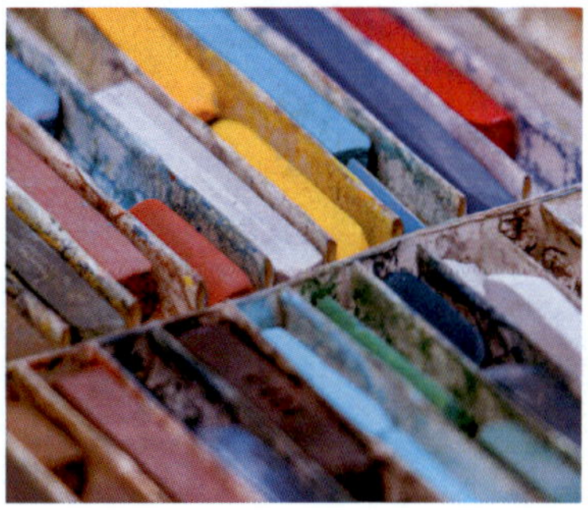

https://adventureswithart.com/how-to-darken-colored-pencils/

PASTEL BLOCKS AND PENCILS - As with colored pencil there are medium specific methods of blending different kinds of pastels to work your tonal values and saturation and as long as you have learned some of these, you will be able to make your wheels, strings and practice making harmonious relationships.

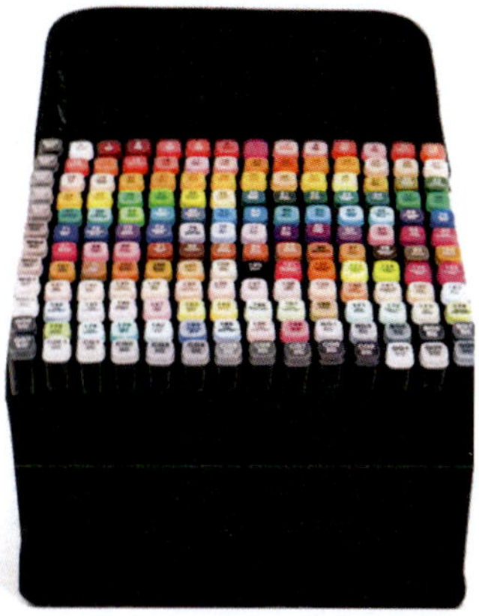

ALCOHOL MARKERS - Copic and similar colored markers come with blending markers and there are multiple tutorials online about blending with them. Your abilities to get the shades on all of your hue strings will rely somewhat on the range of hues and values in your kit. You will get great benefits however from undertaking the color harmony exercises and learning how to use color relationships and arrange more harmoniously. (use marker appropriate paper, as it does bleed through regular paper).

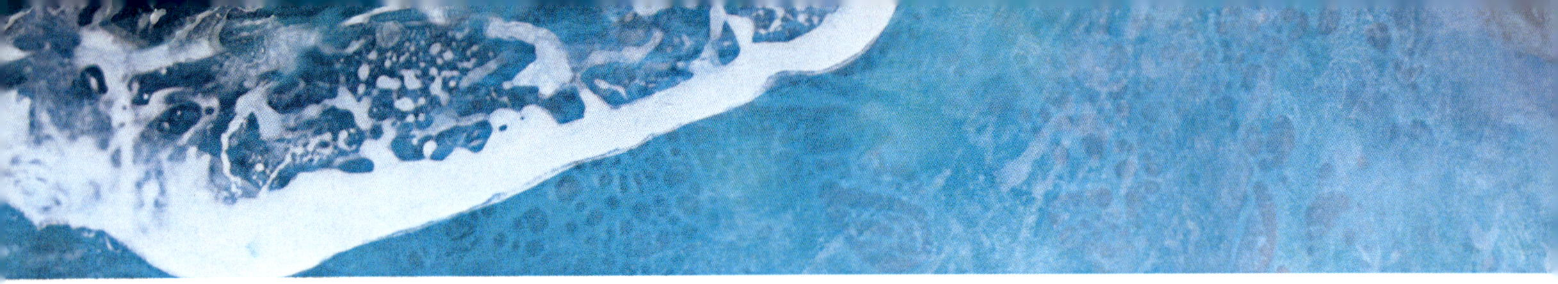

TOOLS AND MATERIALS TO USE WITH YOUR COLOR WORKBOOK

Whichever medium you are learning to paint in could be used to practice color mixing but the workbook exercises are based around contemporary acrylic pigments as they are the most convenient, dry quickly, (unlike oils), won't heavily buckle the pages, unlike watercolors (plus acrylics are also quite commonly used to start out with now by art students).

In watercolors, gouache or oils, many of the pigment names are the same but it is most practical to focus on the basic primary hues (and the pigment numbers suggested) that you have already or get for your kit and use medium-specific papers to carry out your exercises. (when dry, you can even collage them into your work book which you can use as a helpful reference for all your creative years to come.) Numerous convenience colors could always be purchased later once you have mastered basic color mixing.

Synthetic hair flat brushes

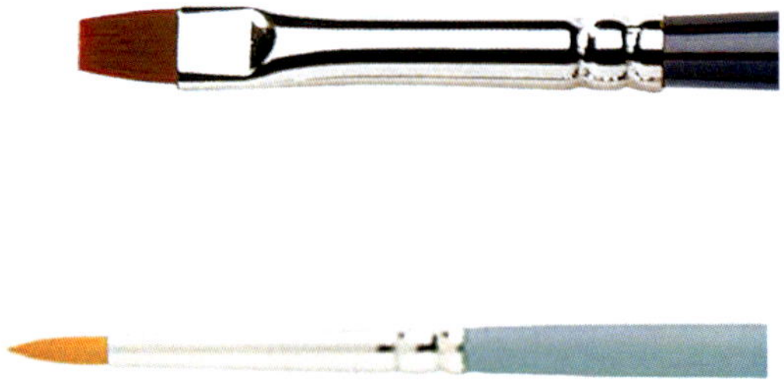

Basic Equipment

- 2 - 3 small flat brushes, one little pointer
- water (just for wash-up - use your acrylic paints thinly but undiluted in this book)
- Visit our **online studio** (public links in black) on melbourneartclasses.com.au to get more information on brushes. NB: Get the hues right on your palette first before adding to the work book .(or let dry, cover with a thin white and do it again). Sometimes our mistakes teach us the most. This all takes practice for everyone, so be prepared to do a wheel (or several) for every medium you get into. Repetition is the mother of skill and all that.
- Paper towels, old bathroom towel (keep brushes clean between colors)
- Spray mister bottle - you can get a cheap bathroom travel kit from the pharmacy or dollar store and use the little spray mister bottle to keep acrylic paint from drying out on the palette.

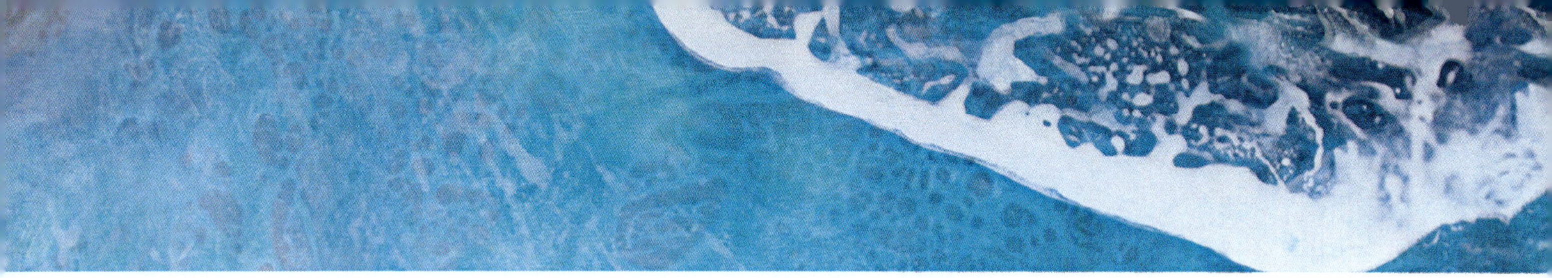

■ Palettes - there are several examples of the kinds of palettes you may choose to use. Ideally, mixing colors on an achromatic gray surface of a light to mid-tone is said to be the easiest when learning because any color will look darker on white and lighter on black. The value as well as the hue and saturation are being measured and estimated by eye as you go about your color mixing exercises and prepare to mix any color you want or need. Having said that, we don't necessarily recommend the 'easiest' way because when you apply your colors to a background (of any color, value or saturation) these relative

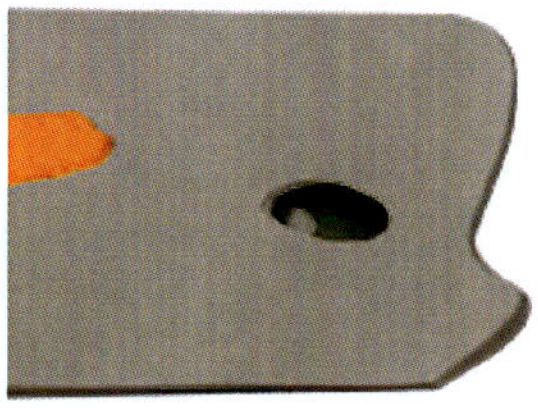

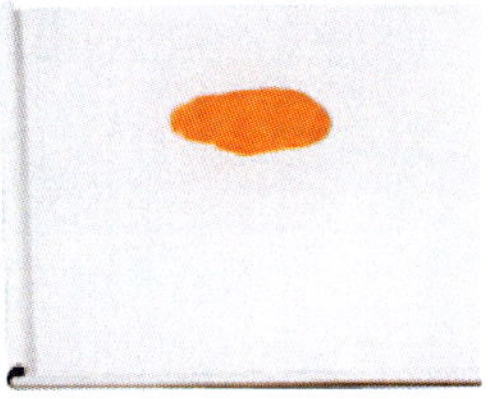

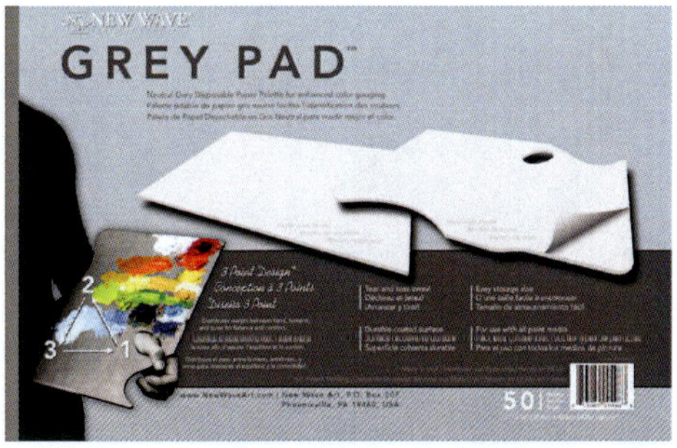

effects will occur (you will learn about simultaneous contrast later on) , so getting your eye in for assessing and measuring all the dimensions of the colors you are mixing and knowing how to easily balance them according to the background they are going onto is a skill that is being practiced right from the palette (if you choose to use a white palette).

ACRYLICS AND OILS - Rip-off palettes which come in white or neutral gray, or use smooth white plastic plates (not paper ones, they absorb the moisture from your paint), or baking paper. These are cheap, disposable and effective palettes for acrylics Think about stay-wet options too, DIY examples in next pages. We see students buying the little watercolor palettes for use with acrylics, but they are the less ecologically sound option as left over paint seems to get washed down the sink (scraping it out of the little round pans is very hard to keep them clean once it has dried). Good for watercolors though although white plastic plates are good for that too.

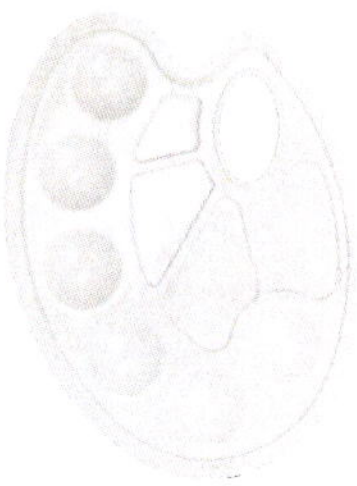

Art paper - There are some good versatile papers that come in a pad and are for watercolor, gouache, acrylics or even oils. You can print or draw up the wheel template and the other string strips for undertaking the color mixing and relationship exercises on your choice of paper or you can't paint directly into your workbook with acrylic undiluted (liquid paints cause buckling of the book's paper). Oils take too long to dry and will hold you up unless you create them on oil paper and collage them in after they dry. (naturally you will need a solvent to clean up if you use oils, unless you use water miscible oils, which we highly recommend, as they wash up in soapy water.) Windsor and Newton Artisan range are excellent. I learned in Windsor and Newton traditional oils from age 11yrs and I can vouch that this modern water-miscible formulation of oil pigments are as vibrant and beautiful to use with the joy of soapy water wash-up (no-one would ever stop by my room as a student for a coffee due to the solvent fumes, and actually many people are really quite sensitive, even to the so-called 'odorless' kinds of solvents).

At our studios, we block in with high quality acrylics, add a coat of matt varnish and complete in water-miscible oils (when teaching oil painting we don't often use traditional oils).

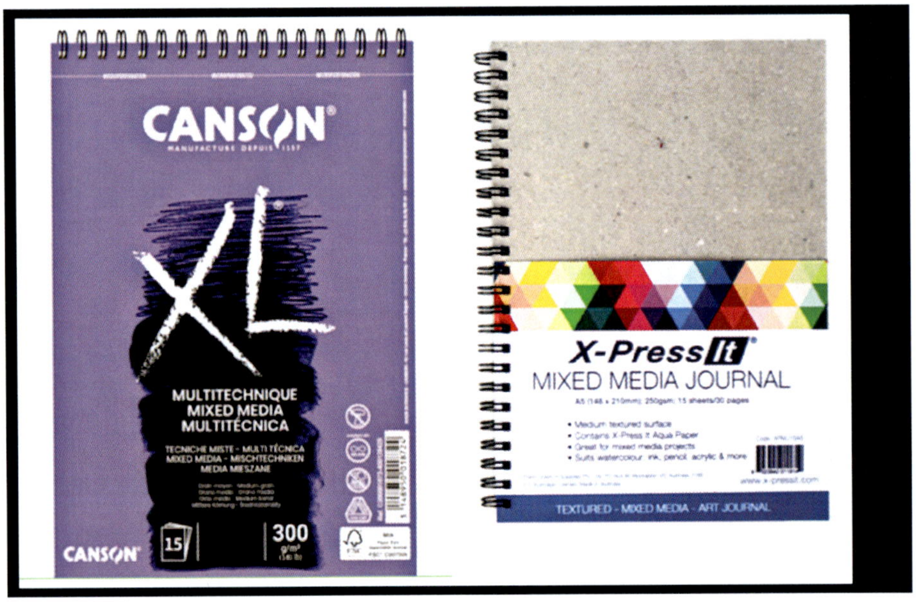

DIY PAINT STAY-WET STORAGE SYSTEMS

MATERIALS TO HELP YOU SAVE PAINT

Wasting dried up paint is a common but unnecessary problem. There are a number of ways to DIY plus use recycled materials and save your paint mixtures simultaneously.

- Firstly, mix acrylic or oils with a long flat metal spatula on a glass palette (or other flat waterproof surface). Mixing on your painting palette with a brush is ok for single use small amounts but in general there is no waste if you mix it, then pick it all up and place in a little pile in your stay wet storage system, taking from there when you need more.

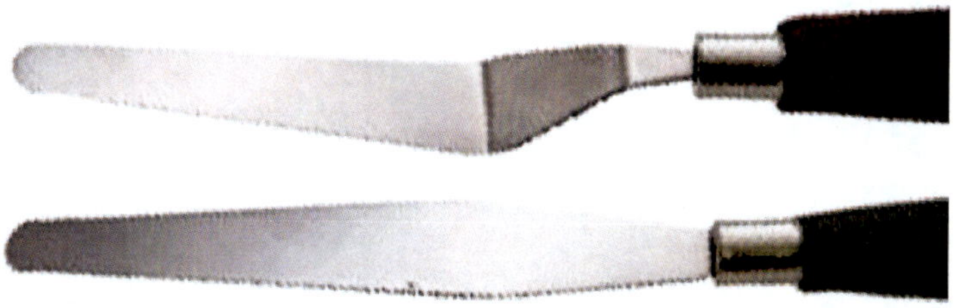

- There are commercially made Stay-wet palettes you can buy, but since they are relatively$$$, you might prefer recycling where possible and having varying amounts for favorite secondaries, tertiaries and your own custom colors. The bead jar tower idea (images in the next pag-es) is great for making a decent amount of your secondaries when you are learning to make shades (rich grays). Then you have the exact complementary opposite to keep and mix, for chromatic shades of your own primary colors. If you are working with liquid acrylics however, use little squeeze bottles for storage rather than bead screw jars (liquids can spill or glue the screw lid shut every time!)
- If you are mixing smaller amounts just for one project, the best recycled concept we have im-plemented at our studios for students is a 'contact plastic peel-off sheet' or A4 plastic sleeve kept inside an XL ziplock bag with a wet Chux cloth behind the closed sheet to keep a nice humid, air-less environment. You can even suck out the air through the last inch of open zip edge to make a vacuum in the ziplock bag.This system lasts well for one or two projects at least, then you can replace the inner sleeve. You can also keep more than one sleeve inside the ziplock bag.(labelled well with what is in there.)

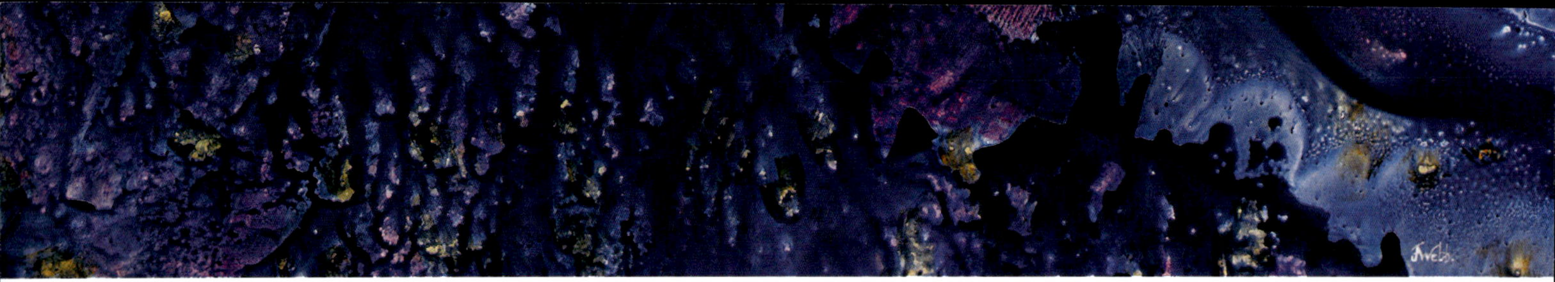

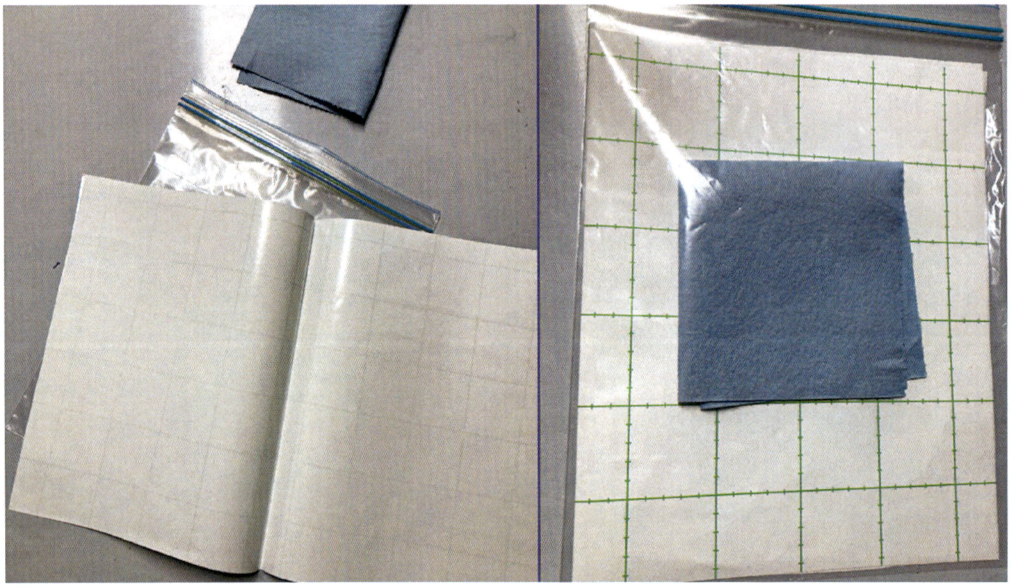

Just be sure to use amounts that wont spill out when the sleeve is closed (having 4-5 small piles closed into one is enough, start a new sleeve if you have more to save. Label them clearly.

For a group or class (or a very frugal organized individual) we have seen many students make the sacrifice of eating an entire box of chocolates, because they have nice little cups to arrange your 15ml (0.5 ounces) or 2-3 teaspoons of each custom color. You need to use a special plastic glue to fix kitchen flat sponge over the whole lid, keep it wet and you have a nice DIY stay-wet system.

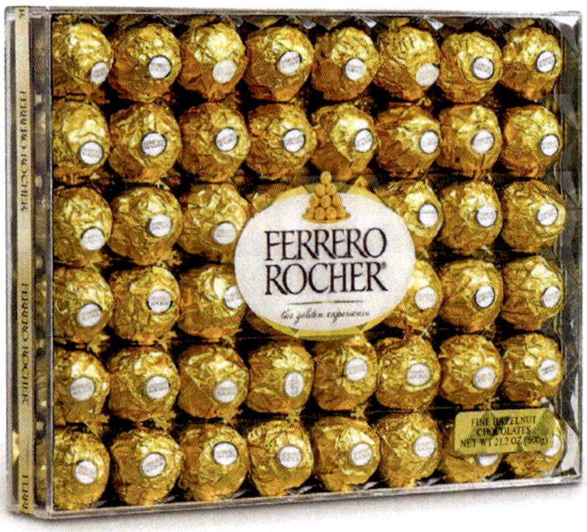

For 10ml or above you can use beading jars. Little towers are the most user-friendly and come in 10, 20, 30, 50, 100 mls (that is here in AU, in U.S. they might be measured in ounces or inches across. Four important things to remember if using this system to store acrylic paints:

1. Spread vaseline around each thread or the paint can glue the jars closed
2. Always add enough pigment to allow only a little air above, as a small amount of pigment with relatively more air above it can lead to drying out.
3. Spray a small film of clean water inside each time you take some paint out to further help prevent any drying out.
4. Don't let your little paint towers roll around horizontally, especially if using liquid acrylics, they are better kept vertical. They are designed for beads after all. Use the squeeze bottles for liquid acrylics.

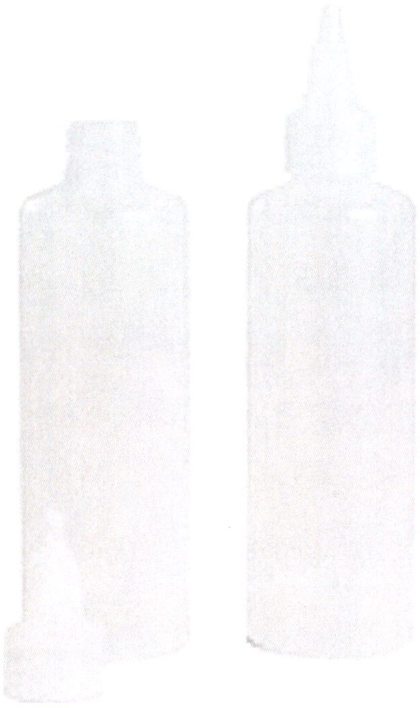

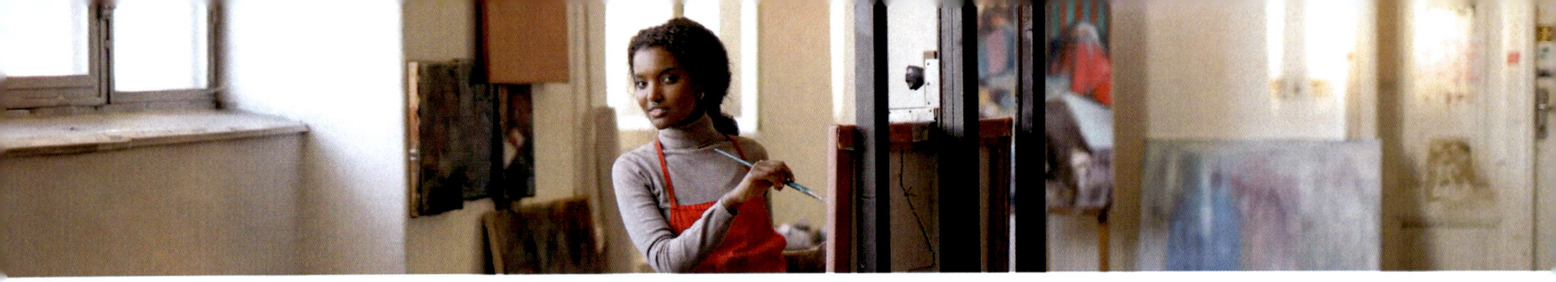

SETTING UP A GREAT PLACE TO PAINT AND USE COLOR EFFECTIVELY

Hardly anyone has a huge light-filled studio at their disposal when they are learning about art, color and design. Natural light is ideal but weather and other constraints mean that clever use of electrical lighting is necessary for many artists and certainly most students. If you could work comfortably in a sheltered area outside, you would be in our idea of lighting heaven. Even a north facing window will still give changing light conditions all day. Many students and artists only get to work at night in any case. (at least we don't have to strap a candle to our head as Michaelngelo did!)

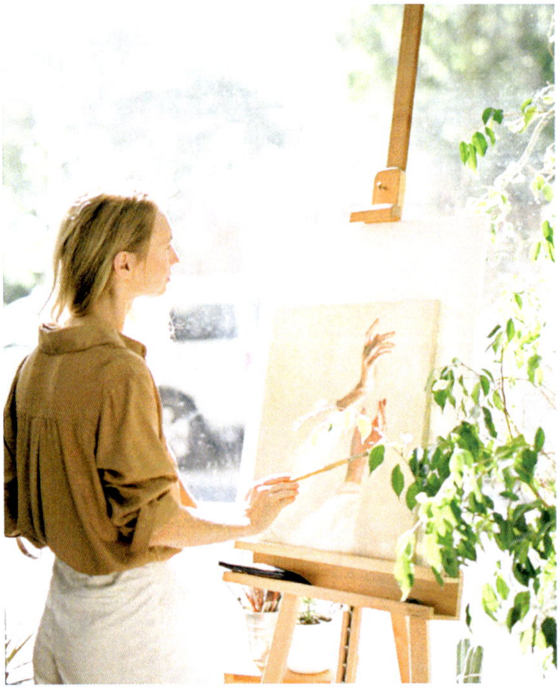

ELECTRICAL LIGHTING

Michaelangelo used that candle strapped to his head whilst up on a scaffold laying on his back working on the Sistine Chapel. Fortunately we have a range of options available to us to help arrange suitable lighting indoors, without such discomfort and struggle. Too much light can cause issues as well. Your enjoyment and progress with drawing and painting is very much contributed to by your physical comfort as are your results in terms of value patterns and color mastery.

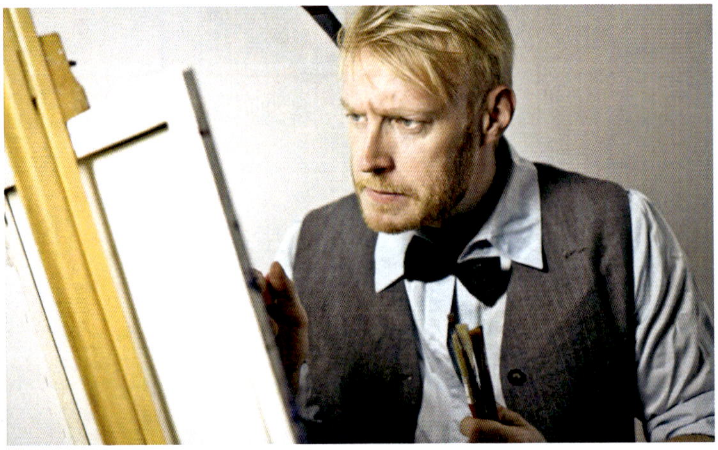

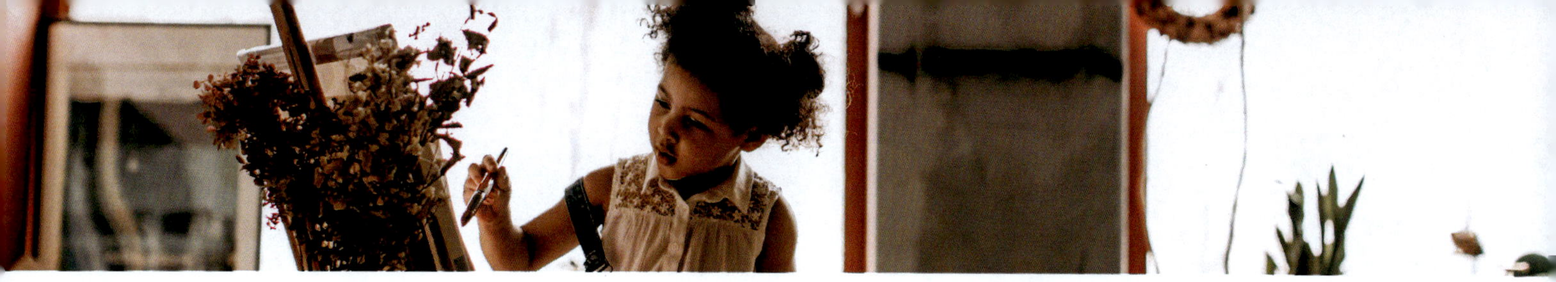

TEMPERATURE AND KELVIN MEASURE

Having a daylight setting (or cooler type) temperature of light is best in your work area. Michaelangelo's candle was about 1800 K, we are looking for about 5000 K (Kelvin)

INTENSITY AND LUMENS MEASURE

Measuring light values (equally important element in your drawing and paintings) can be harder if your ambient light is too weak or too strong. The distance between the light source and your easel or table surface can be adjusted. You can get the white of your canvas or paper closer to what it would be in daylight.

WATTAGE

This will vary depending on size of the room, distance of your easel or table from the light. (Watts measure the power required to meet the functions of the appliance). Wattage is less important than lumens and Kelvin.

ANGLES FOR YOUR LIGHTING

At 45 Degrees from the side and behind is the ideal angle to avoid glare or shadows.

DISTANCE

Ideally get a portable tall lamp stand (can be moved as required), or you can move your easel to be in a better location/distance/ angle to your light source(s) if that is all you have.

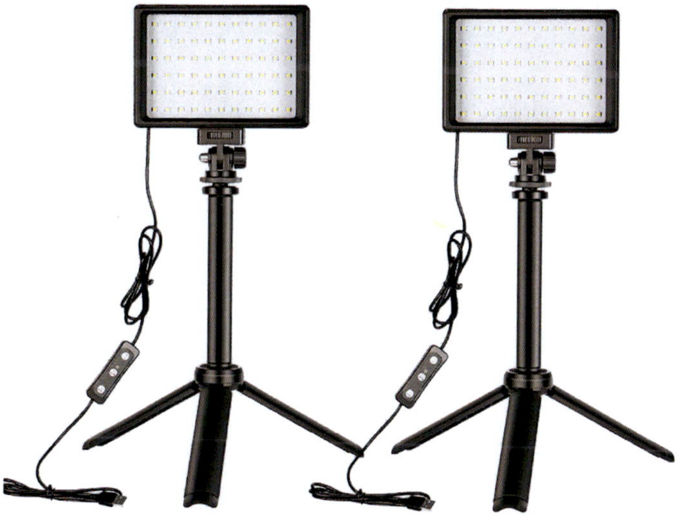

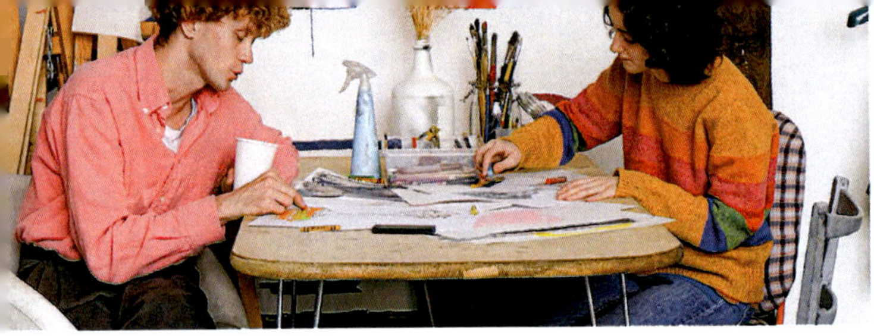

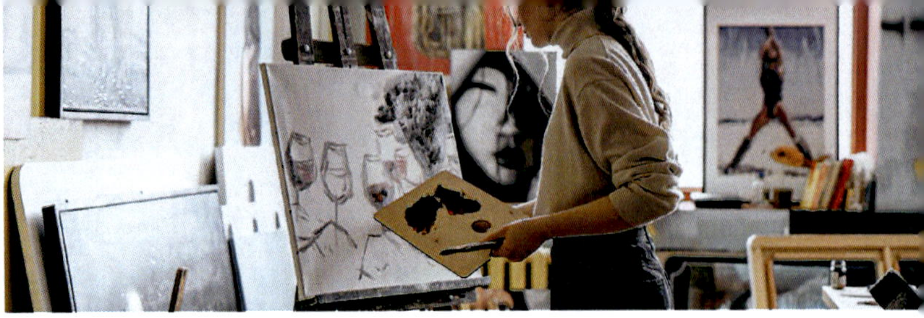

One light on either side is ideal, but suspended above a desk if you paint flat is a great option too if you find yourself in a spot where you could practically arrange and fit this (having said that, tilting your canvas or pad a little with a book or similar, at least 30 degrees is better for equally visualizing the proportions properly).

TYPES OF LIGHT FITTINGS

LED PANELS - Since I moved into my new studio (where the electrician who: quote- "knows how to light a studio" installed wall mounted spotlights (!!!) I have since installed portable LED panels on the ceiling, but you can also get these from hardware and electrical suppliers with a stand and they come with options of warm, cool and daylight (that way if you are setting up in a bedroom, lounge room or similar, they can easily be tucked way after use).

CFL BULBS

If you only have the option of using current fittings and putting a better bulb for the job, look for Compact Fluorescent Light Bulbs eg. 45W , 5500 K, CFL Daylight bulb (Emart). Then move your desk or easel around to avoid glare, shadows or then uneven spread of light.

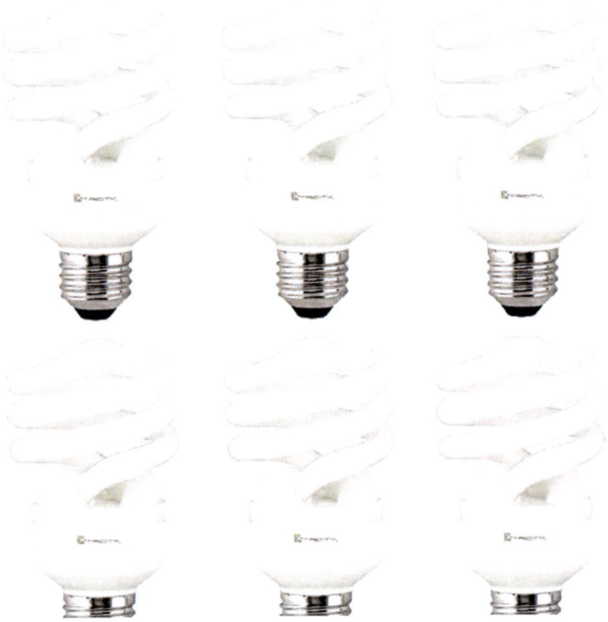

EASEL, WORK STATION OR DESK?

Many people have a picture of a 'real' artist toiling away at an easel, so one of the first things they out on their shopping list is an easel. Outlined next are a few alternatives.

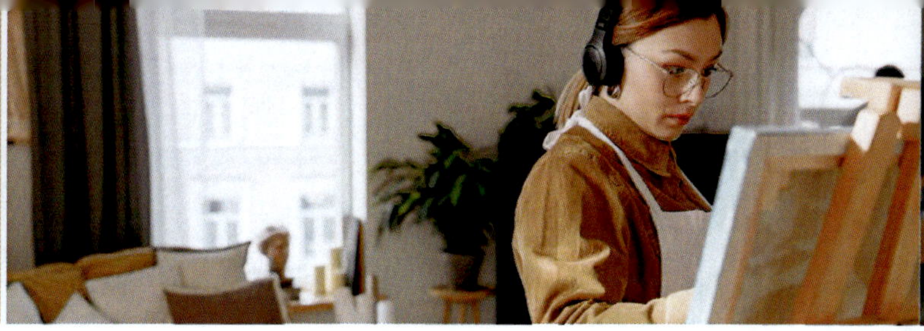
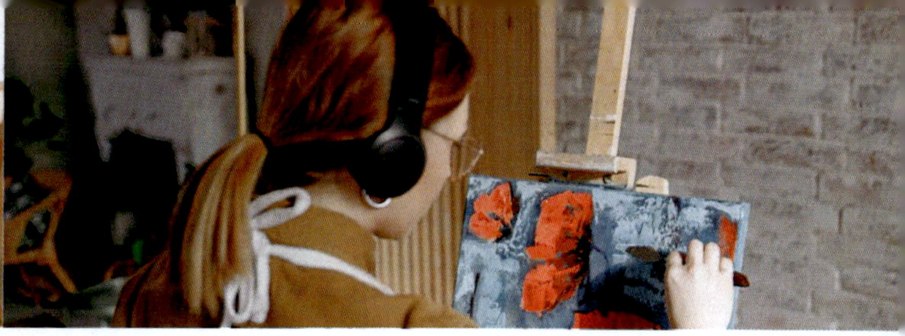

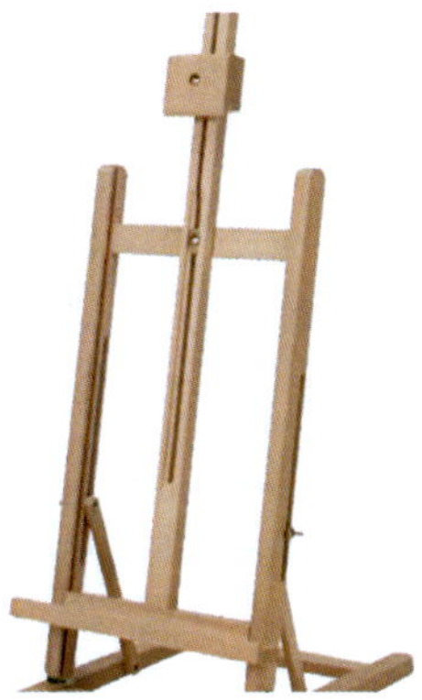

Before discussing easels, let me just point out that millions of excellent paintings and drawings have been created on a table, desk, on the floor or even hanging on the wall, so if you don't try all methods you may end up with an easel when you actually prefer to work another way.

DESK EASEL

These can be found fairly affordably but many students claim that they get a tired arm when starting out (not accustomed to holding their arm up for long periods). One advantage of a desk/ workstation is the arm resting capability which is also great for fine motor control that requires a lot of practice when starting out. You can also rest all of your arm except thewrist and fingers if you use a book or wedge on the table)

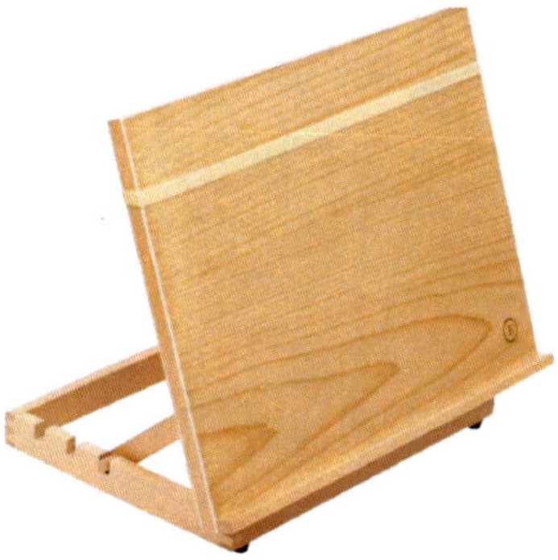

STANDING EASELS

These come in endless sizes and designs and in most cases can be adjusted for you to either sit or stand. Oil painters tend to use a 'mahl stick' to rest their painting hand on, mostly to not drag it across wet areas, but in effect it is also a way to rest and stabilize their arm/hand.

Prices vary enormously. Types include simple A-frame, tripod (good for outdoor paintings trips and if you need to store in a tight space.)

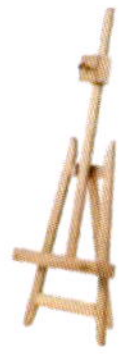
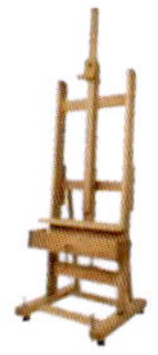
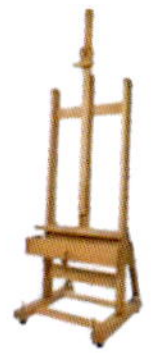
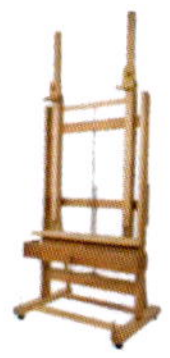

and solid portable ones on wheels, ideal for larger canvases (and you can move them to follow the natural light around!).

When we get questions about 'art stations', we suggest one that has a horizontal space as well as the tilted desk part (for palette, brushes, water etc), as the others (right) are best mainly for drawing media and drafting.

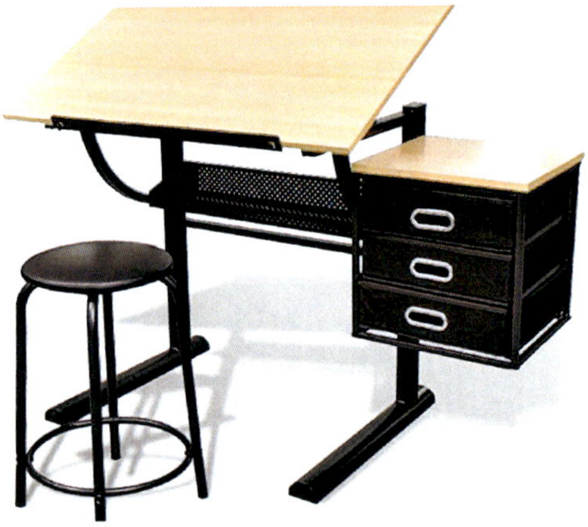

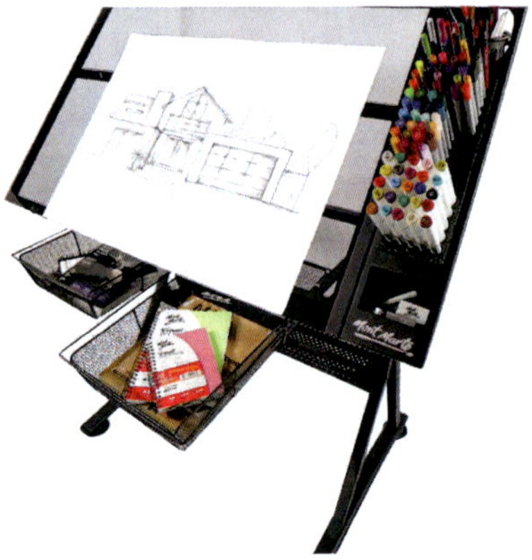

FLAT STUDY DESK

If you just have a desk available, cover the desk, make a strong cardboard angled wedge or use a fat book(s) to lean your canvas on (and don't put your glass of wine or your cup of tea near your water jar or you know what you will end up washing your brushes in!!) He-he...I have almost done it!

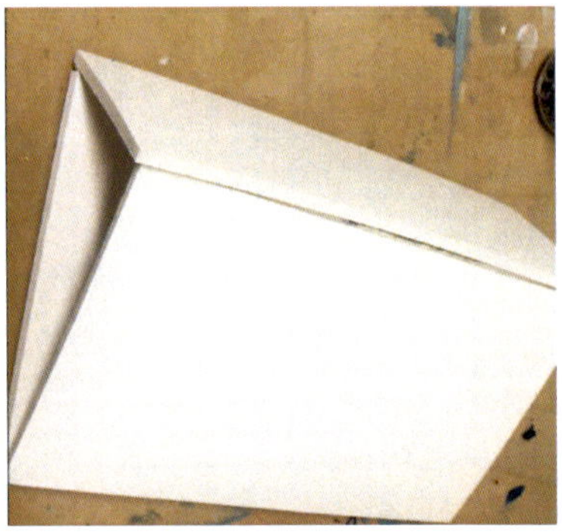

THE WALL

I lived by the beach in Brazil for a time and worked upstairs looking out over the ocean (those were the days my friends). I used to hang the large canvases on the outside wall and for the few small ones I undertook, they leaned on a 45 degree angle on the table.

FLOOR PROTECTION

If your 'studio' is also your shared lounge or other household room, use waterproof floor coverings (like house painters use) if you want to avoid paint or painty water from causing a new permanent (unwanted) look. If you get to use the garage, you could worry less (and there would possibly be more framework options for hanging LED light panels above.)

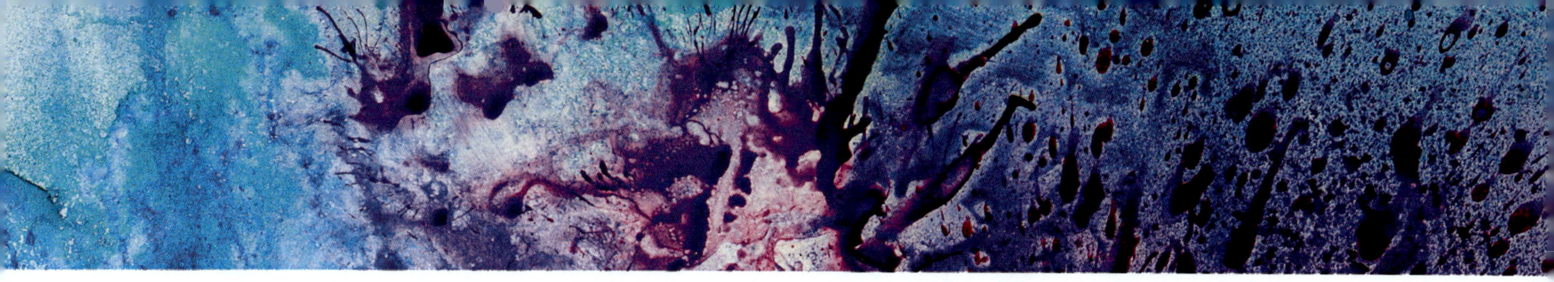

THE STUDIES OF PSYCHOLOGY & BIOLOGY OF COLOR

Psychological studies tell us that each color group has varying psychological influences for humans (? and some animals). Note: Color psychology is also considered a theory and not an absolute and many of the studies are quite anecdotal.

The whole concept has become extremely popular in marketing, art, design, fashion, and many other areas where colors and emotions are thought to be important. Here I have collated some ideas from different sources. Do some more research if it is interesting to you.

It is my conclusion that the 'emotions of color' are actually very personal, subjective and also highly swayed by cultural influences, although there are some general commonalities.

"Colors, like features, follow the changes of the emotions." **Pablo Picasso**

BASED GENERALLY ON ON COLOR PSYCHOLOGY STUDIES OVER MORE THAN TWO CENTURIES

The generally accepted model of color psychology relies on six basic principles:

All Colors can carry a specific meaning.

Color meaning is either based in learned meaning or biologically innate meaning.

The perception of a color causes evaluation automatically by the person perceiving.

The evaluation process forces color-motivated behavior.

Color usually exerts its influence automatically.

Color meaning and effect has a lot to do with context as well.

SOME STUDIES declare that even the color of a placebo pill can actually influence the 'effects' on the subjects in a study of pharmaceuticals. I will mention a few of these study's suggestions over the next pages but none of them reflect an absolute irrefutable finding.

Generalized findings about each color are shown.

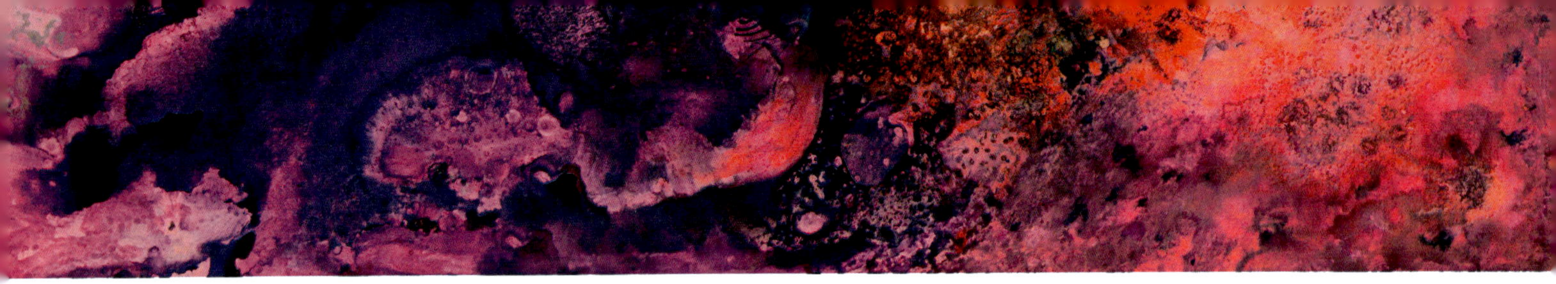

THE STUDIES OF PSYCHOLOGY & BIOLOGY OF COLOR

MAGENTA - (Pink) Our primary color (in modern triadic color theory). - associated with uniqueness, confidence, compassion, maturity, femininity, playfulness, cuteness, love, romance, joy, kindness, sincerity, sweetness, certainty. (it is worth noting that different shades (from light to dark) have variations in their common perceptions. Also not known by many, pink was not perceived as a feminine only color (in American, European cultures at least) until the 1930s-40s -50s.

Biology - (Pink is not appearing in a lot of the research, but it has been implied that pale pink can lower blood pressure, whereas red can raise one's blood pressure. Go figure!!

"Now I really feel the landscape, I can be bold and include every tone of blue and pink: it's enchanting, it's delicious."   Claude Monet

RED-ORANGE - called just 'red' in most studies, not to be confused with primary red (magenta), vibrant fire-engine red has associations with energy, excitement, heat, passion, love, lust, blood, power, danger, strength, courage. Red symbolises luck in China and yet mourning in South Africa. In general, dark, medium and light shades of colors seem to imply quite varied symbology.

Biology - Red is said to increase appetite. Scientific studies did not confirm the anecdotal signs that this color raises blood pressure or rate of respiration. (Biological studies seem to be mainly undertaken on red, green and blue)

"If one says 'Red' – the name of color – and there are fifty people listening, it can be expected that there will be fifty reds in their minds. And one can be sure that all these reds will be very different."   Josef Albers

ORANGE - seems to average symbology thats a little cross between red and yellow, said to symbolise individuality, creativity, youth, enthusiasm, warmth, acceptance, and positivity, ruggedness, excitement, encouragement, optimism, self-confidence, affordability, creation , autumn (fall)

"Orange is red brought nearer to humanity by yellow." Wassily Kandinsky

BROWN - reliability, stability, wholesomeness, honesty, sincerity, wisdom, comfort , grounded, protected, grief (on the negative side grief, boredom, timidity, predictability) Dark brown is strong, but sometimes also sad and depressing.

1946 -on trying to paint a pale blue sky...

'I cannot pretend to be impartial about the colors. I rejoice with the brilliant ones, and am genuinely sorry for the poor browns.' Winston Churchill

YELLOW - Competence, happiness, hope, spontaneity, Also inexpensive, low quality , the mind or intellect, logic, new ways, uplifting, energy, cheerful, hopeful, fun, happiness (too much yellow? -cheapness, anxiety, nervousness, caution, visual fatigue, agitation, apprehension, impatience, criticism, cowardice, deceit)

Biology - can increase appetite (it is stated that people lose their temper more and babies cry more in yellow rooms)

"How wonderful yellow is. It stands for the sun." -Vincent Van Gogh.

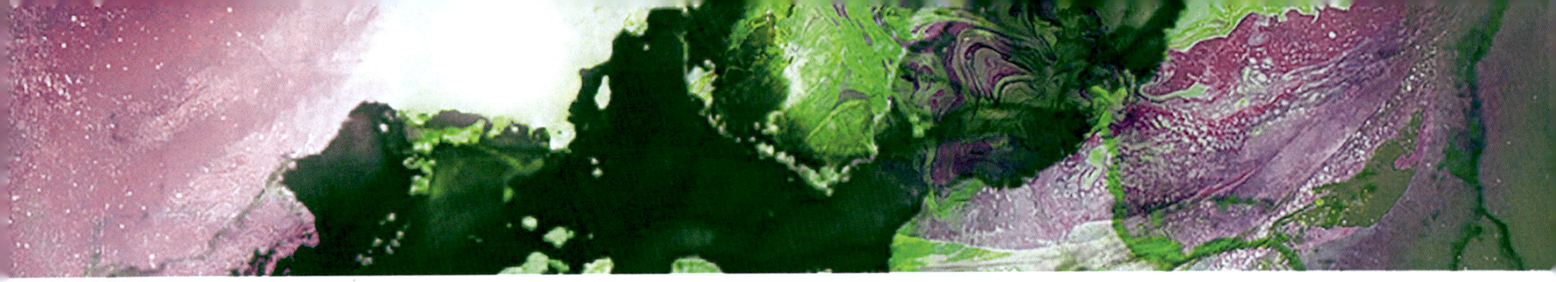

THE STUDIES OF PSYCHOLOGY & BIOLOGY OF COLOR

GREEN - good taste, good luck, eco-friendly, nature, growth, balance, health, harmony, healing, stability, rebirth, organic, freshness, money (?too much - envy, greed, jealousy, selfishness, nausea).

Biology - relieves stress, promotes healing, promotes memory, also said to relieve migraines.

"Absolute green is the most restful color, lacking any undertone of joy, grief, or passion. On exhausted men, this restfulness has a beneficial effect, but after a time it becomes tedious."
-Wassily Kandinsky

YELLOW-GREEN - (commonly referred to as Chartreuse in design circles.)
The tertiary color yellow-green is generally perceived to be an exciting and vibrant shade, inspiring feelings of joy and cheeriness. Chartreuse is said to represent enthusiasm, happiness, growth, nature, and youth. Like standard green, chartreuse is associated with the blooming of spring. Some sources combine a mixture of attributes normally given to green or yellow.

"The world is exploding in emerald, sage, and lusty chartreuse - neon green with so much yellow in it. It is an explosive green that, if one could watch it moment by moment throughout the day, would grow in every dimension."
Amy Seidl

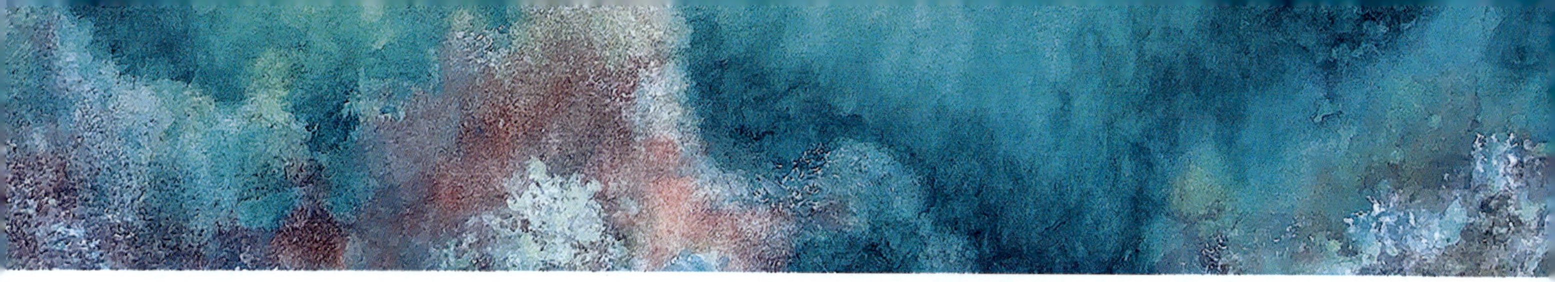

BLUE-GREEN - (aqua, teal, turquoise) sea, health, peace, calm, abundance
Biology - Exposure to light in the morning, and blue/green light in particular, prompts the release of the hormone cortisol which stimulates and wakes us, and inhibits the release of melatonin. In the late evening as the amount of blue light in sunlight is reduced, melatonin is released into the bloodstream and we become drowsy.

'My personal symbolism for blue-green (turquoise) has always been joy and happiness (like they say yellow is a symbol of this for most)'. **Jennifer Webb**

A British study on how color affects the brain found that after painting London's Blackfriar Bridge blue-green (it was raw black iron), suicides from the bridge dropped by a noticable 34 per cent. A similar Japanese study on suicides had even more striking results.

BLUE - Sophistication, trust, honesty, competence, high-quality, corporate, reliability, serenity, peace, conservatism, solitude, predictability, intelligence, responsibility, dependability, calming (?Navy - can appear boring, rigid, conservative.) Blue can sometimes seem icy, distant, or even cold. Too much blue is associated with sadness (Think about paintings that feature swathes of blue, such as those produced by Picasso during his 'Blue period', they can seem so lonely and sad.) What about when they 'sing the Blues', definitely about the down side of blue.
Biological - slowing the pulse rate and reducing appetite. (anecdotal evidence only).

"Sun-bleached bones were most wonderful against the blue – that blue that will always be there as it is now after all man's destruction is finished." – **Georgia O'Keeff**

THE STUDIES OF PSYCHOLOGY & BIOLOGY OF COLOR

INDIGO (Blue-violet) - Generally, it's stated that Indigo seems to represent our deepest thoughts and spiritual wisdom. The blue in Indigo implies reliability, communication, meditation and peace while the Violet speaks to the higher self, mystery, inspiration, intuition.

VIOLET - (not exactly purple), the word is derived from a word Greek via Latin (purpura) for a red-violet color derived from sea snails, so violet is essentially the secondary color alongside purple (see red-violet). Violet, in our triadic 12 part color wheel, is slightly more towards blue than what is commonly known as purple) They are studied as one in psychological terms it seems.

Commonly signifying: royalty, wealth, luxury, sophistication, spirituality, fantasy, ambition, imagination, creativity, deep thinking (?too much- immature, impractical)

"Color is the keyboard, the eyes are the harmonies, the soul is the piano with many strings. The artist is the hand that plays, touching one key or another, to cause vibrations in the soul."
Wassily Kandinsky

RED-VIOLET -(purple) warmth, sophistication, power (darker shades can represent sadness and frustration). In some parts of Europe, purple is associated with death and mourning. In writing, the phrase "purple prose" is sometimes used to describe writing that is extremely imaginative or even prone to exaggeration, hyperbole, or outright lies.

Mauve is just pink trying to be purple. ~James Abbott McNeill Whistler (1834–1903)

BLACK - happiness, sophistication, exclusivity, power, elegance, protection (negatives: fear, expensive). Can be seen as cool, intimidating and unapproachable.

"Before, when I didn't know what color to put down, I put down black. Black is a force: I depend on black to simplify the construction. Now I've given up blacks." -Henri Matisse

WHITE - purity, virginity, sincerity, minimalist simplicity

Biology - An all-white room with fluorescent lights can strain your eyes to the point that just being in the room can lead to headaches and anxiety (and the subsequent release of the stress hormone cortisol, which has it own health implications).

"Such a magnificent sky, and it's nothing but white paper!"
Pierre-Auguste Renoir

No indisputable scientific evidence was discovered yet but there are many broadly agreed upon generalizations across cultural boundaries.

https://www.sciencealert.com/does-colour-really-affect-our-brain-and-body-a-professor-of-colour-science-explains
https://99designs.com.au/blog/tips/color-meanings/
https://www.verywellmind.com/the-color-psychology-of-purple-2795820

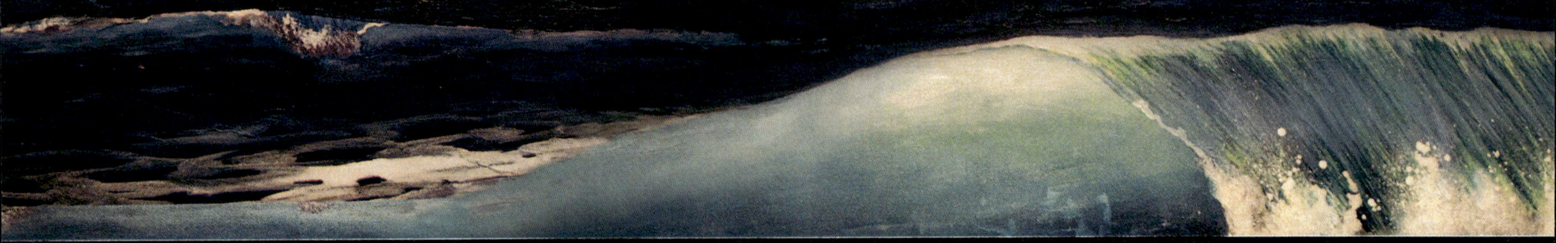

CREATE SOME STRINGS FOR THE 12 HUES AROUND THE WHEEL

QR login is on p.177 to download extra templates for practising more strings and wheels. Print some for each medium you need to practice in. You can also watch some video demonstrations of mixing. Mixing tints and shades of all hues is great preparation for creating your wheels.

NB. We have no control over the printing process, but we expect if you have the paperback workbook, any orange or violet will appear a little neutral compared to the e-book, which is in RGB. Just mix yours as vibrant as your pigments allow. String and wheel printed colors are a hue guide only.

A 'string' is commonly made by mixing gradations of white with a hue, resulting in successively lighter tints of the hue. We also make gradations of shades (darker tones of a color or hue).

YOU HAVE 3 WAYS TO MIX A SHADE OF A HUE

Advanced method - needs some practice but the most harmonious chromatic grays are created as shown in the next pages by determining the exact mixing hue partner .

To the left of the main hue are two gradations of tints, made by adding a little white, then a little more. To the right you need to discover the perfect complementary hue to make gradations of neutral shades on the way to a rich gray for each hue.

Quick Hack Method - you can try both ways in these next exercises and make your own comparisons. Make your own 'Natural Black' with dark brown (Burnt Umber) and Ultramarine Blue. Add a little, then a little more until you reach the darkest shade of each hue in your shade strings.

The Dirty Harry Method - add a bonafide black pigment PBk7, 9, 11, little by little. It was how many artists have done it over the years, as their pigment ranges were more limited.

Try out your mixes on a spare palette or paper first, then add to your workbook. Use medium specific paper for any other medium you want to use for color mixing practice.

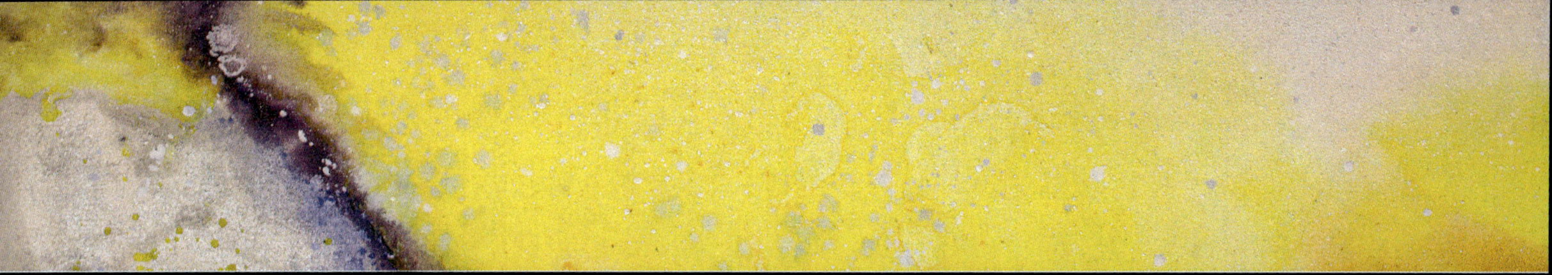

MIXING A YELLOW STRING OF TINTS AND SHADES

First, make your complementary color for yellow. ie. secondary violet. Use Ultramarine blue and primary red (Magenta) in amounts that end up making a violet with no obvious red or blue bias. You will know it is a good partner for your yellow when it mixes to a nice neutral rich chromatic gray. This may take some back and forward, and this is normal for everyone learning. Do your strings of all of the partner pairs at the same time, it's a logical tactic to save time.

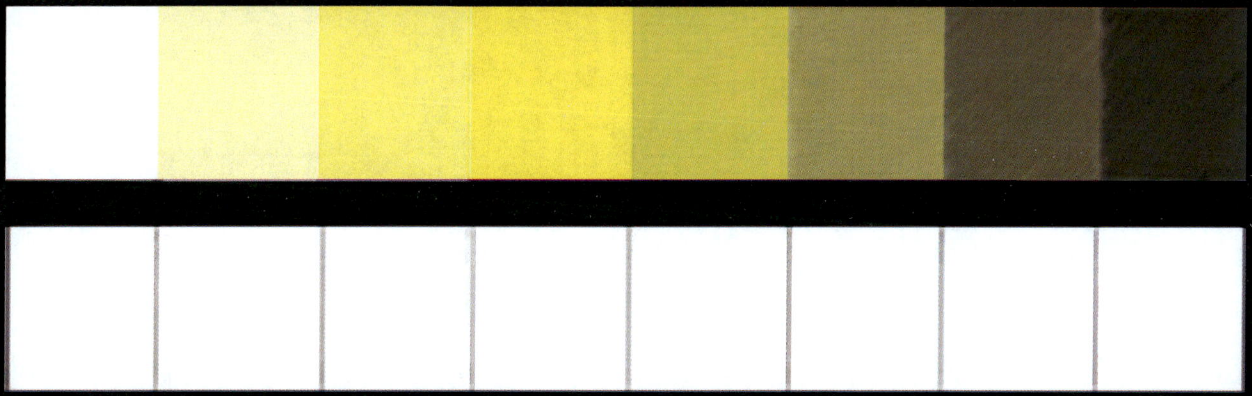

TIPS

- If you get a greenish gray, this means that the violet you mixed has a blue bias Just remember that green is opposite magenta on the wheel, so add a tiny bit more magenta to your violet now and test again in a new area of your palette. Always add tiny amounts, mix, test and repeat until you get the gray you are aiming for.
- If you get a brownish gray, (blue is opposite the browns, which all come from orange, yellow-orange and red-orange) so add a tiny bit more blue to your violet mix and try again in a clean area of palette (with a clean brush).
- Once you get a gray-ish hue with no heavy bias towards green or brown, make up at least 20 ml of that exact secondary violet, store it in a small jar and label it and add a swatch.
- All violets can all appear harmonious included with yellow in a scheme, but only the true secondary violet for your yellow is going to make nice rich shadows for primary yellow subjects.

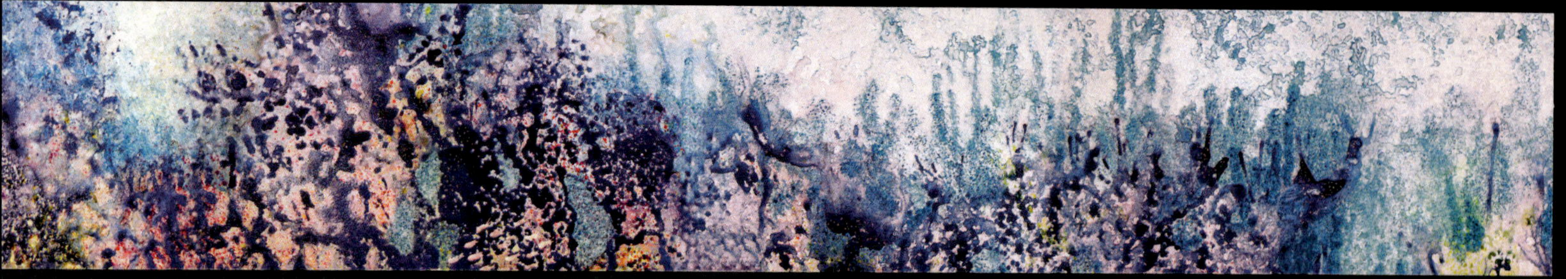

MIXING SECONDARY VIOLET TINTS AND SHADES

Since you have already made a mixture of secondary violet when you were doing the exercise for a Primary Yellow string, this one will be very straight forward. You will simply add your primary yellow in small increments until you have the rich gray for violet. There are a few important tricks here to get the darkest shade (since your yellow is opaque it will not give the very darkest of gray, and you may be wanting this at some point). For a very dark gray related most harmoniously to violet, you can:

- Use your natural black (made with Burnt Umber and Ultramarine Blue), in fact this hack is the standard go-to for many who want to darken any hue without using the direct complement.(as opposed to the old black hack (with Mars or Carbon black) which deadens the color somewhat more (do a comparison some time and decide for yourself)
- Use a transparent yellow (eg. PY3 Hansa , PY150 Azo or PY42 Transparent Yellow Iron Oxide to create the shades (once you have a transparent pigment for each primary, not essential to get started). You will use a whole lot more pigment this way though.. One day, when you find yourself using a lot of violet(s) and you want to buy a dedicated tube or pot, you will not find one that sits exactly opposite your primary yellow. No probs! You now know how to balance the resulting bias when making shadow mixes and in a scheme it will harmonize well enough as long as it is vaguely opposite. Pay attention to the lightfastness ratings of single pigment violets and red-violets.

Actually one of the most lightfast secondary violets is the one you can mix yourself with your Ultramarine Blue, PR 29 and Quinacridone Magenta PR 122. A Dioxazine violet PV 27 will need a little blue added, as it leans a bit into Red-violet. (PV23 is not as lightfast). In each medium, there are dedicated violet pigments, just check for lightfastness and opacity, buy those you love the look of (but it's always advisable to see it spread thinly if you possibly can)...maybe not all visitors to art stores do this but we have gotten away with it for decades! We want to see its undertones and transparency/ opacity so we ask and they allow usually.

Fig 2   The chrome cocktail shaker in this still life (from one of our advanced students) was executed in rich dark grays with the violet and yellow from this tetradic scheme.

NOTE-the image does include a small amount of green (technically not in this planned tetrad) but because they neutralized it very well, it does not interfere in the overall harmony. Think about all the possible uses for a rich gray from violet and its complementary partner yellow. (including the shadows on the fruit here).

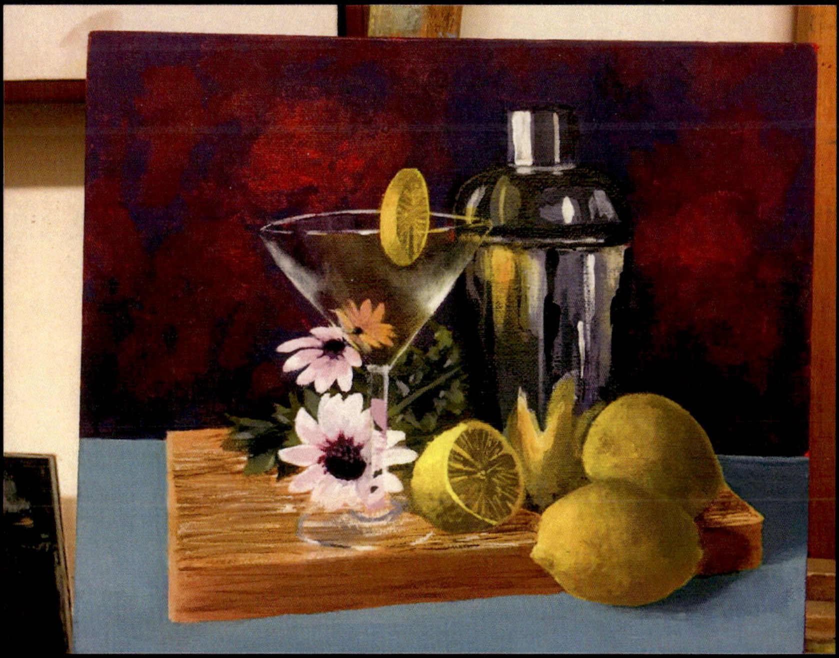

MIXING A BLUE-VIOLET STRING OF TINTS AND SHADES

Sometimes referred to as Indigo, Tertiary Blue-violet is opposite Yellow-Orange on the triadic color wheel. Ultramarine Blue, for example, sits just inside this sector of hues, so adding a touch of your primary red can take the hue toward the middle of this range (of course too much will take it over more to secondary violet or on to red-violet).

The common challenge is deciding which tertiary to add some blue or red to (your own mixes of Blue-violet and / or it's partner yellow-orange can both be tweaked so that the grays are not too brown or too green. (as usual if it gets to a brownish gray, simply add a little more Ultramarine to your Blue-violet mix and try again. If it ends up a greenish gray, you could add more magenta to either as it is plays a part of each these hues.

Indigo (the dye) has a dark history, being responsible in part for fueling of the slave trade and even trade wars. From the plant indigofera tinctoria the color is very lightfast, lasting well past the yellows and reds of many old tapestries.
Considered "Blue Gold." It died out along with legal slavery.

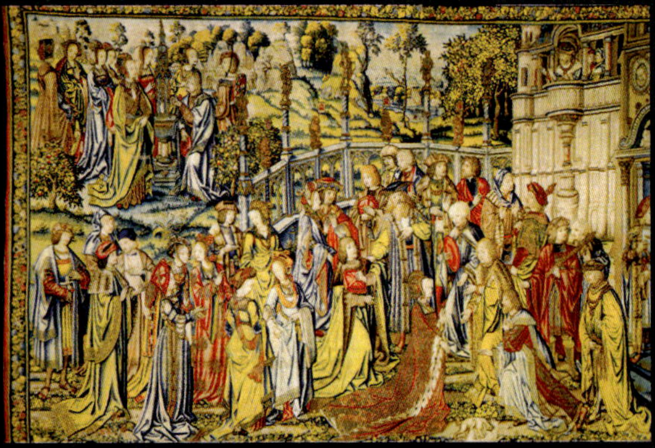

MIXING A YELLOW-ORANGE STRING OF TINTS AND SHADES

Follow the instructions as above for a blue-violet hue as the partner for your yellow-orange (you could use the same violet if you already made up a jar and add some more Ultramarine blue to a sample).Then add a tiny bit of magenta to the yellow to make some yellow orange.

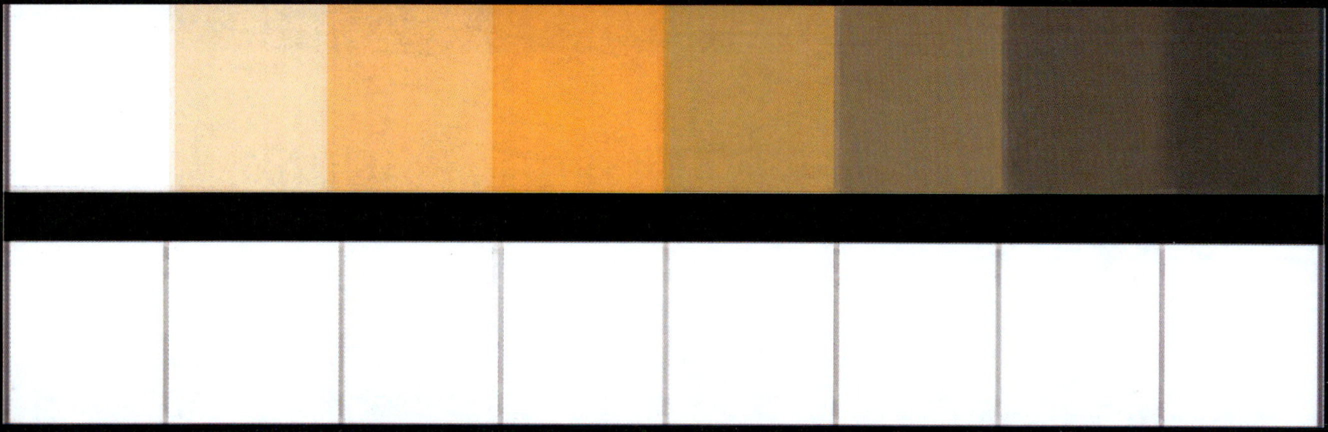

Now you are testing two tertiaries, so if your gray is greenish, a little red could be added to either mixture, if it has a brownish bias, more blue is required in your Blue-violet.

Fig 3

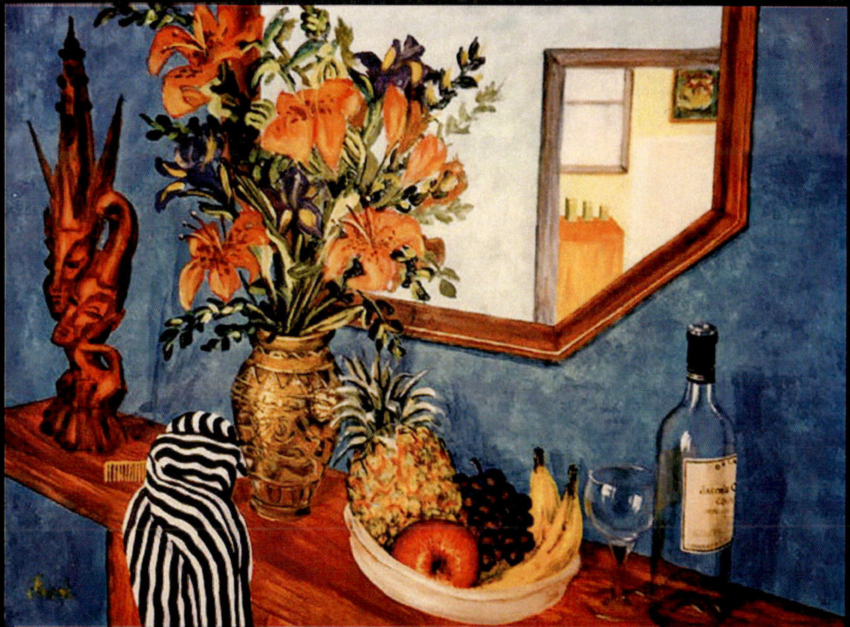

Making an object look metallic can be made easier with a nice pre-mixed string. (of course any reflected colors can appear as well and add to the realism)

This brass vase was made using a yellow-orange string of tints and shades.

MIXING A SECONDARY ORANGE STRING OF TINTS AND SHADES

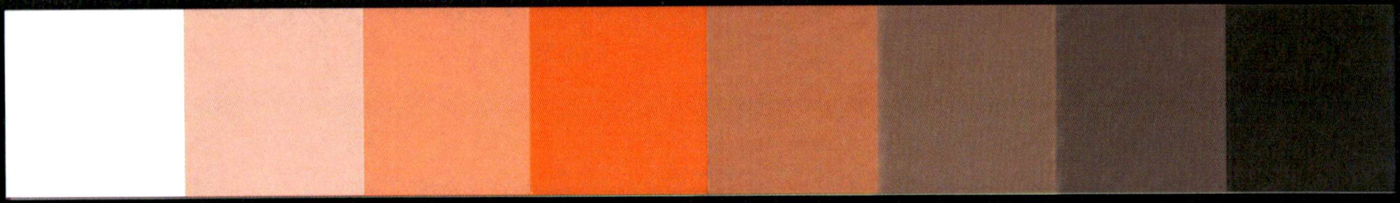

Essentially, you could choose any blue you love to call your primary, but what is most essential (when mixing shade strings etc.) is that your secondary orange is made to perfectly mix a chromatic grey with your chosen primary blue.

Add yellow to your Magenta until the orange you are mixing can make a chromatic gray with your chosen primary blue.

You can mix this orange into a new little jar, name it, also mix the blue and call that your Primary Blue

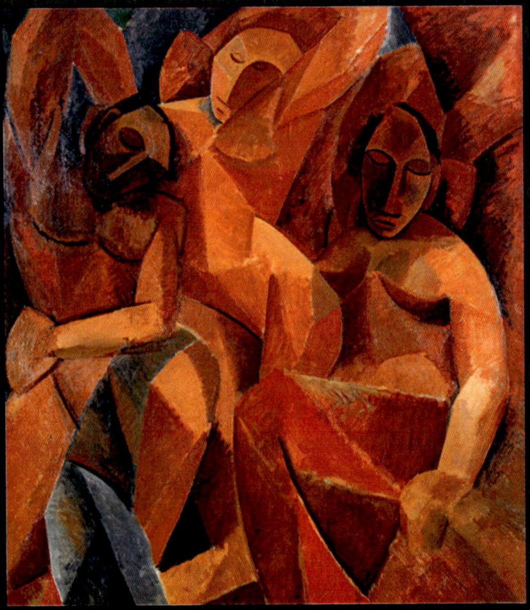

NB. Phthalo Blue (PB 15:3 can be a bit hard to work with due to its strong green bias). It is stunning in mixing turquoises, but makes dull violets.

Use your primary blue and the orange that you mixed with your red and yellow (either magenta, or the red-orange you already mixed plus a little more yellow). As you saw in previous string mixing exercises, the most neutral gray is achieved by balancing any bias when you are testing your two partners.

Fig 4

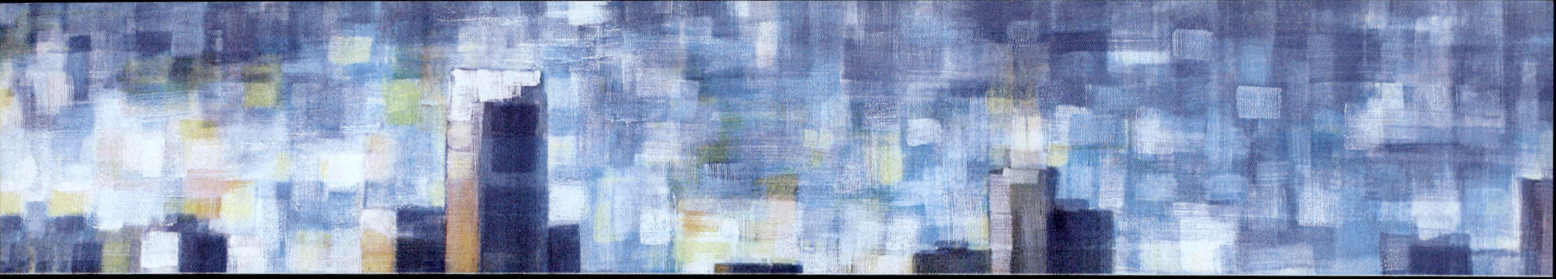

MIXING A PRIMARY BLUE STRING OF TINTS AND SHADES

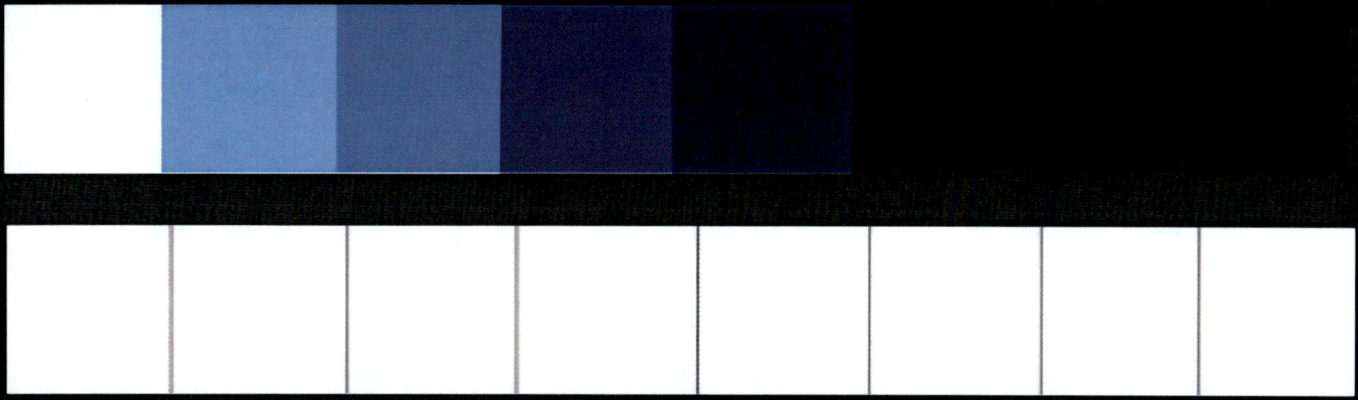

While preparing for the tints and shade strings of orange you would have arrived at your choice of primary blue (by reaching a nice rich grey with the two partners).

If you have just one blue pigment to call your primary (and it is lighter in it's mass tone than a Phthalo Blue eg. Cerulean or Cobalt), there will be no way to make nice deep blues or deep rich grays. This is why we suggest that your first priorities for blues could be (untinted) Phthalo Blue 15:3 and Ultramarine PB 29, then make a mix of both : 1 part Phthalo Blue to 4 parts Ultramarine. They are both dark in masstone so you can mix a greater range of tints and shades, plus you now have a warm blue, a cool blue and new blue mix that is somewhere in the middle.(or if you can get only one blue you could get red-shade phthalo Pb 15:1, it is less red shade(violet bias) than Ultramarine Blue and at least it is dark in masstone).

If you have a bigger budget for more Blues, you could splurge on many hues eg. Cobalt blue, Cerulean blue, Indanthrene blue (not available in many brands), or all the turquoises and indigos and any number of them depending on the medium you choose...BUT.... to learn the most and mix the most by buying the least to start, my vote is for Phthalo Blue-green shade and Ultramarine blue. (4 things for the cost of 2, ie. darkest masstone (more value/tonal options), a cool blue (better for mixing blue-greens), a warm blue (best for mixing violets) and when mixed , another blue hue close to 'Primary' to partner with your orange).

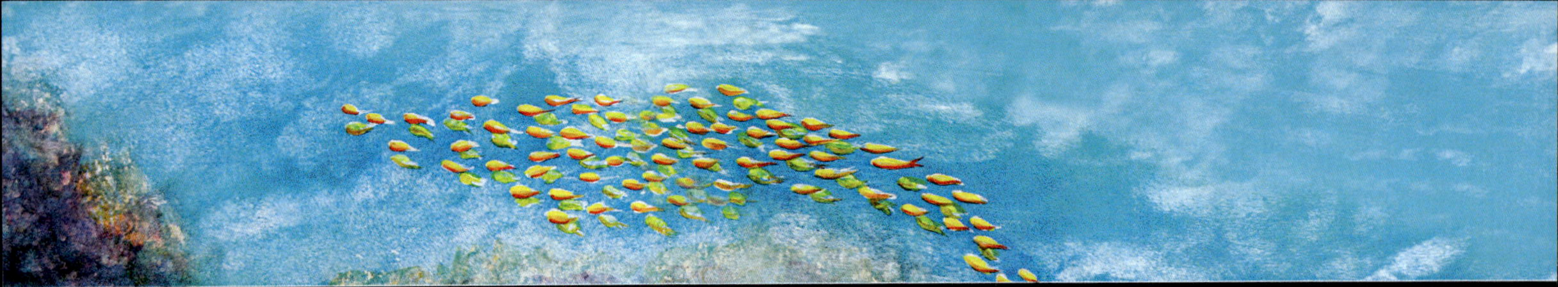

MIXING A TERTIARY BLUE-GREEN STRING OF TINTS AND SHADES

What is not to love about turquoise, teal, aquamarine, robin egg blue! Blue-green is my happy hue. Maybe it is one of the reasons that I object so vehemently when I see a commonly available color wheel turn up so many times with new students who assumed that if it was put there for sale it must be able to truly help them find mixing partners well!

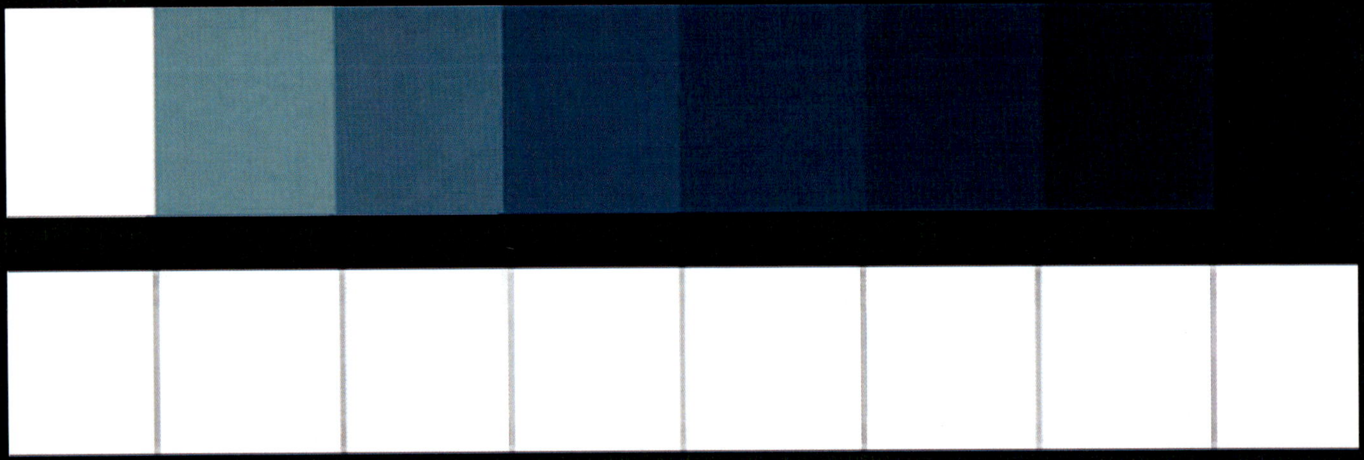

Assuming that all beginners are wanting to know how to mix great harmonious deep values (shades) for their paintings (among many other things), the proposed secondary green found printed opposite the red-orange on these commercial color wheels sold out there must (in my mind) be the single most common reason for the mud mixing challenges of many beginners. Magenta doesn't exist for these wheel manufacturers!

Those fire-engine reds (misleadingly named 'primaries') are screaming out for a mixing partner that is within the blue-green sector of the 12 part triadic color wheel. I am no massive fan of Magenta (was encouraged to girly up and wear it as a kid!) but I do know from years of practical evidential results, that Magenta is the primary red on the triadic wheel and the partner for my beloved blue-green is in fact red-orange (a tertiary by definition since it can be made by adding Yellow to Magenta.)

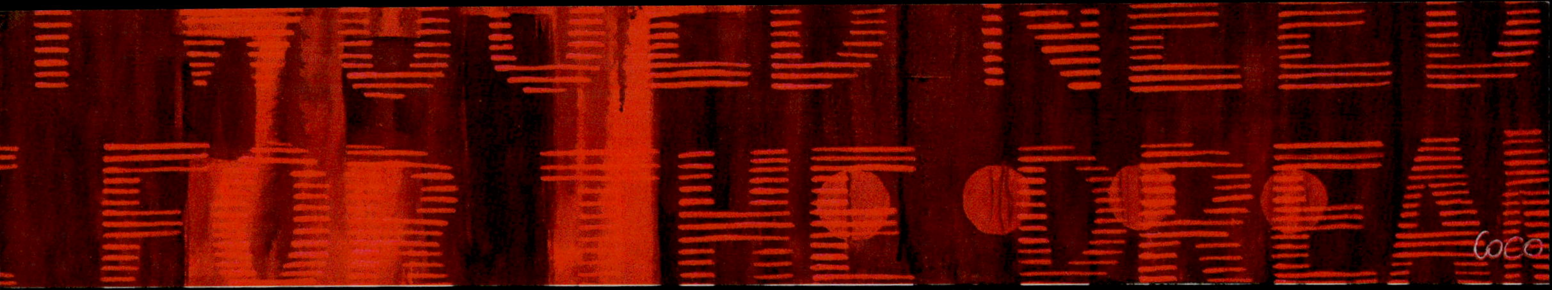

MIXING A TERTIARY RED-ORANGE STRING OF TINTS AND SHADES

To make tertiary red-orange, you need to mix yellow into your primary red (Magenta). You will know you have a good partner when your red-orange makes a rich gray with your blue-green. Too green? Add a touch more primary red to your red-orange mixture until it makes a rich gray with your blue-green partner. Too brown? Add a bit more blue to the blue-green mixture.

Create your strip here using your red-orange and blue-green mixtures.

An example of when an artist could want to deepen and darken a tertiary red with a dark version of it's complement (blue-green).

Fig 5

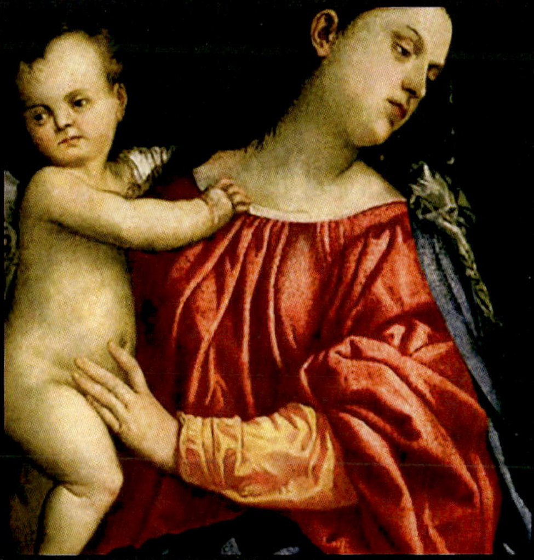

This is a small detail from a Titian work, and actually the clever old masters often glazed the reds transparently in layers over a grisaille (achromatic value-modeled underpainting).The resultant 'luminance' gives a velvet or satin look. Today, most realists would know to find a chromatic shadow color with the complement.

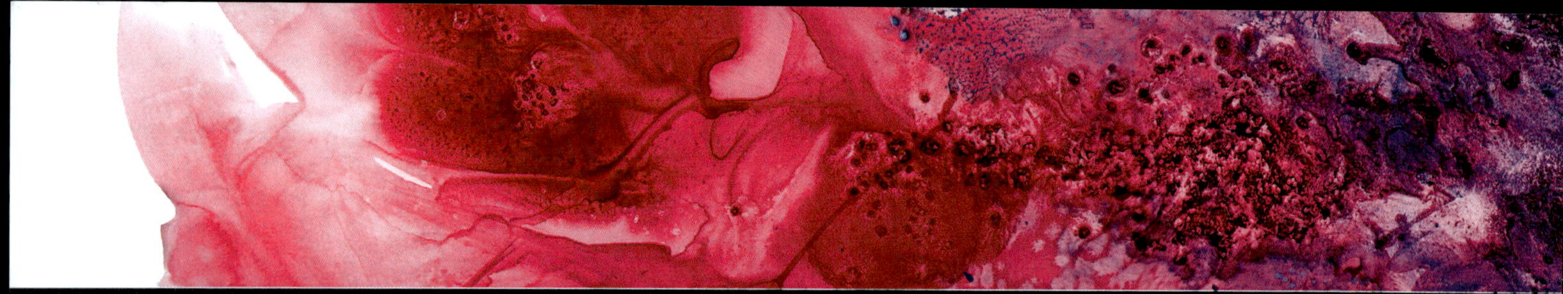

MIXING A PRIMARY MAGENTA STRING OF TINTS AND SHADES

This is where you get to test out your secondary green (assuming you followed our suggestions not to buy a ready-made green). You use Phthalo Blue (green shade) and add yellow until the resultant green makes a rich gray with your magenta (or you would need to adjust for whichever red you chose as your primary), then add successively more magenta to get the shades coming backwards. Of course, just add successive amounts of white to your magenta for the tints.

Refer to the color wheel to remember how to correct a strong brownish tinge in your grays.

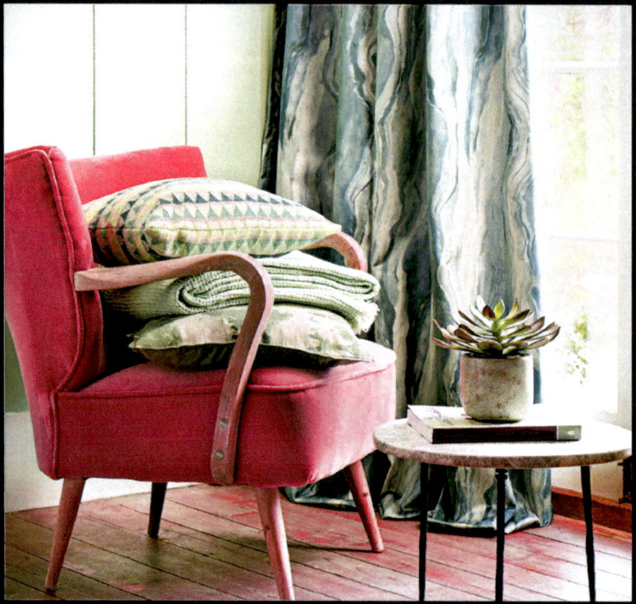

If this was a photo reference you were using to paint an interior scene and you were aiming to show the light, medium and dark tones of pink, mixing a string as you are in this exercise would be a really good plan.

**Abstract schemes benefit as much as representational ones too), from the inclusion of harmonious grays and neutral shades of a hue.

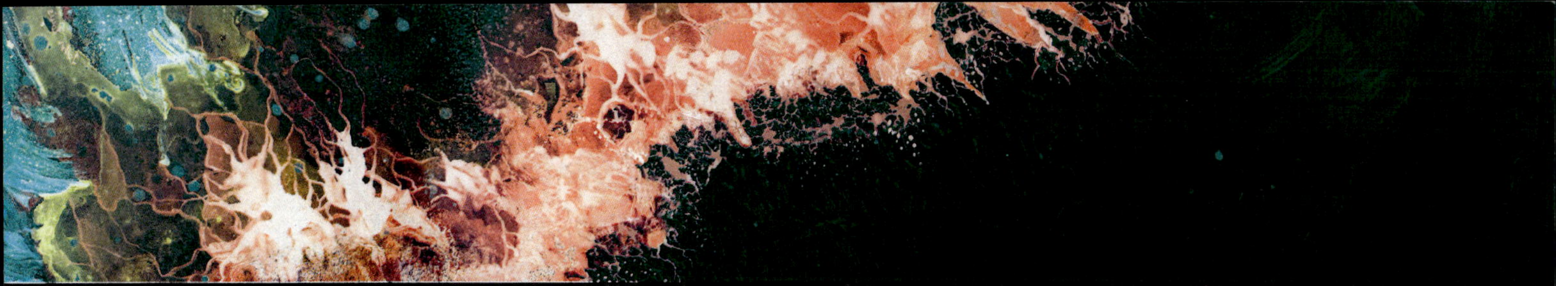

MIXING A SECONDARY GREEN STRING OF TINTS AND SHADES

Your secondary green is going to be the hue that doesn't appear more towards yellow or to blue and will also successfully make a rich gray shade with your primary red (Magenta).

When might you want to mix a succession of grayer versions of a hue? What about in landscape painting? Background and middle distance foliage is never as saturated in hue as is that seen at the very foreground. Values, contrast and detail all vary as well. Studying up on atmospheric or (or aerial) perspective will lead to a desire to learn to create different saturations and values of the same hues.

Fig 6

Renoir has used three greens, Yelow-green, Secondary Green and subtly slightly blued green in the background. There are neutralized versions of the first two which give the shadow areas.

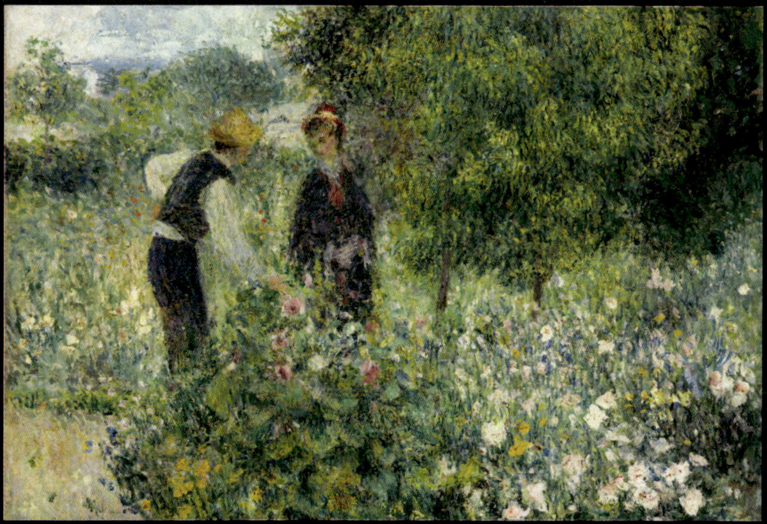

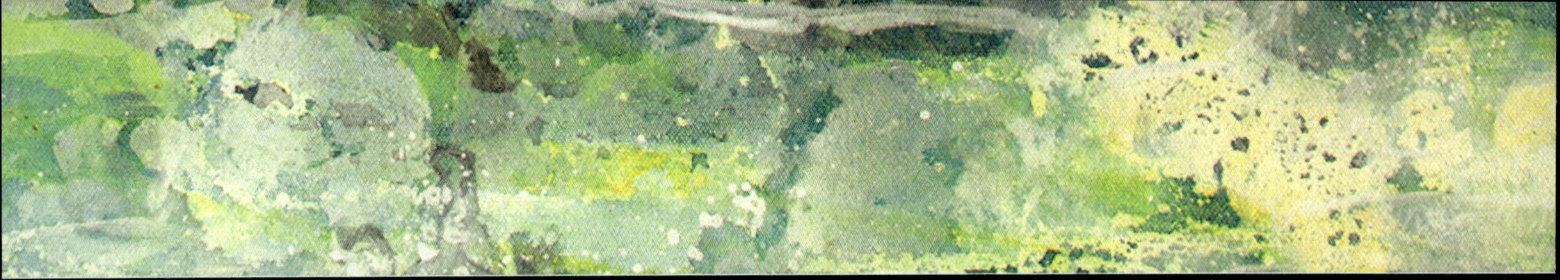

MIXING A TERTIARY YELLOW-GREEN STRING OF TINTS AND SHADES

Your Tertiary yellow-green is going to be the hue that appears more towards yellow than to blue and will also successfully make a rich gray shade with your tertiary red-violet which sits opposite on the wheel (in our case, to start, made with Magenta and Ultramarine Blue). Because both have blue in them, you can adjust either or both to have a bit more blue if your rich grays are looking a bit brownish. Just add successive amounts of white for the tints.

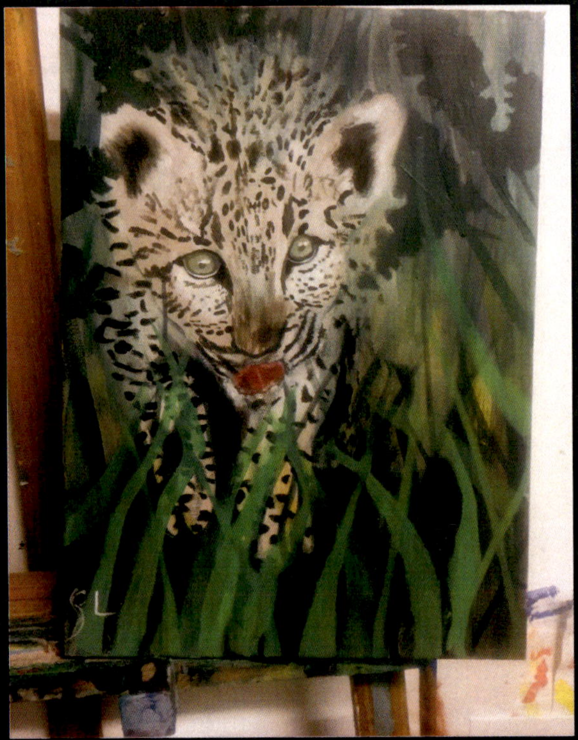

When might you want to mix a succession of grayer versions of a Yellow-green hue? What about in landscape painting? Background and middle distance foliage are never as saturated in hue as the ones seen at the very foreground. Values, contrast and detail all vary as well as saturation.

This little piece was the (demo) result of a group kids holiday workshop on painting wild cats. Kids lap up this kind of knowledge (how to mix complementary colors to make rich grays). Of course they love baby animals too!!

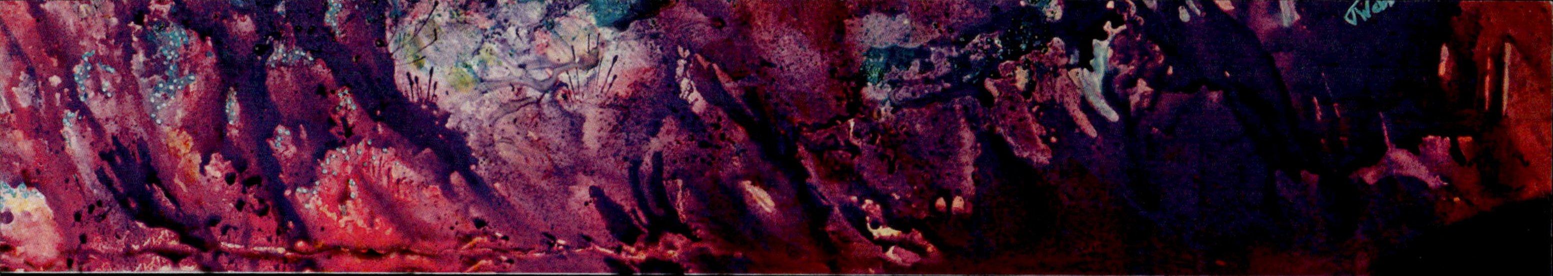

MIXING A TERTIARY RED-VIOLET OF TINTS AND SHADES

You have no doubt realized by now that you will need to mix a tertiary Yellow-green hue to create the shades of the string for Red-violet. So when it comes to balancing the bias of the rich gray, the blue you may need to add (to balance out a brownish look in your shadow gray) could be added into either mixture since they both contain it in some amount. If your chromatic gray leans to green, keep adding tiny bits of red-violet etc.

We should consider ourselves so lucky to have access to amazing red-violet pigments and blues and reds that make great red-violets. There was a time when the effort, time and expense of making this hue (by crushing tons of molluscs) made it only possible for rich patrons or Royals to include it in their art commissions Actually the punishment for using "Tyrian purple" during Caligula's Roman rule was death. It was allowed only for the Emperor Caligula.

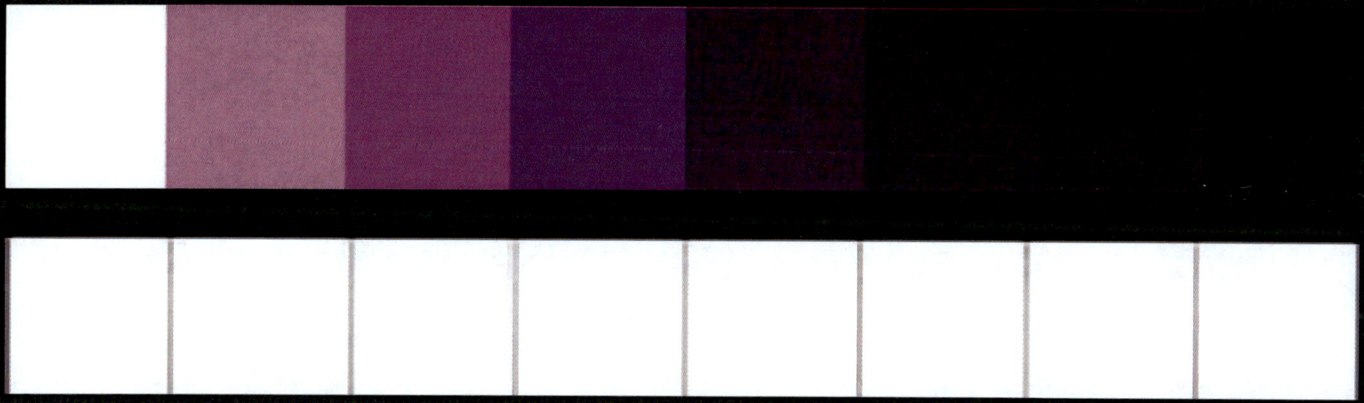

The source we trust the most (especially for researching and selecting watercolor pigments).

Other great links on the subject are in the Resources section Some nice, saturated and lightfast violets are obtained with a mixture of ultramarine blue (PB29) and quinacridone magenta (PR122). So add a bit more red and you get an equally lightfast Red-violet, more Ultramarine blue for a blue-violet.

PV 15 Ultramarine Violet is a good single pigment red-violet as well..

Any violet made with magenta and Phthalo Blue 15:3 will be quite de-saturated.

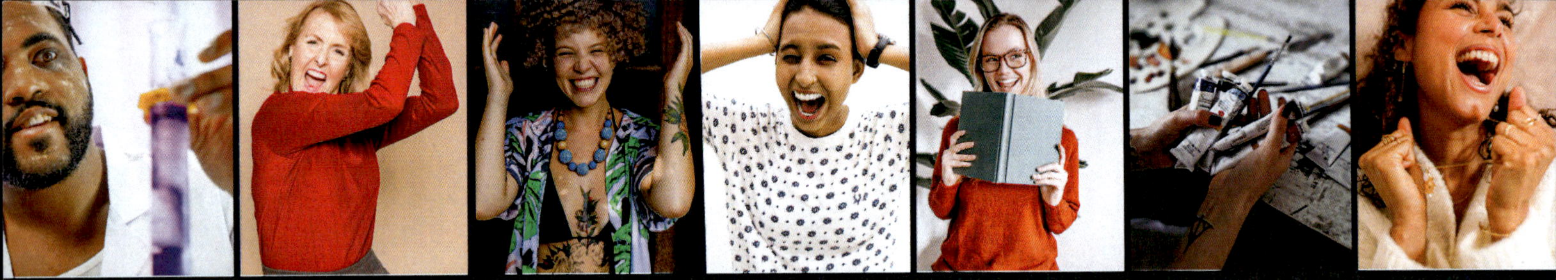

MAKING YOUR OWN COLOR WHEELS AND CREATING SOME HARMONIES

IF THERE WAS A CLIMAX IN THIS WORK BOOK...THIS NEXT SECTION IS IT!!

- Here in your own color workbook, empty wheel templates are provided (for undiluted acrylics or colored pencils) and in addition, once you use your bonus login for the online templates, you can download and print as many wheels as you need. We make one for any medium we work in. If your printer takes watercolor paper and/or A3 paper, you can upsize your wheel and have it on medium specific paper if you wish. You can also laminate it after or keep it protected in a plastic sleeve (in which case you can add to it later). You could also hand copy the outlined format onto your own paper or board if you can't print it.
- A few images of some completed wheels in different brands and mediums are shown.
- If you want to truly master color, it is recommended to create a wheel regularly, certainly whenever you start with a new medium. The way we (for professional work) select/buy our pigments for each medium varies (especially if you are trying to select for lightfastness and longevity) because the ratings can vary for certain pigments depending on the carrier of the particular medium.

1. Empty Basic Triadic 12 part Color Wheel with neutrals and rich grays towards center.

Sample created by Melbourne Art Classes with mostly student grade Watercolor pigments

2. Empty Comprehensive Triadic 12 part Color wheel featuring DIY Pigment Mapping:

- Add your Tints towards the center on this template.

Neutrals and rich grays go towards the outside (this wheel also has a place for tints of grays).

Lined space top and bottom for your own pigment mapping information. Whenever you buy a new pigment, paint a bit on paper and stick a tiny bit where it fits on your wheel plus add it to your mapping lists.(as shown on some examples from our studios)

Sample created at Port Art studios with Chroma A2 Pigments (lightfast student grade)

3. A nod to Johannes Itten - Designed as above but with further star divisions The empty spaces can be utilized for dots of various hue alternatives, made or bought, mapped by you.

EXTRA TIPS FOR COLOR WHEEL SUCCESS

- In a 12 sector triadic wheel, there are still many possible subtle variations for each saturated hue, each neutral range and rich grays too. Remember that color, like all elements, is relative. Pigments available to buy all vary somewhat from one manufacturer to another, from one medium to another and even within the same pigment number. If you decide on an 18 sector wheel there is a place for an extra 6 tertiary variations or intermediates.

- As long as your primary color is fitting somewhere into it's hue sector, the most important thing is to choose **the ideal mixing partner to sit opposite it**. As this is the partner you will know to choose when you want a nice gray harmonious shadow color.

- As you find yourself with mixtures of the hue that fit slightly to one side or another, there are color mixing pages (p.96-101) for each hue family of the wheel so you can always put a swatch there, note the ratios of any pigments in the mix and take a bit aside to tint as well. It is helpful to see analogous hues and their variations all on one page. Give them each a name too if you like because they are unique to you (eg. donkey brown, avocado green, watermelon red, you decide.)

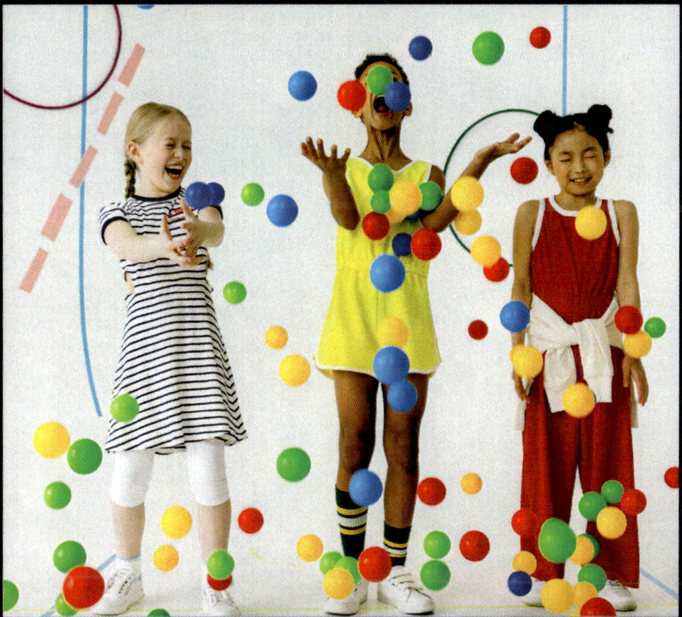

It's not accidental or random child's play once you know how to use color!

The color mixing exercises pay off no matter how many times you need to repeat them. You now will have the ability to predict what will result from a mixture and balance up what does not look as you wanted.

SIMPLE TRIADIC COLOR WHEEL -(primaries) MAGENTA, YELLOW, CYAN

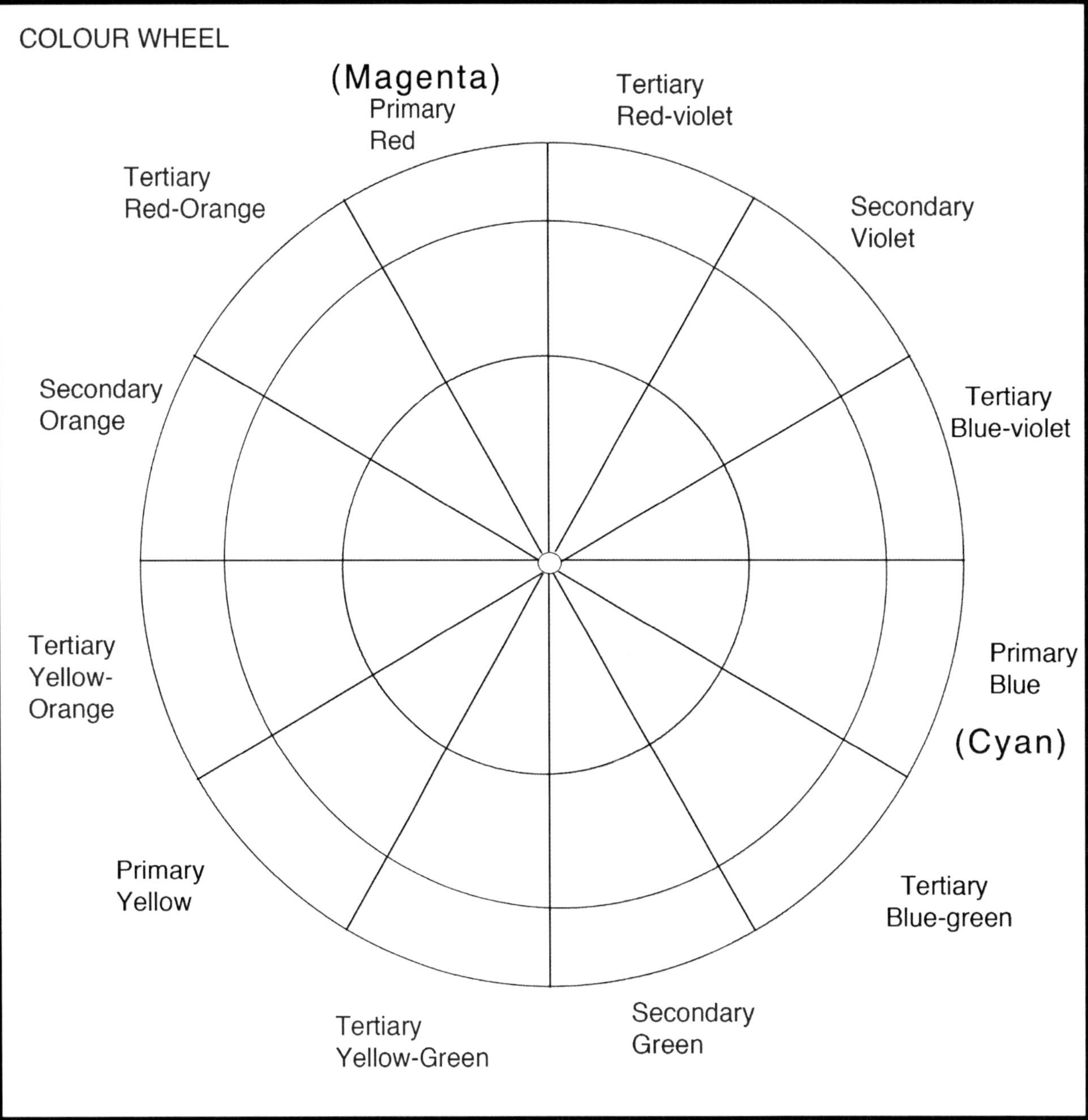

Use the outside ring for a tint of each hue, the middle ring for the saturated hues and the inside for a chromatic gray (rich grays that we need for shadow colors, to neutralize and darken a hue). You can draw in another ring by dividing the middle one if you want to show another neutral on the way from saturated hue to arriving at the chormatic gray for each hue.(or use the more comprehensive templates shown next .You can print more anytime using your QR login. USE UNDILUTED ACRYLIC IN THESE WORKBOOK PAGES and your medium specific paper for other mediums you are using now or in the future.

(STUDENT WATERCOLOR PIGMENT) COLOR WHEEL

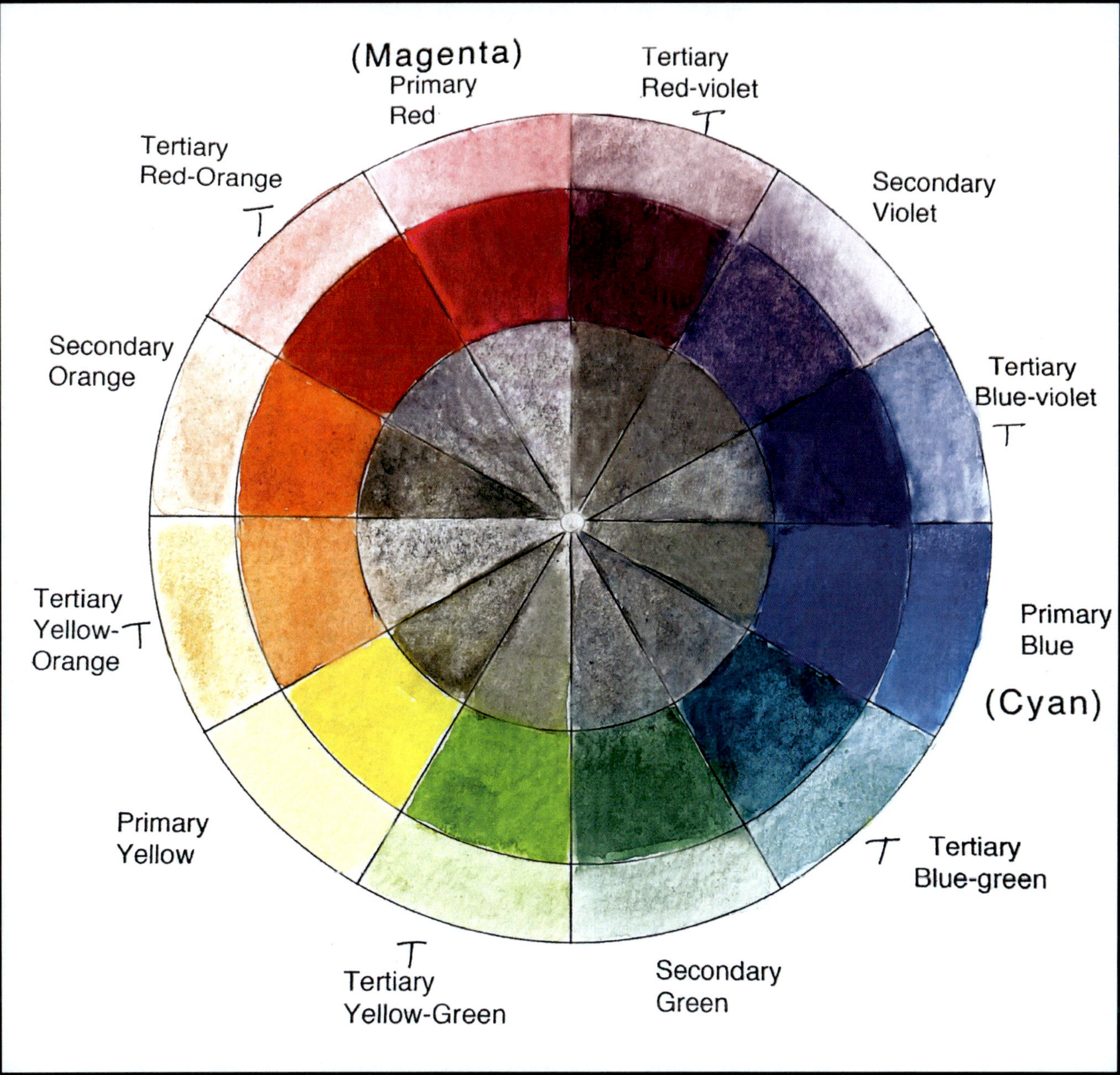

Pigment results will vary from different manufacturers, grades and also within different mediums or carriers.

This wheel template was printed onto watercolor paper. The Micador student watercolors were used in this student wheel, with the exception of primary red (they used Permanent Rose for the Primary red as the student red was too orange biased) and for the Primary Blue some Cobalt blue was added (from Art Spectrum range) with a little Cool blue (it's green bias was balanced up a bit back toward the primary spot with the warm bias of the Cobalt.)

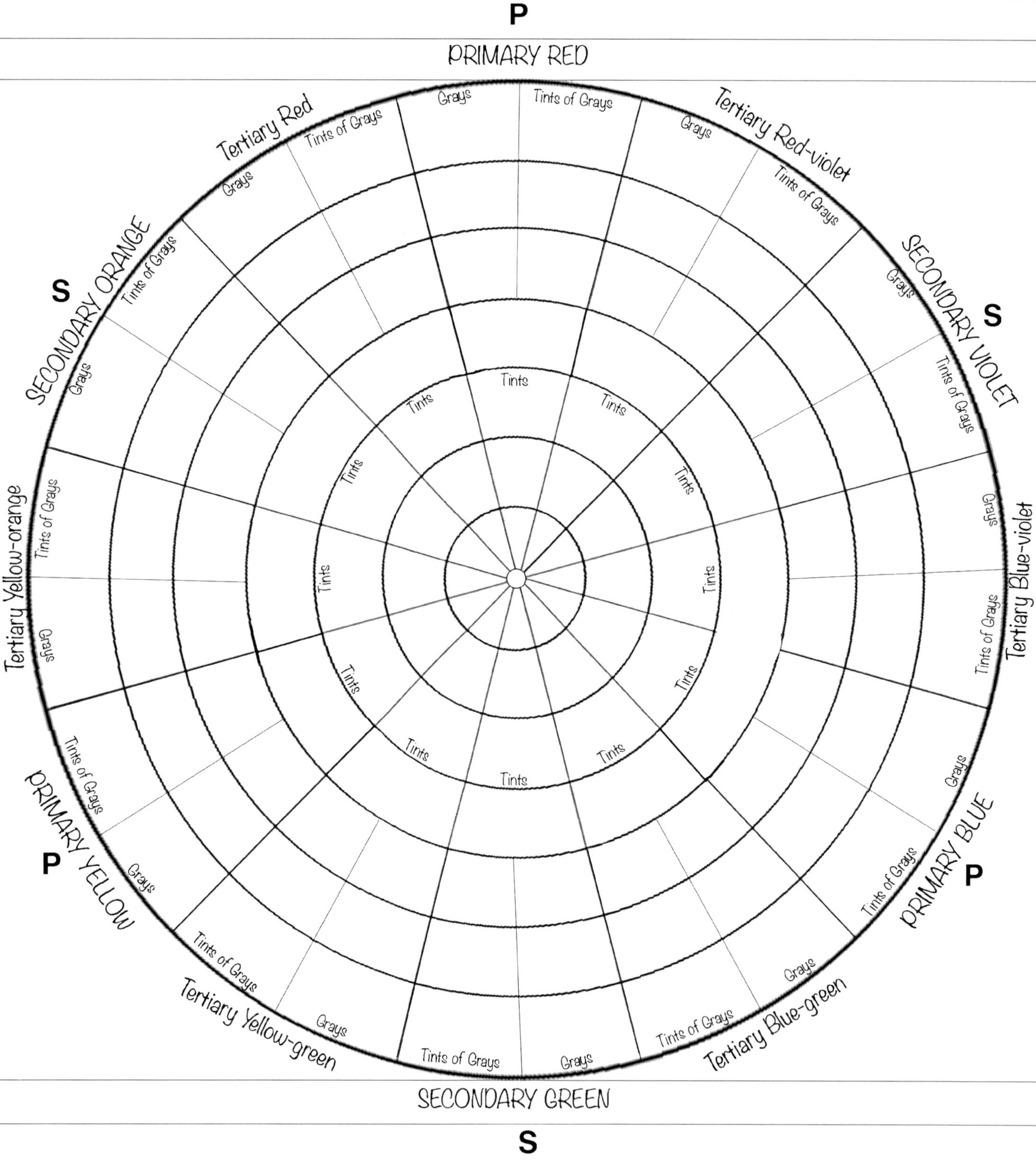

COPYRIGHTED MATERIAL

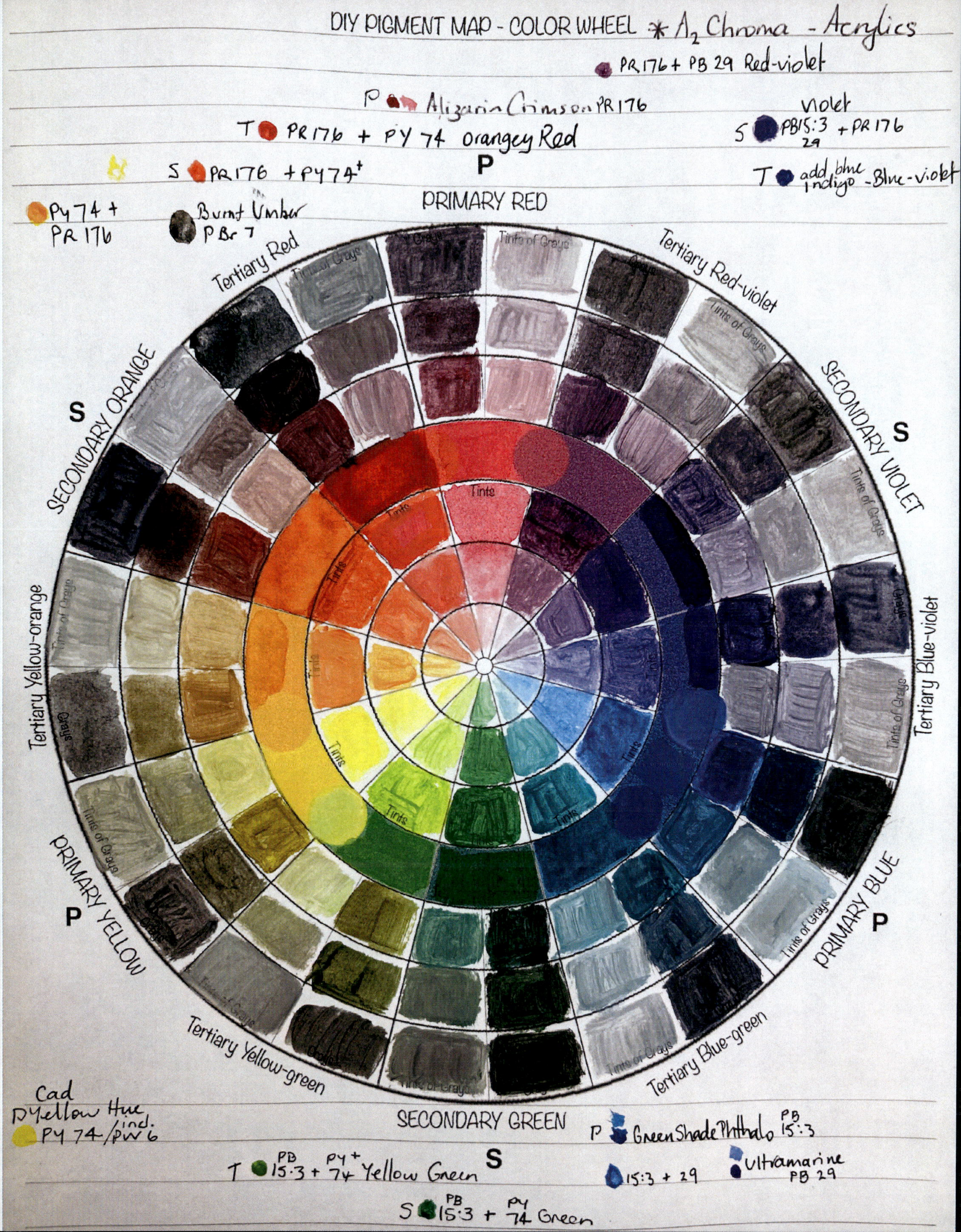
DIY PIGMENT MAP - COLOR WHEEL * A2 Chroma - Acrylics
PR176 + PB 29 Red-violet
P Alizarin Crimson PR176
T PR176 + PY 74 orangey Red
violet
S PB15:3 29 + PR 176
S PR176 + PY74+
P
T add blue indigo - Blue-violet
PY 74 + PR 176
Burnt Umber PBr 7
PRIMARY RED
Tertiary Red
Tertiary Red-violet
S
SECONDARY ORANGE
SECONDARY VIOLET
S
Tertiary Yellow-orange
Tertiary Blue-violet
PRIMARY YELLOW
P
PRIMARY BLUE
P
Tertiary Yellow-green
Tertiary Blue-green
Tints of Grays
Grays
Tints
Cad Yellow Hue ind. PY 74 / PW 6
SECONDARY GREEN
P Green Shade Phthalo PB 15:3
S
T PB 15:3 + PY 74+ Yellow Green
15:3 + 29
Ultramarine PB 29
S PB 15:3 + PY 74 Green

MAKING YOUR OWN COLOR WHEELS AND CREATING COLOR HARMONY SPINNING SELECTOR GUIDES

You can make a handy Spinning Scheme selector which facilitates easy selection of scheme hues for the more complex arrangements: Triads, Double Split Complementaries and Tetrads. There is a short video on the online pages (once you use the QR code in the last section and login, you can see how quick it is to make a protective cover for your wheel(s) and use the spinning guide to select new harmonies.

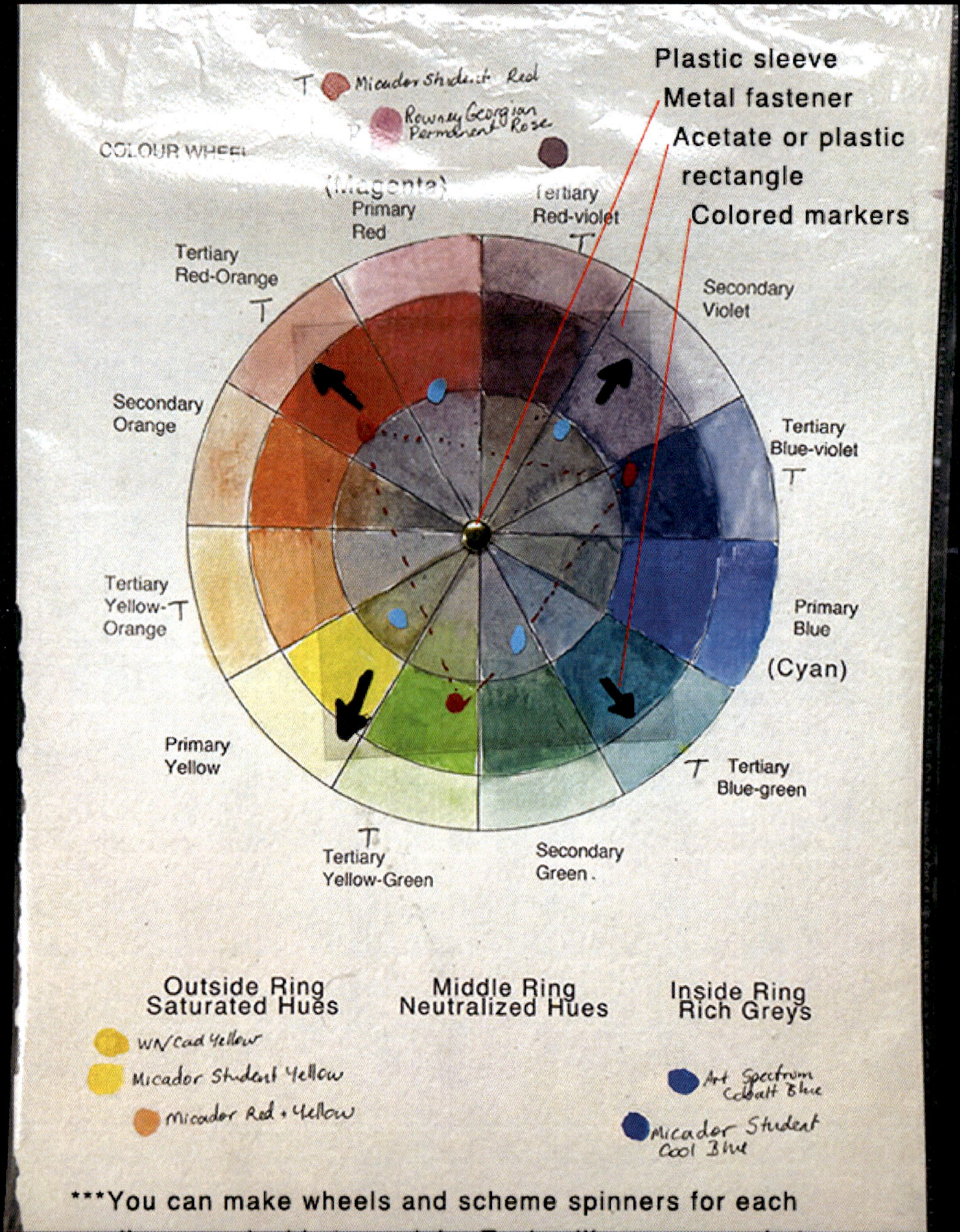

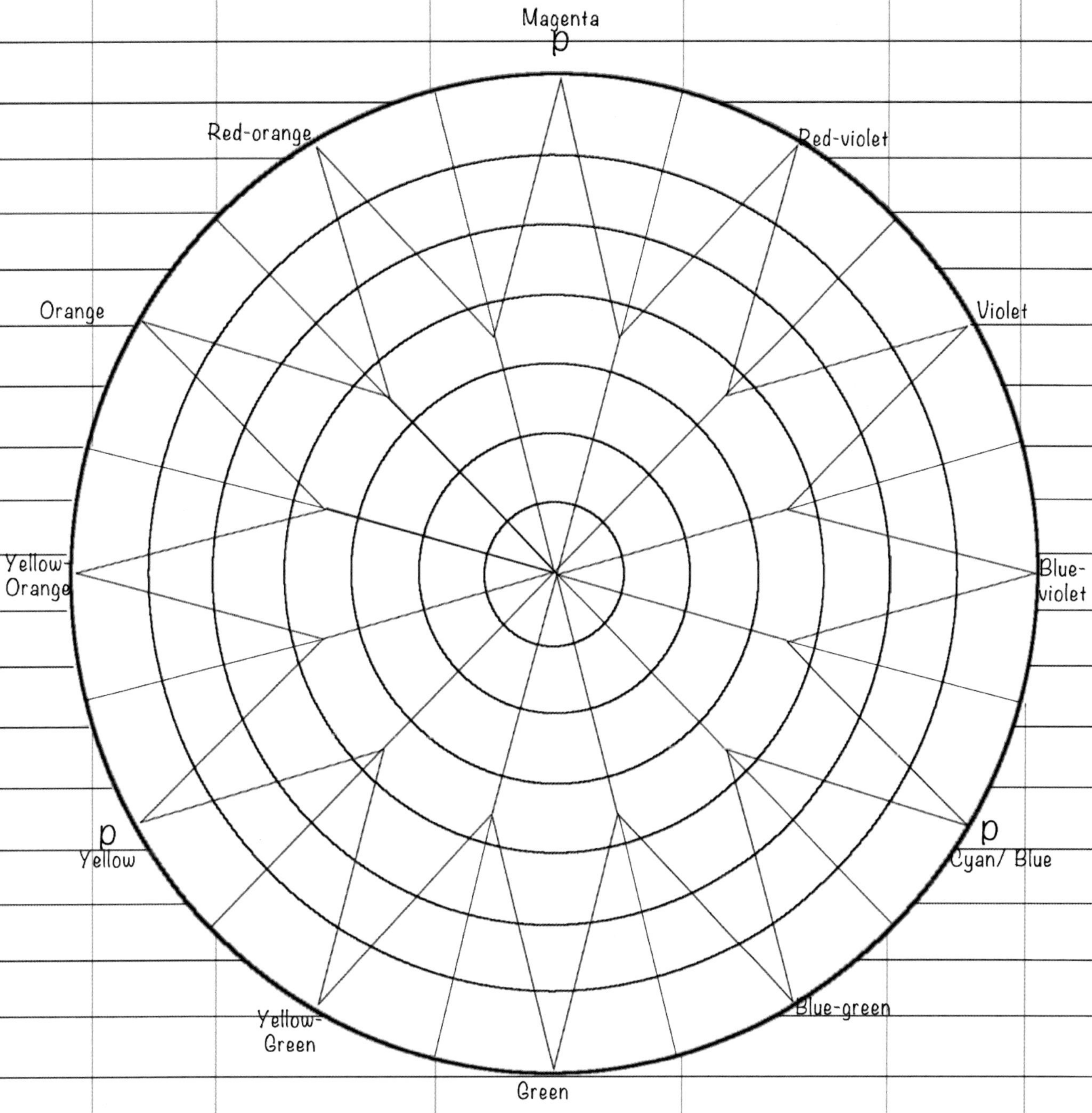
Magenta
p
Red-orange
Red-violet
Orange
Violet
Yellow-
Orange
Blue-
violet
p
Yellow
p
Cyan/ Blue
Yellow-
Green
Blue-green
Green

MIXING A FEW DIY CONVENIENCE COLORS

There is not a huge list of color "recipes" here and this is why:
We are of the confirmed belief (and we have found in practice) at our studios that every learner and every artist grows substantially in their color mastery by practicing color mixing by eye and learning the principles of color relationships and mixing, thereby developing the independent skills of making any color they need and knowing how to harmonise cleverly.

TIPS FOR MIXING YOUR CONVENIENCE COLORS AND SAVING THEM

- Have little spare storage pots or bottles for those colors that you are going to want with more frequency (they may also come in handy as a starting point for other future colors you want to adapt slightly). If the color is just for one project, have a zip-lock stay wet palette ready (p. 56) to keep the paint from drying up.
- Always add tiny amounts at a time until you feel (looking by eye) that you are arriving at the hue, saturation and value you were aiming for. If Phthalo blues or green are involved, make it even tinier dots as they are very bossy to mix with.
- Make your own color charts in the mixing pages here, or on cartridge paper, place a sample of the new color and write down your own 'recipes' as you measure and make them, keep your records for future mixes that you may need again. (Sometimes the 'mistakes' will turn out to be just what you want for another project. Some may be 'mud', add them to a pot of 'spare random brown'). Keep name, number, proportions and brand(s) recorded.
- Remember that there are three dimensions of the color you are aiming to achieve : Hue, Saturation and Value. (and work in daylight or close to it when you are mixing).
- When you are thinking of mixing a new convenience color, look through the neutral stages of your hue strings (of tints and shades), to see if there is one in there that looks close to the color you are aiming for. eg. for a 'plum' color, take a look at the red-violet string of grays, find a mauve in the tints there. Look on strings of family members too for variations or highlight colors. For a 'Broccoli color, look at the strings of green and yellow green. (of course!) Have fun!!

WHY ARE THEY CALLED CONVENIENCE COLORS?

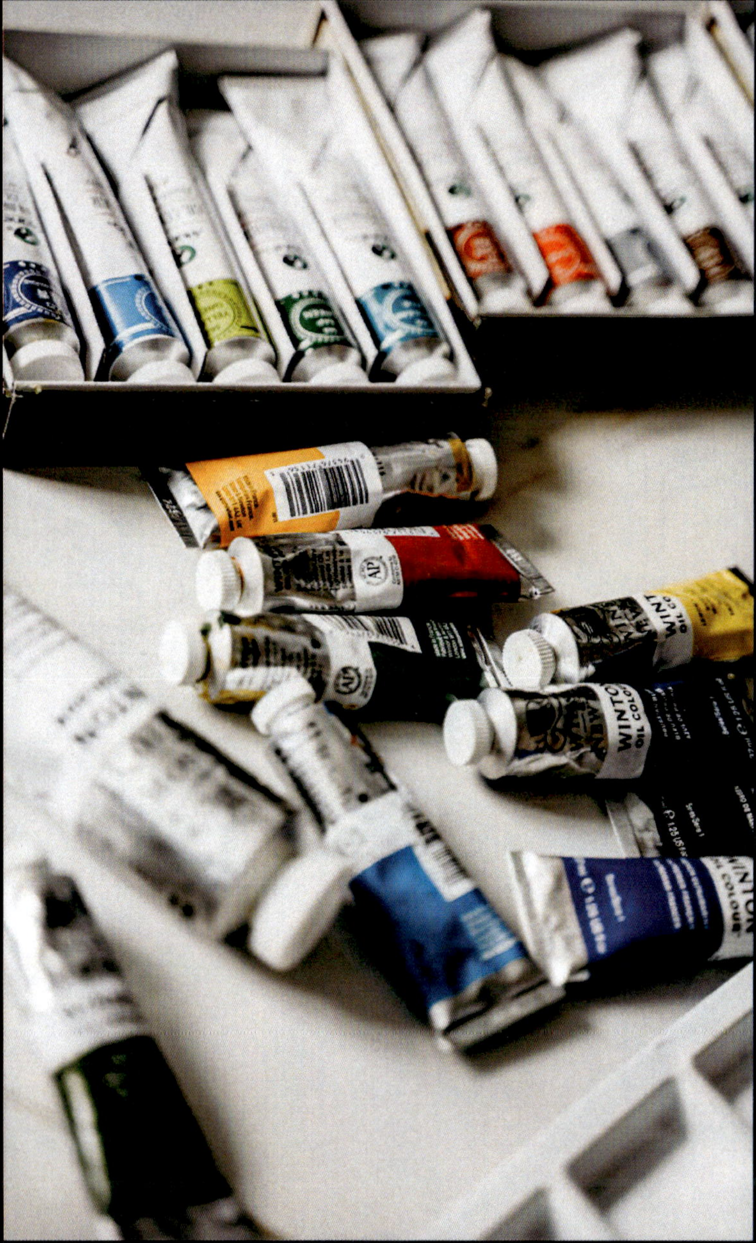

- Single pigment colors are prized by professional artists as the lightfastness and hue can be defined more simply. (all control is in the hands of the artist.)
- Other artists value the ease of not having to mix commonly used favorites every time. So it is the 'convenience' that they enjoy of having pre-mixed colors.
- When paint manufacturers create mixtures using several different pigments they often bring down the lightfastness of the new color by including a cheaper addition. On top of this, the more times they or you mix more hues together, the more chance of muddy mixes (whenever all three primaries are mixed in random combinations, a muddy color can very easily result.)
- Some artists complain how hard it is to exactly mix certain traditional hues eg. Naples Yellow, Indian red etc. Just remember, there are variations of these colors between paint manufacturers even if they use the same pigments by numbers, and your version of any hue is just as valid if it works for you and fits nicely into your cleverly planned harmonious schemes.

Burnt Umber
PBr 7
Very dark brown

Ultramarine Blue
PB 29
Dark warm blue

Natural Black
(a version of "Payne's Grey")

Mix this yellow-orange by adding a little red to your primary yellow

Natural Black
(a version of "Payne's Grey")

Yellow Ochre
PY 42 or 43
(can also be tintied with a little white)

Take some of the yellow ochre you made already, add white until it looks a bit like the swatch on the right (hard to get it exactly as all manufacturers use a varied combination of pigments)

Titanium white
PW 6
(you may want to add a tiny dot more yellow)

Naples Yellow Hue

(historically made with toxic lead and antimony, but the cadmiums replaced it mostly)

Take some of your Yellow Ochre hue that you already made

Titanium white
PW 6
+
A dot of the Natural Black you already made

Buff Titanium

Mix red-orange (add a little yellow to your primary red) or use your opaque red

Natural Black (a version of "Payne's Grey")

Burnt Sienna
Siennas and umbers are mostly different versions of PBr7

eg. cadmium, pyrrole

Take your tertiary red-orange that you already mixed (or some cadmium type hue which is opaque)

Add your natural black in small amounts until you reach the value seen there, then add a dot of magenta as required to get it to the hue you see

Indian red ochre

eg. cadmium, pyrrole type hue

Mix secondary orange (add some yellow to your primary red)

Natural Black (a version of "Payne's Grey")

Raw Umber
Siennas and umbers are mostly different versions of PBr7

For a transparent version of this hue use Phthalo Blue 15:3 or 15:1

with Transparent yellow-orange Tr. Yellow Sienna or oxide

HOOKER'S GREEN

(always start with the other when mixing with Phthalo family as they are very bossy, add a tiny bit at a time until you reach the hue you are after.)

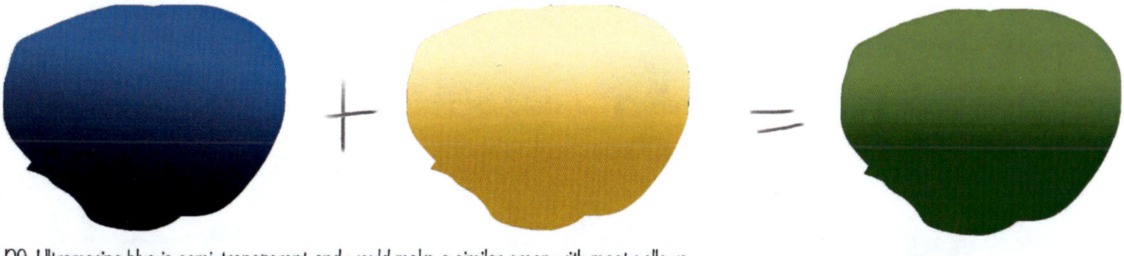

PS. Ultramarine blue is semi-transparent and would make a similar green with most yellows

MIX AS MANY ORANGES AS YOU CAN - Revisit the secondary orange, yellow-orange and red-orange from your strings and wheels practice. Tints and neutrals and subtle variations, all good. Keep the last row for metallics (copper, gold) and/or transparent variations of oranges (transparent oxides and siennas) and any convenience colors that you may buy and include later on. They can all play a part in your harmonious designs that include these analogous neighbors (and the browns that come from them of course). Add the hue to the circle, tint the lower half, use the rectangle for pigment details/ ratios etc.

MIX AS MANY YELLOWS AS YOU CAN - Refer back to the practice for this when you mixed the yellow, yellow-orange and yellow-green hues in the strings and the wheels. Save the last rows for future pigments that also fit into this corner of the wheel. Use the rectangles for your own notes, these are your personal mixtures, give them a name if that helps (eg.chartreuse, corn, mustard, cookie....have fun with this). There may be colors repeated from orange and green pages, doesn't matter, its good to have analogous colors together in a chart of your own making.

MIX AS MANY REDS AS YOU CAN - Revisit when you mixed the magenta , red-orange and red-violet hues in the strings and the wheels. There are many red family pigments out there that you can buy later if you want a whole lot of ready made variations (including transparent, metallic etc) after you have mixed as many you can with your basic essentials. They are all potential analogous partners, just remember they all have different shadow mixing partners. Save some spots in the last few rows for future reds you may add to your collection .eg. Naphthol, Pyrrole, Cadmium, Iron Oxide red etc.

MIX AS MANY BLUES AS YOU CAN - You can make a decent array of blue hues with your two blues in your essentials kit, (anything with blue in it, blue-green, blue-violet, primary blue and all tints, neutrals etc). There are amazing unique blue pigments out there, that fit into the same hue sections that you are creating with your two blues, each have a unique combination of dimensions not quite possible with just any blue. In the future, use the last rows for any new blue pigments that you purchase.(or start a new journal for your own mixtures or opther blue pigments eg. Indanthrene, Cobalt,Cerulean.

MIX AS MANY GREENS AS YOU CAN - If you are a huge fan of the hue green and all of its variations, you may well seek out some green pigments including pure and convenience mixes. Don't underestimate the variety that you can personally make as you have two blues and a yellow (plus magenta to further vary the saturation, if you bought the bare essentials as we recommended) and white to tint. Make as many greens as you can, who knows when a landscape might appeal or a red-violet might be crying out for a new partner in one of your harmonious schemes. Variety is the spice of life (and also in our art).

MIX AS MANY VIOLETS AS YOU CAN - refer back to your Violet, Blue-violet and Red-violet strings. This is where you can see indigos, mauves, mulberries and any other name you wish to make up for the colors you create that come from the violet corner (have violet in their sector name somewhere). Keep in mind to use warm Ultramarine blue for vibrant violets as the green-shade cool Phthalo Blue makes dull violets .

SIMULTANEOUS CONTRAST - (COLOR CASTING)

Optically, a color will cast it's complement eg. A stroke of what appears to be a neutral gray mixed on your palette, then painted onto a stretch of cool blue will appear warmer (brownish), as the blue casts it's complement (orange) onto the stroke of paint.

Artists use complementary combinations to add drama (eg. blue makes orange appear more 'orangissimo', hence complementary!!) Vincent Van Gogh often lay yellow alongside violet, orange with blue, etc. He was entranced with simultaneous color contrast.

A great way to feel this wonderful phenomenon doing it's thing is by painting varying background colors, let them dry, then mix the one tinted rich gray color or a beige and see how different it looks on each color background, but placing a small stroke in the middle of each one. Here are some color shapes , each with a stroke in the middle. Squint and stare at the cross in the middle of all these color shapes and then one by one, look peripherally at each one, start to see the subtle variations in the appearance of each dot (which are all actually the same beige color.)

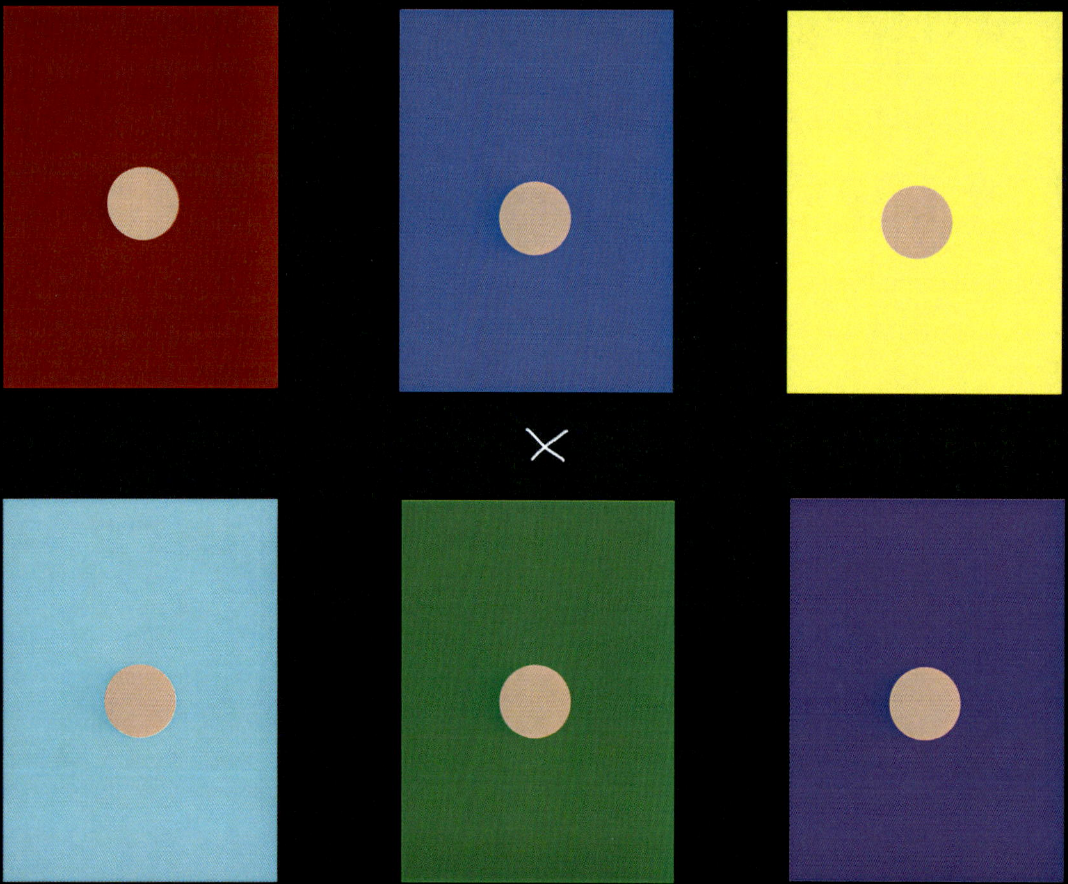

CHEVREUL'S LAWS OF SIMULTANEOUS CONTRAST

- The old Renaissance boys knew about Simultaneous contrast.

Said Leonardo: "Of colors of equal lightness, that will look brightest which is against the darkest background, and black will display itself at its darkest against a background of greatest whiteness. And red will look most fierce against the yellowest background, as do all colors surrounded by their directly contrary color."

- Not just hue is affected by this phenomenon. Saturation, Value and Hue are all subservient to this phenomenon
- Chevreul looked into this phenomenon a bit more and published a book about it.

The Law of Simultaneous Color Contrast' 1839

- If two color areas are seen close together in space or time, each will shift in hue and value as if the visual complementary color of the neighboring or preceding color were mixed with it.
- Cool colors look cooler when placed next to warm ones.
- Warmer colors look warmer when placed next to cool ones.
- A dark color juxtaposed with a light one makes them both look brighter.
- Dark next to bright (saturated) makes the bright one look brighter. (One reason I chose to create our work books with white and colors on black pages).
- Dark next to light makes the light seem lighter and the dark darker.
- A bright color next to a muted color makes the muted one look more dull.
- If two colors are of a similar brightness, both look less bright when placed next to each other.
- If you use a comb or brush on your hair, there is less time for the study of color behaviors. Chevreul had his priorities sorted! "Thanks Michel Eugene !"

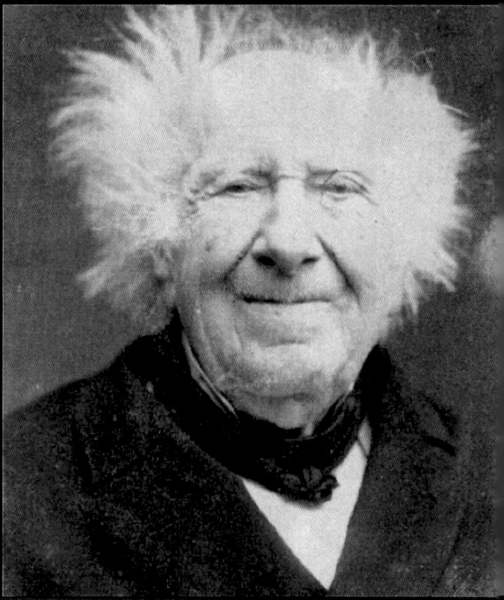

Josef Albers (studied and taught at the Bauhaus school) is thought of by some as the most influential in the area of color theory dealing with Color Interaction. Albers put practice before theory and prioritized experience. 'What counts,' he claimed 'is not so-called knowledge of so-called facts, but vision ie. seeing.'

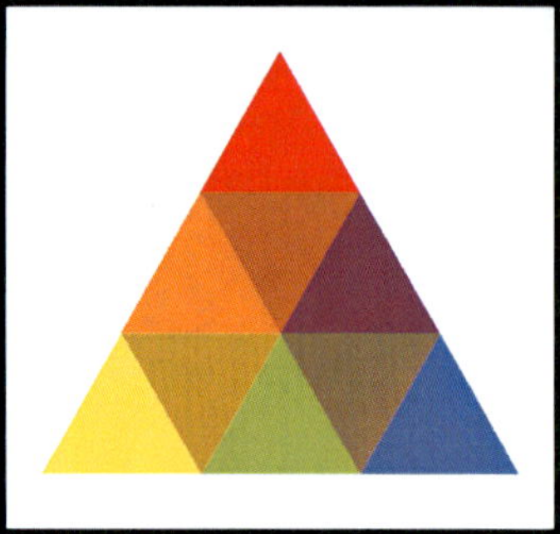

He used a color triangle (he did a lot of optical blending,and teaching with colored papers not as much (realism) paint mixing, I am sure that making mud was never an issue for him clearly, so spectrum red was still his primary). CMY took over as the primary model more recently.

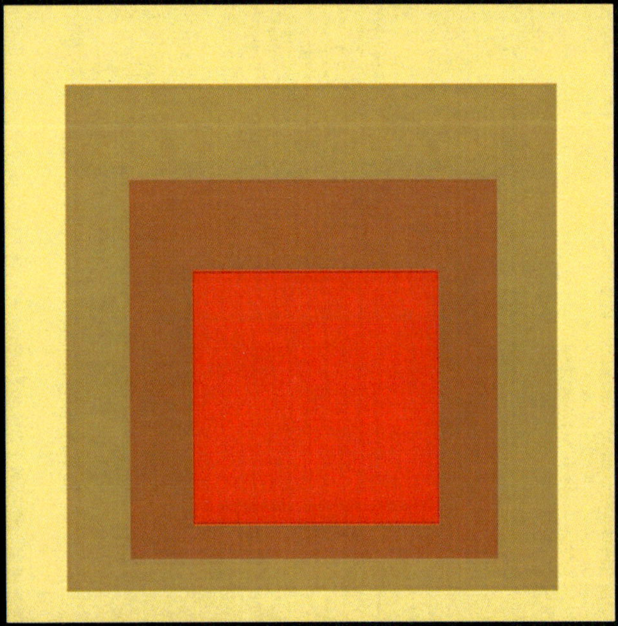

Fig 7

Albers created more than a thousand art works in the series 'Homage to the Square'.

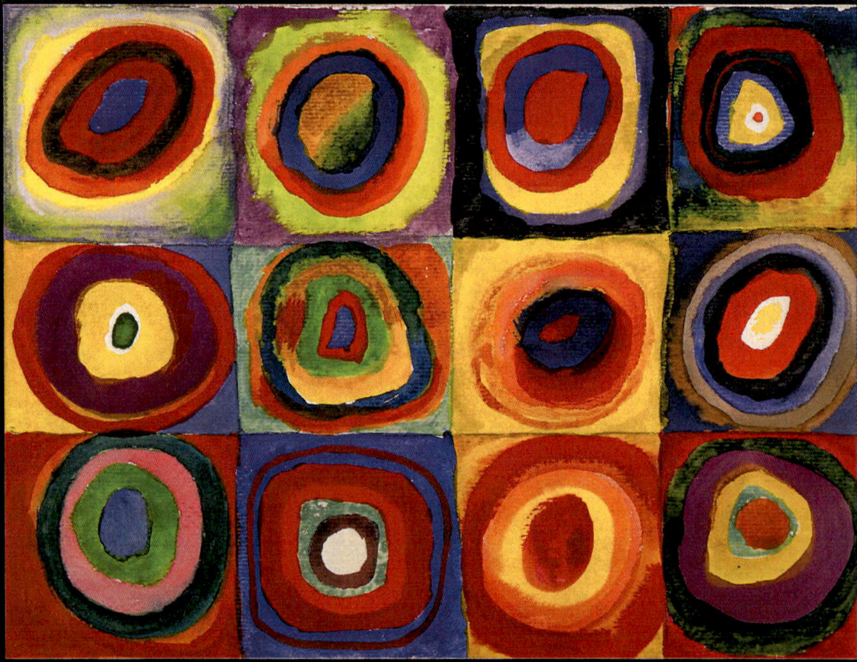

Fig 8

When I first came across the work of Joseph Albers, I was already familiar with the works of Wassily Kandinsky and I thought 'Wow...this guy was really influenced by WK', and in actual fact, turns out, they were both at the Bauhaus School together, one left for the US and one for France (in 1933 with the rise of Nazism.)

When this magical (some say surprising!) Simultaneous contrast happens as you are creating a painting, you will be able to predict it and know how to balance it within the mixtures you are using. . Have a go at our 'cloud scumble experience' on the next page. See for yourself.

An example we never get tired of watching is a student mixing a nice rich gray from their orangey earth color and their blue sky color (orangey-brown + blue = rich gray) to scumble (lightly scrub in with a stiff brush) some tinted version of this onto the sky for cloud shadow shapes which they are then planning on blending white highlights into.

The shock that a beginner gets when their perfect rich gray (mixed successfully on their palette) turns up on their blue sky as a brown color is all the practical lesson that most students need to understand simultaneous contrast, and yet experimentation with many color interactions can lead us all to new inspirations.

If optical illusions and these more tricky aspects of the relative behaviors of color inspire you, head to the next pages and do some more for your own practical discovery.

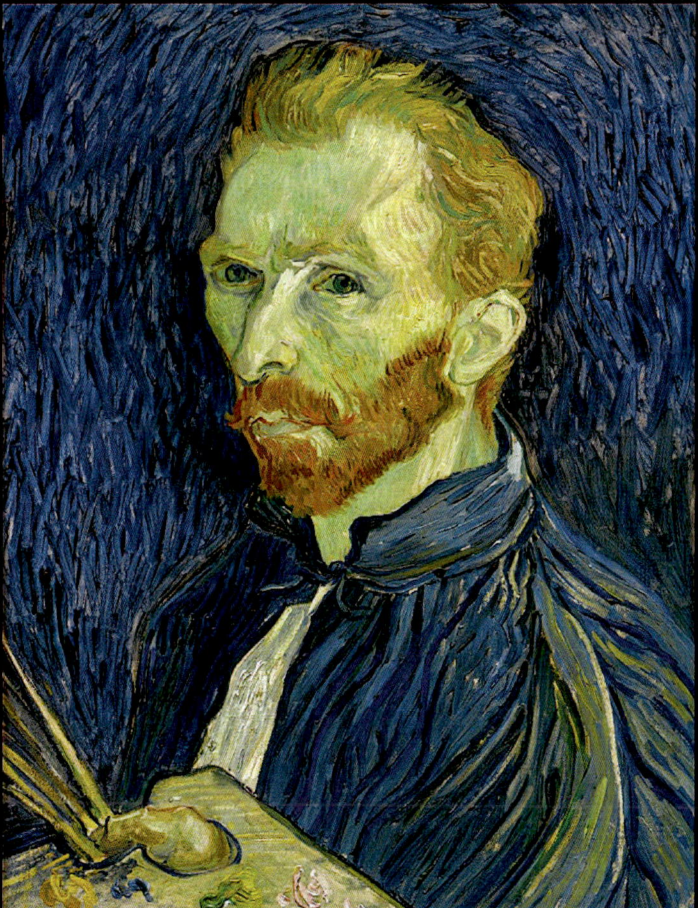

"To exaggerate the fairness of hair, I come even to orange tones, chromes and pale yellow... I make a plain background of the richest, intensest blue that I can contrive, and by this simple combination of the bright head against the rich blue background, I get a mysterious effect, like a star in the depths of an azure sky." Vincent Van Gogh

Fig 9 - Self Portrait 1889

IMAGINE YOU ARE IN THE EARLY STAGES OF A LANDSCAPE PAINTING

You have a block in of an earthy foreground fading to the horizon and a gradient in the horizon with your blue color. You are planning on scumbling in some fluffy cloud shadow shapes and then highlighting them with white (let's say the sun is overhead so the cloud highlights are going to be on the upper sides of the cloud shadow shapes).

- Mix a tint of very neutral rich gray made from your secondary orange and your primary blue. Aim to have it of a value that is darker than the horizon blue and lighter than the upper blue. Mix this tint of rich gray on a clean white (or neutral gray) palette until it has no brown or blue bias to it (like you did in the strings and the wheel exercises).
- Now scumble or paint in some cloud shadow shapes. How does the light gray differ when painted against the blue? (compared to how it appeared on your empty palette).
- For the solution: to keep it looking neutral gray as you had planned, go back to the blue or orange string exercises to see what you added to the mix to tweak it to a more neutral gray. (Hint: How would you have neutralized a brownish gray?)

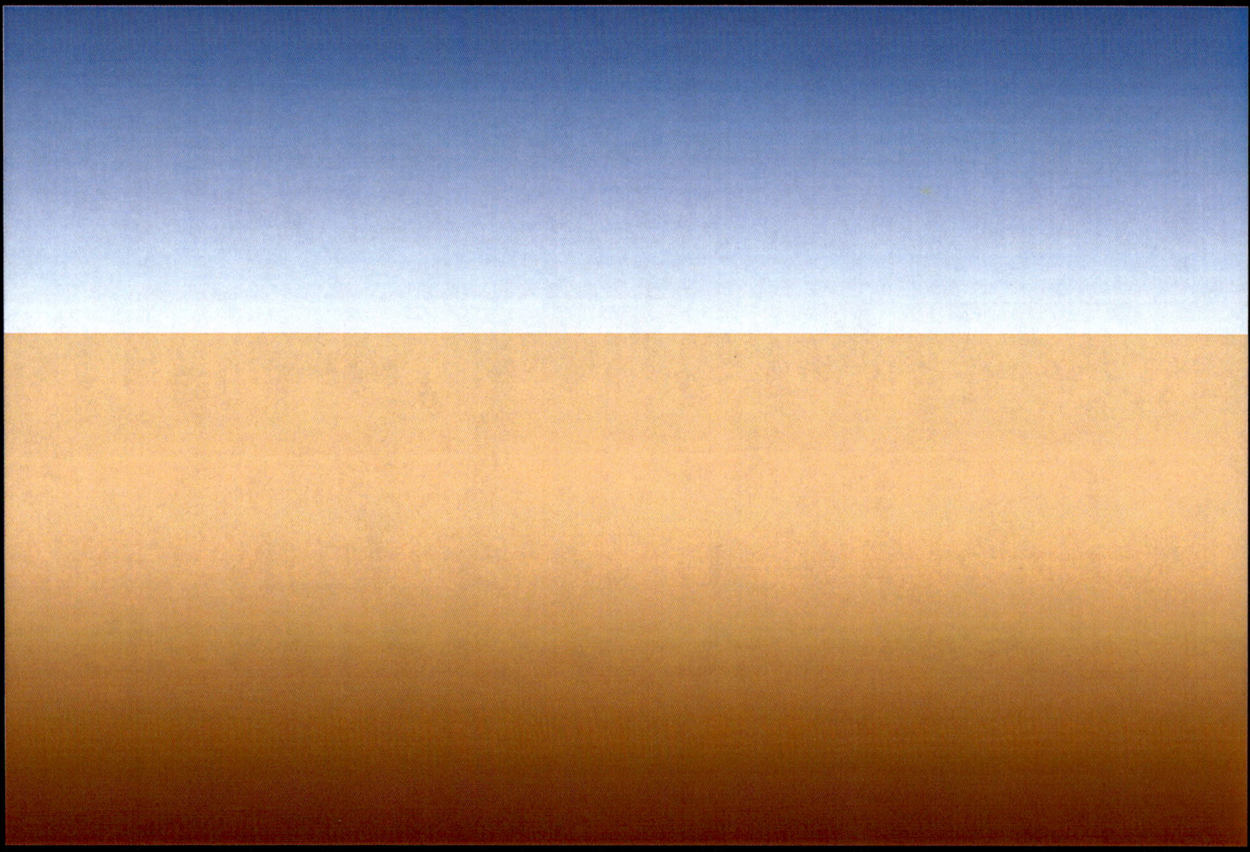

DISCOVER AND THEN MIX SOME HARMONIOUS SCHEMES

Use the line drawings and value sketches provided for quick scheme practice, then create a few simple line drawings of your own to block out some more ideas for harmonious color arrangements of each type. Over time certain 'palettes' may emerge as more pleasing to you for your purposes (or you may get more pleasure out of constantly creating new schemes for each project or series).

- Hopefully you have already made your own color wheel (s), so you could now add a spinning scheme picker (as shown). This will make planning new schemes fun and easy.

- Using your 12 or 18 point triadic wheel, explore all and any versions of each hue section as they will add variety to your plans (various values, degrees of the hue, saturation of the hue, various pigments fitting within each zone, (if you build on your kit later as well).

- If you have some ideas in mind already for compositions, try out some basic shape sketches and create some color test runs with some common scheme types. Planning the scheme (and all of the hues,values and saturations required in it) is a very good part of a solid creative planning process along with other compositional and design planning. (there is a Foundation module available dedicated to this area) on our Online Studio.
https://melbourneartclasses.com.au/online-art-classes/theory-modules/composition-design.html

- If you havn't made a scheme spinner yet, all you need is a little metal fastener and ideally a removable plastic sleeve to protect your wheel. Any marker or paint pen is ok to make triangle, square and rectangular markers (a brief video is found on the online pages when you login to download templates and watch a few videos).

An Achromatic scheme is one with no color (black and white)

Fig 10

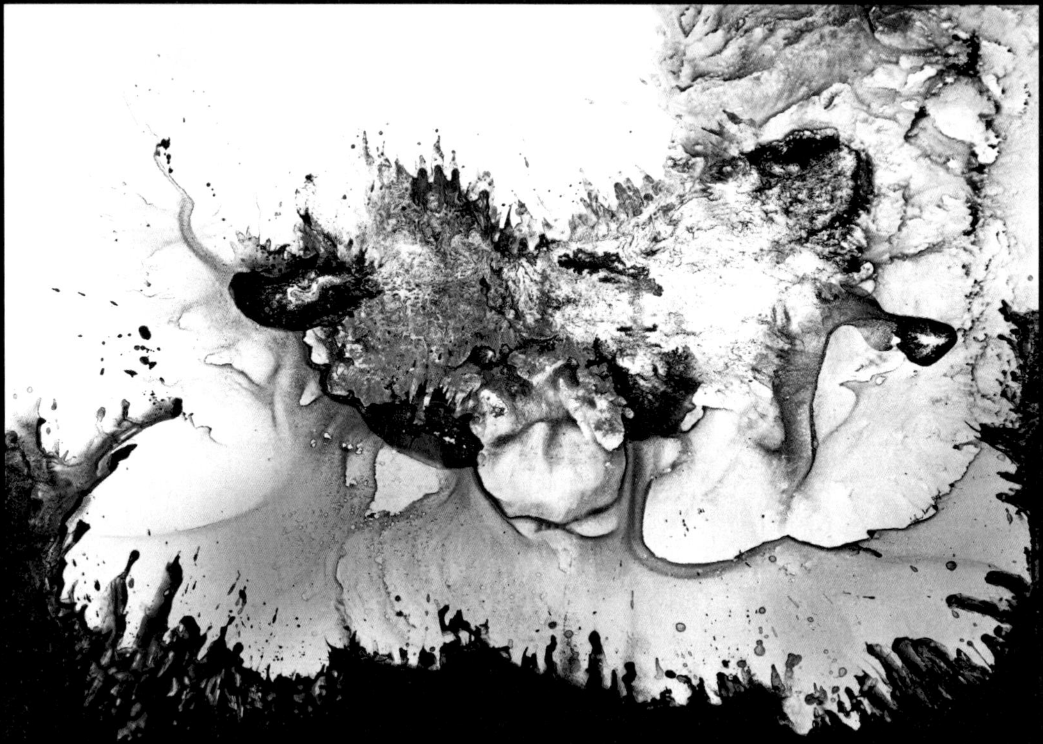

- Those who love color and long to use it masterfully often ask "how does an artist create an effective and powerful art work without the use of any color?"

- Color is just one of the elements (design tools). Line, Shape, Form, Space, Value, and Texture are some of the other potential contributors to the visual message that an artist seeks to get across. Try a little still life study in acrylics with just your natural black and white.

- Stay tuned on our first readers list as the next work book to be published is all about Value, Contrast, Light and Shade.

Often used for black and white imagery (technically this is achromatic), the term monochromatic scheme actually refers to varying values of one hue or color.

Fig 11 - Black and white do not participate greatly in the color influences of a scheme. (although they will in it's notan, or value pattern).

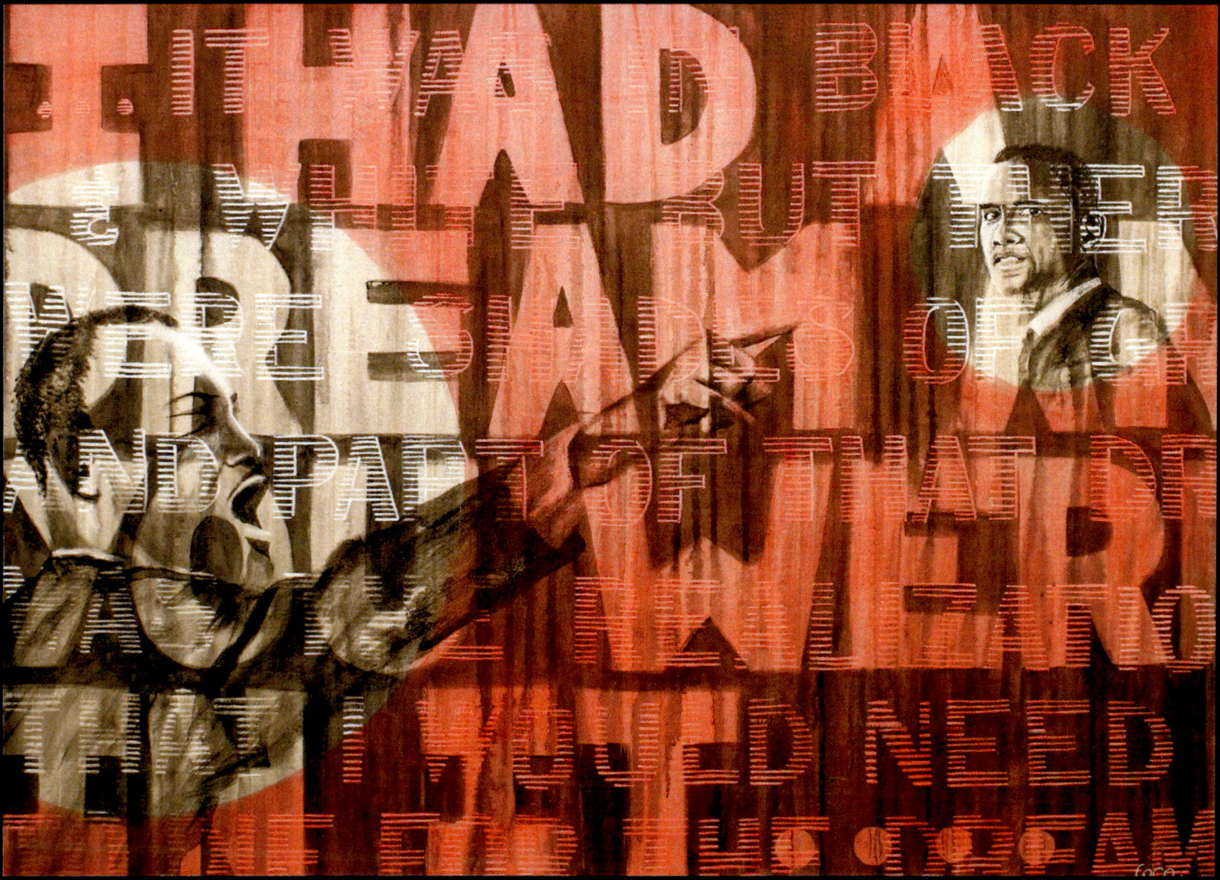

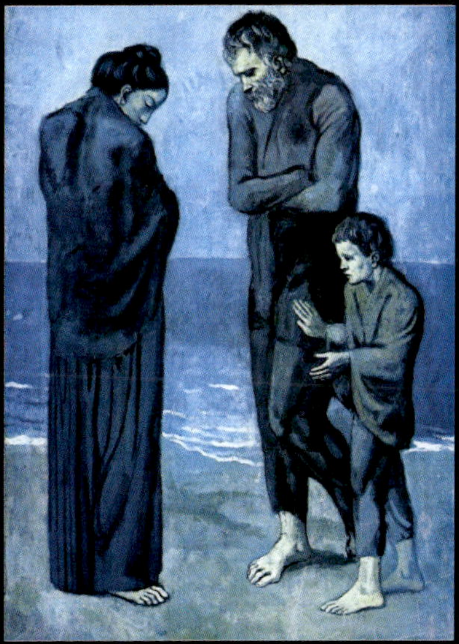

Fig 12 - From Pablo Picasso's 'Blue Period' this scheme is typical of this time in his life. His friend committed suicide, other bad things were happening, he was depressed and not successful at the time, although the artworks from his Blue period are some of his most famous now since his death.

MONOCHROMATIC SCHEMES

Use this page for your own compositional shape sketches and harmonious color planning of some monochromatic schemes. Map it on the wheel and add notes under the wheel as to the pigments, neutrals and chromatic grays/ blacks used.

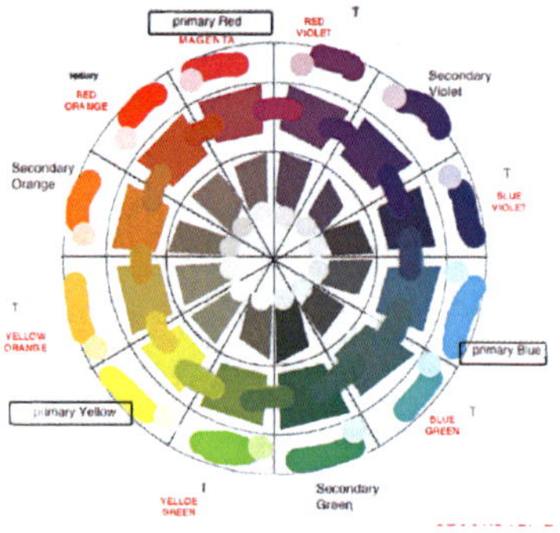

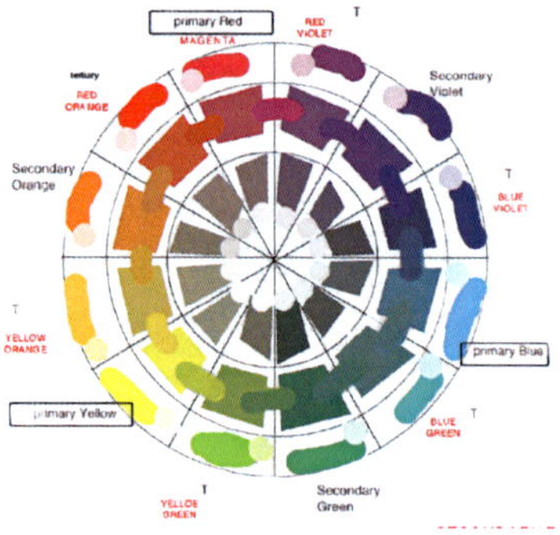

'ANALOGOUS' SCHEME - EXAMPLES

Simply choose 3-5 neighbors on the triadic color wheel (add more and it becomes kind of 'polychromatic', less harmonious or broadly appealing). Generally but not always, the analogous 3-5 hues are all warm or all cool .

Fig 13 Orange, Red, Yellow- Mark Rothko, 1961

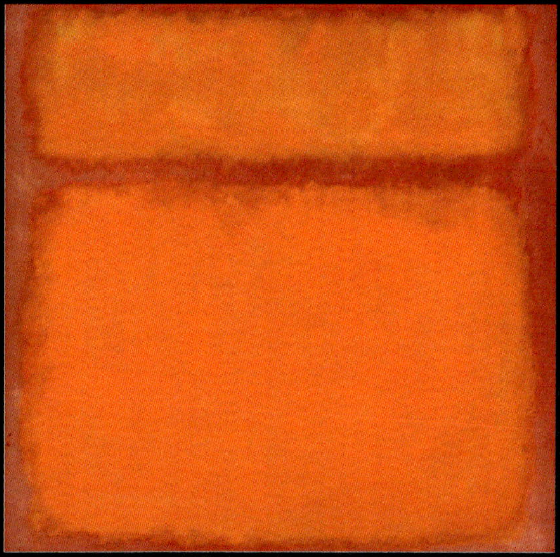

There is less dynamism (movement, activity) in an art work which has a small range of neighborly colors. Without the dynamic pop of a complementary cool color, this primarily warm image is surprisingly calming as it's subtle edges vibrate with the upper orange seeming to hover apart

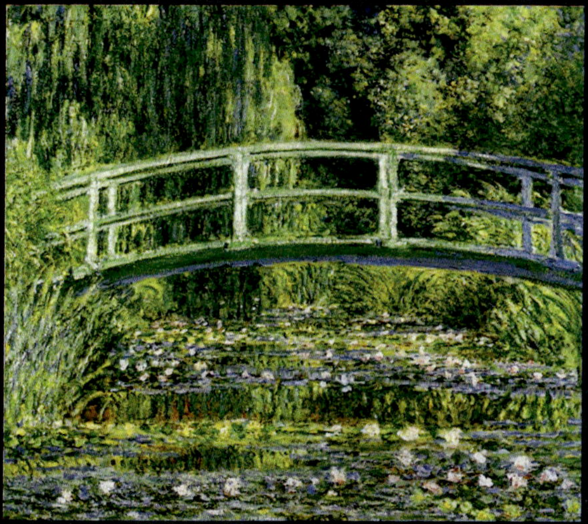

Waterlilies and Japanese Bridge -Fig 14
Claude Monet, 1899

Although there are tiny snippets of pink in this painting, it is analogous on the whole with yellow-green, green and blue

A stray color which is seen minimally or is rather muted (de-saturated) can be included in your schemes without disrupting your planned harmonies.

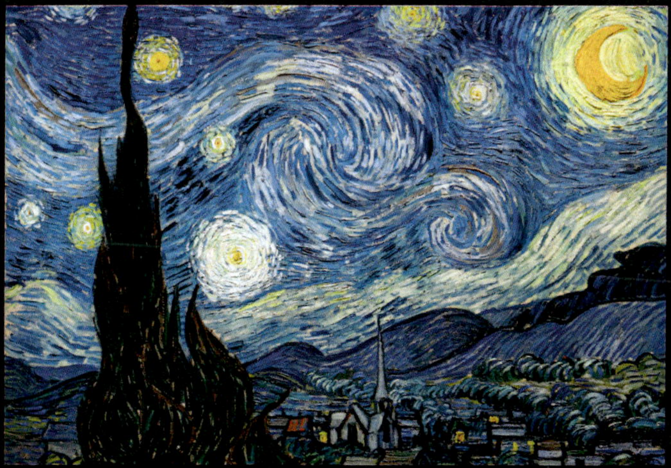

Fig 15 Starry Night-Vincent Van Gogh, 1889

From yellow through to blue, another analogous scheme

ANALOGOUS SCHEME - EXAMPLE

Fig 16

Housed at the Musée d'Orsay , 2 m x 2m in size, this large painting (one of 250 Waterlily compositions that Monet undertook) is a great example of an analogous scheme, with a range of nearby analogous cool hues of blues and greens.

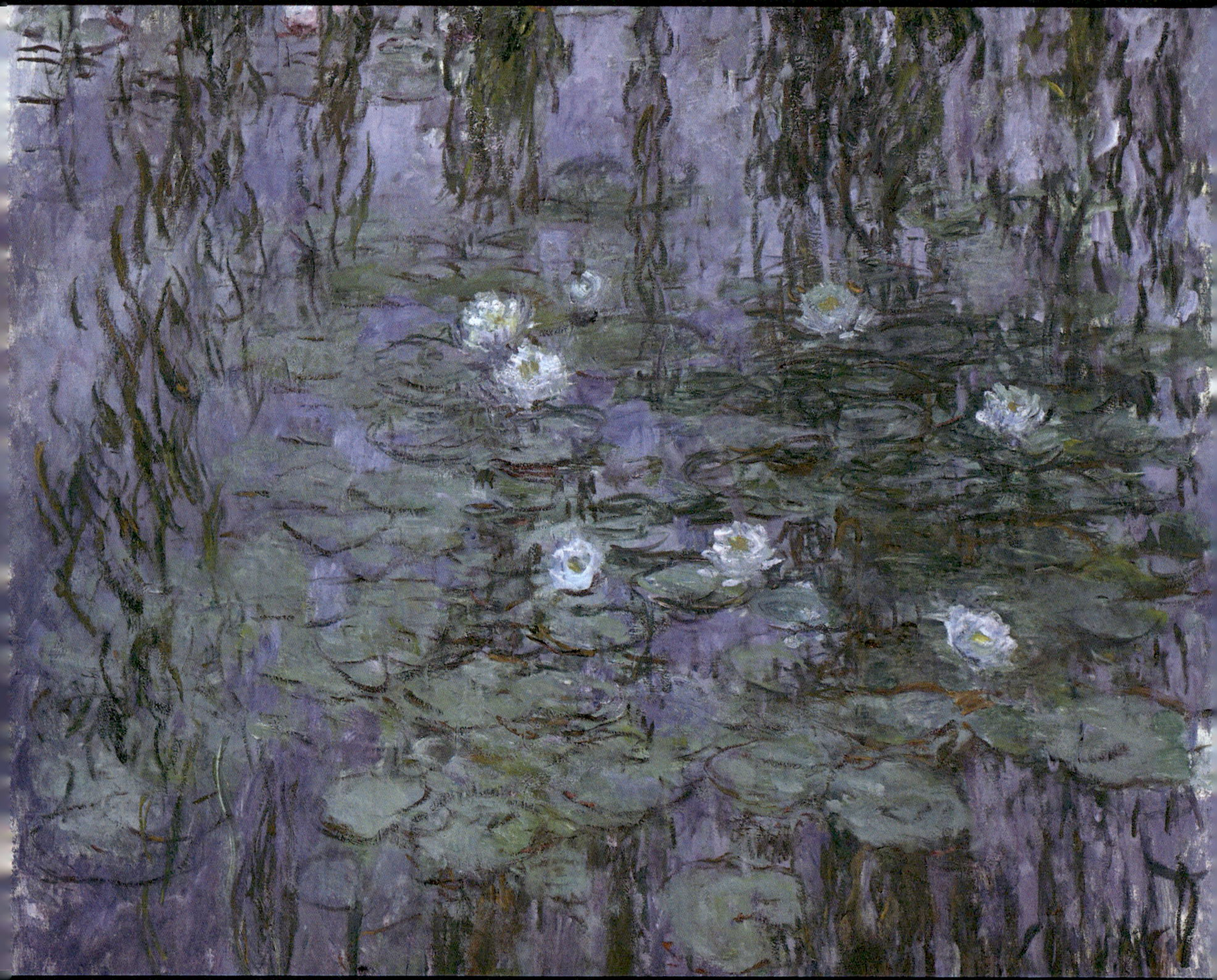

Note how the cool green and blue neighbors convey a sense of calm and peace

ANALOGOUS SCHEMES - COLOR STUDIES

Use this page for trying out your own harmonious color planning of some Analogous schemes. Map them on the wheels, add notes under the wheel as to the pigment names, hues, neutrals and chromatic grays/ blacks used. If you have made some of your own labelled colors, use these names too.

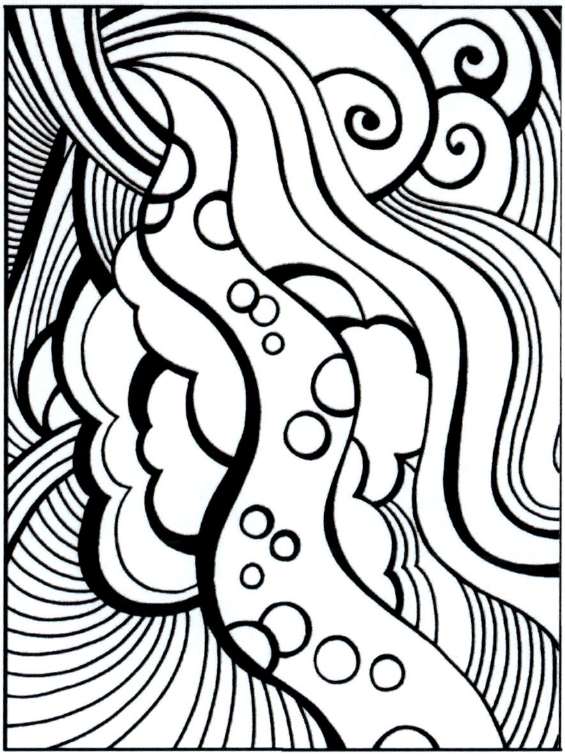

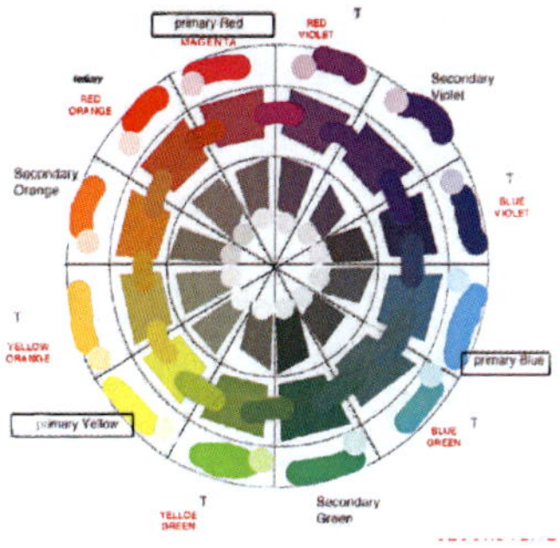

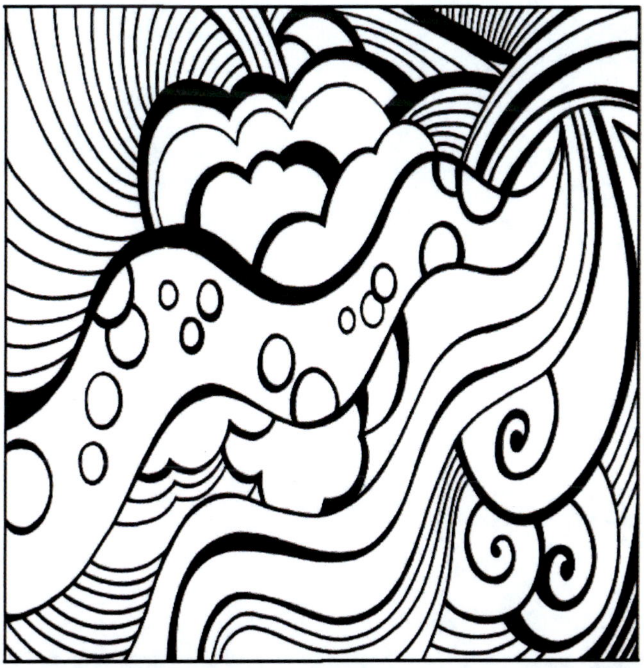

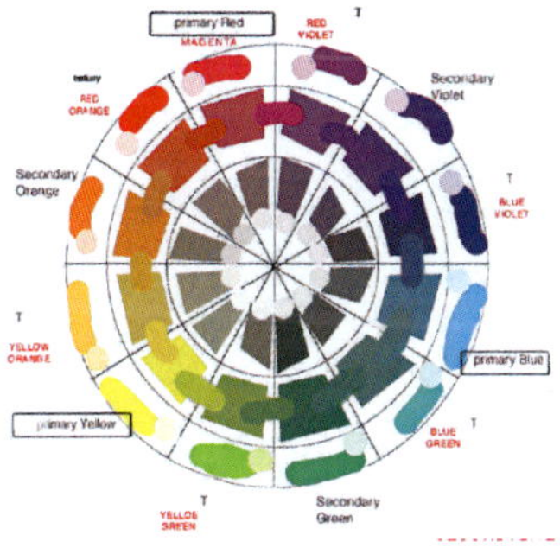

ANALOGOUS SCHEMES

An analogous scheme has more variety in hues than a monochromatic scheme, but not much in the way of a dynamic contrast from the other side of the wheel. How dynamic or serene an analogous scheme is depends mostly on the variety and combinations of saturation, temperature and values.

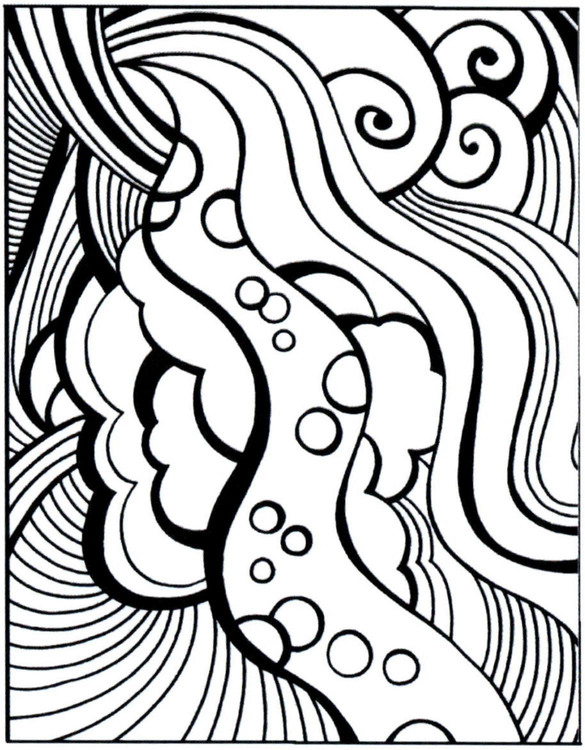

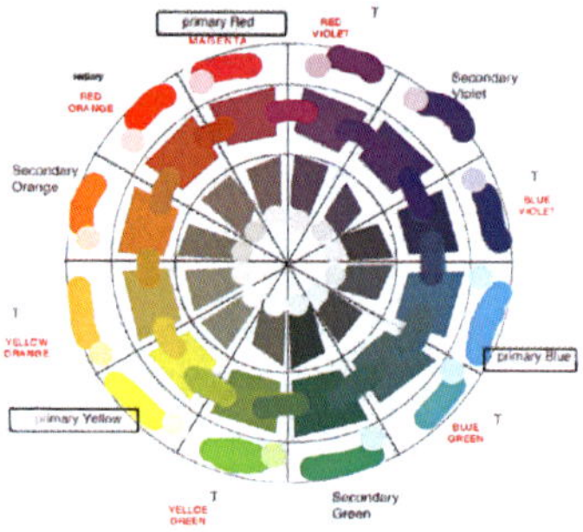

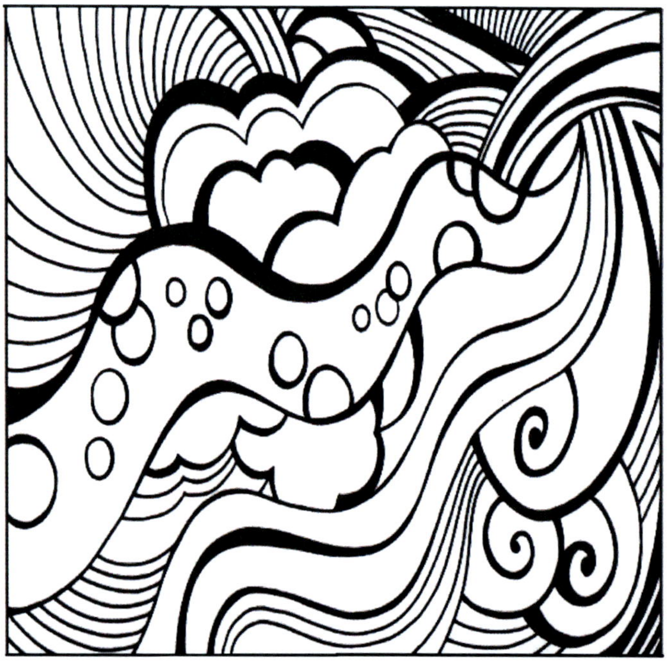

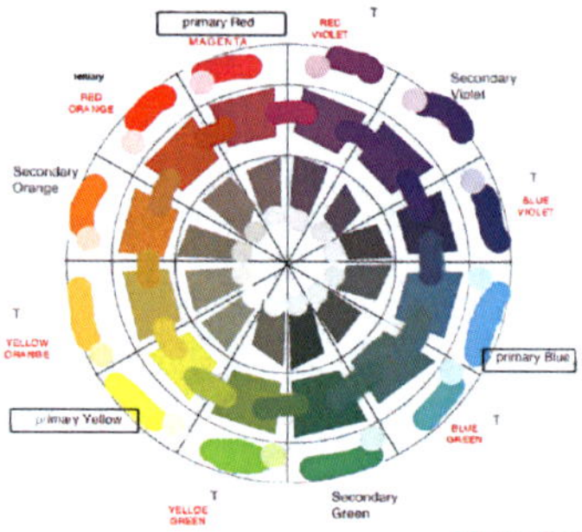

ANALOGOUS SCHEMES

Use these pages for your own compositional shape sketches and harmonious color planning of some analogous schemes Map them on the wheels and add notes under the wheel as to the pigments, neutrals and chromatic grays/ blacks used. (Use your own convenience colors too.)

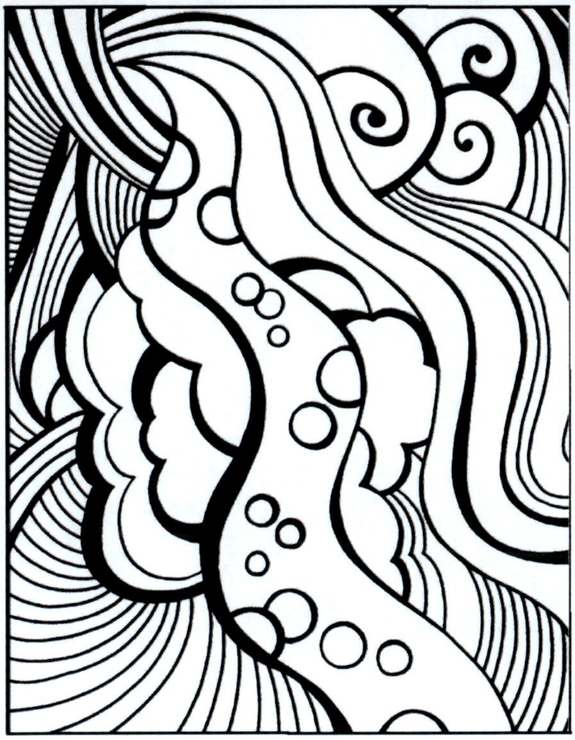

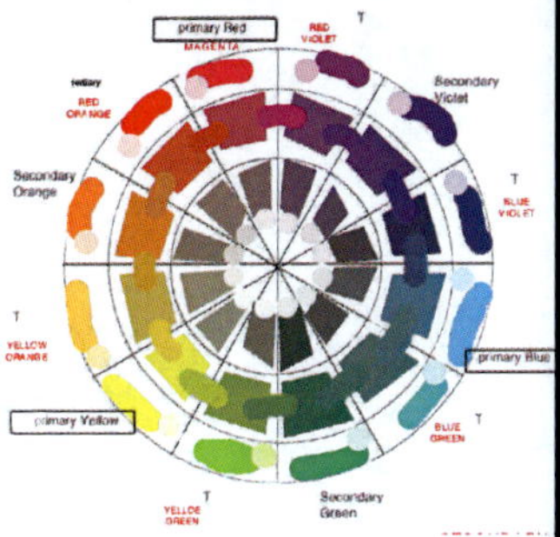

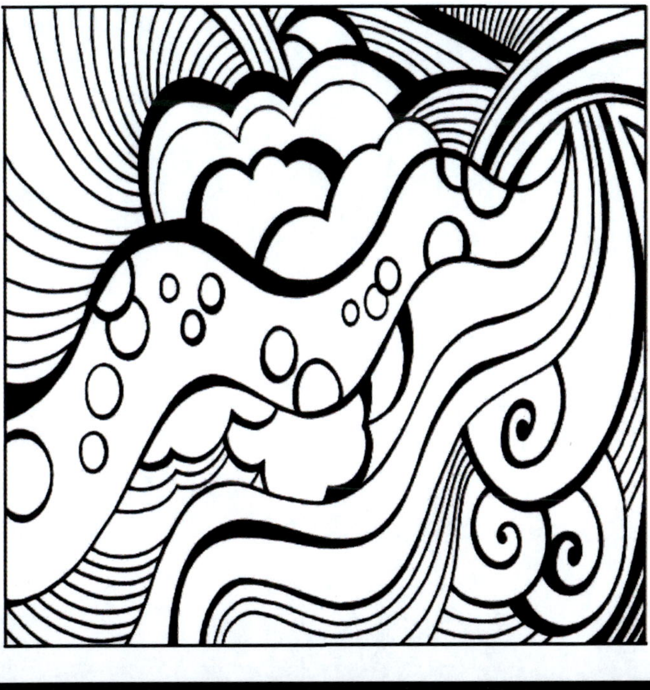

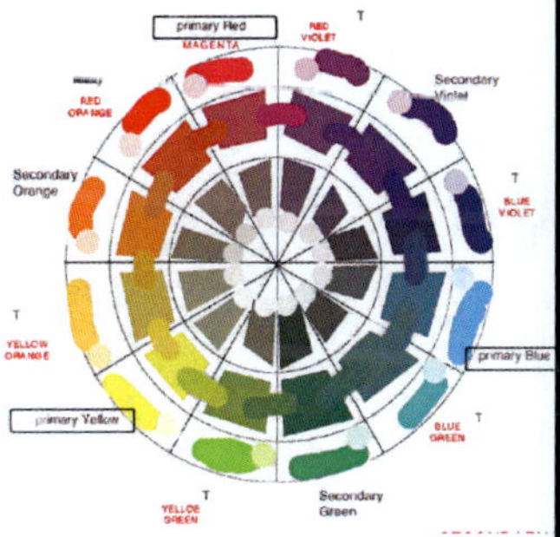

SIMPLE COMPLEMENTARY SCHEMES

Fig 17

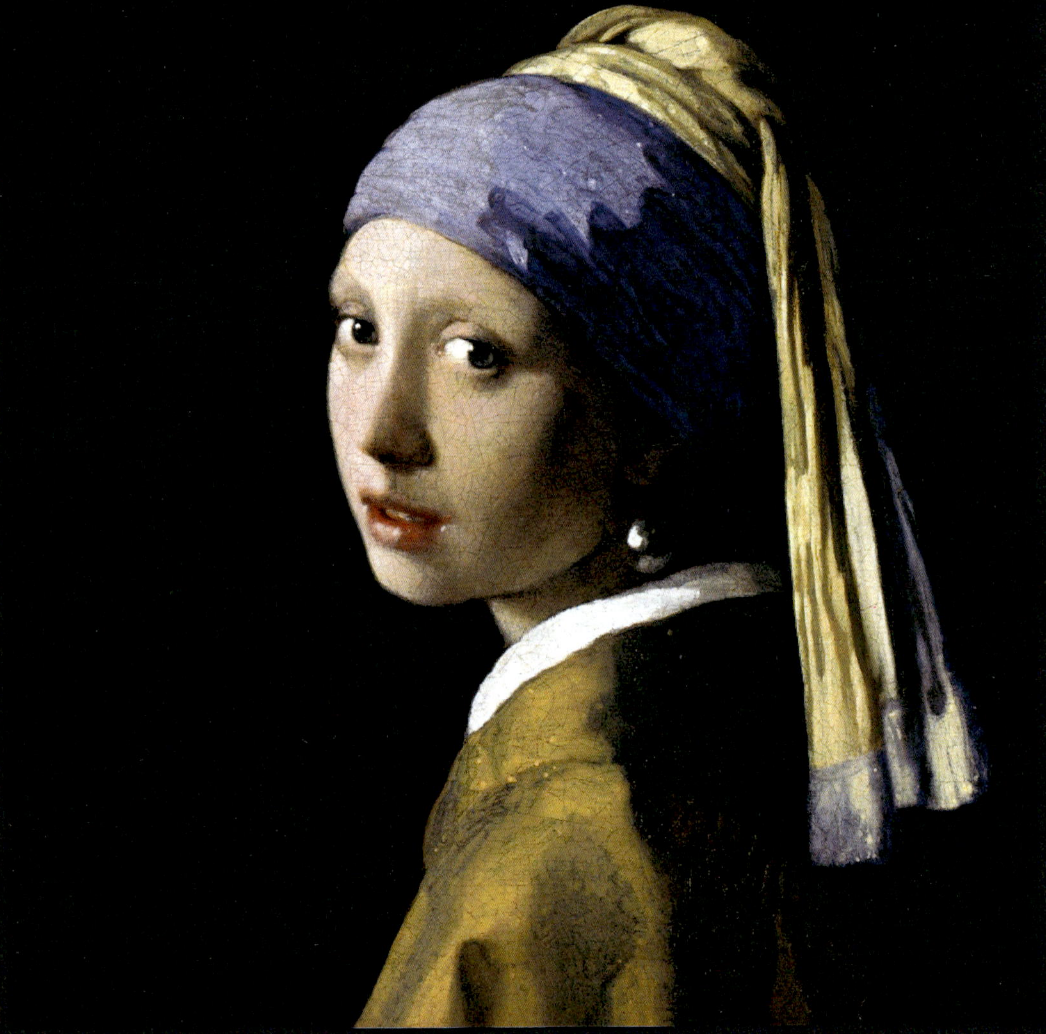

From Vermeer, this famous image holds our intrigue still, timeless in it's classical beauty. Basically a Blue-violet, Yellow-Orange dance going on here (the Red-orange on her lips could see it described as a split complementary scheme) but IMO, the simple scheme is what may very well have contributed to her allure for centuries, on top of her whole 'rich girl chic' look (pearl, expensive blue pigment, who wouldn't love to be portrayed so stunningly!) She has been copied and parodied infinitely since then.

SIMPLE COMPLEMENTARY SCHEMES

Use this page for trying out your own harmonious color planning of some Simple Complementary schemes. Map them on the wheels and add notes under the wheel as to the pigment names, hues,neutrals and chromatic grays/ blacks used.

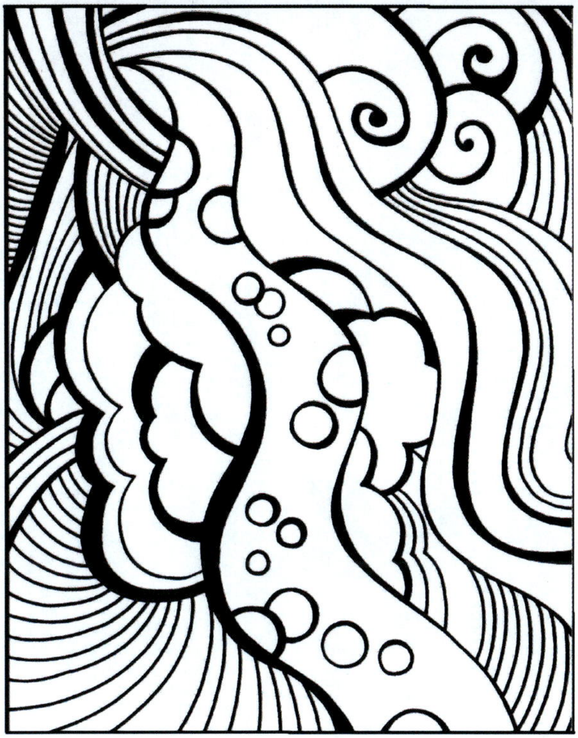

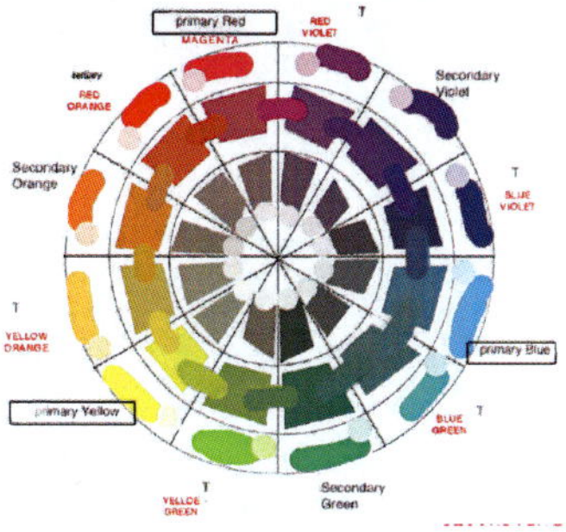

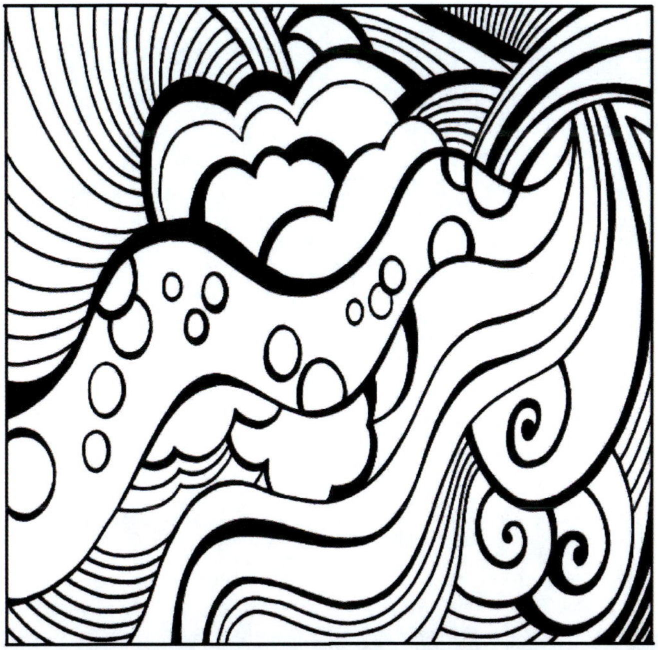

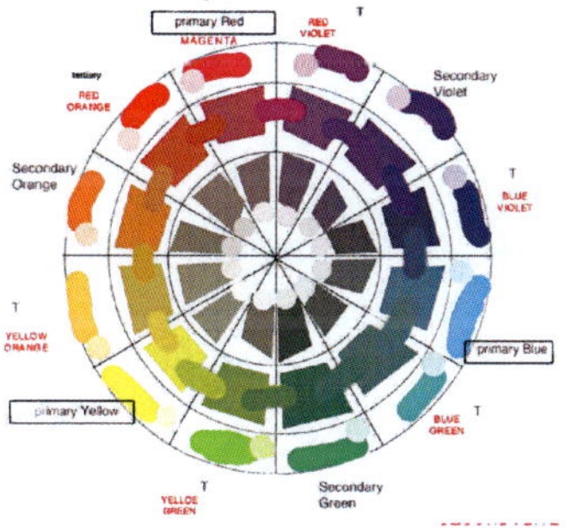

SIMPLE COMPLEMENTARY SCHEMES

Fig 18

Simple Complementary schemes involve colors that sit directly opposite each other on the color wheel. Below is a detail of an image with orange and blue, 'Dreamer i'. The opposite color is called 'complementary' because each color casts it's opposite onto surrounding areas, thus 'amplifying' the other color (simultaneous contrast). They complement each other and yet would cancel each other to gray if mixed together physically. Fascinating! When you set up fairly equal amounts of cool and warm areas, it can create a subtle tension. Mostly, a painting has a balance toward one or the other, not competing, but there are always exceptions, as with any guidelines in art. These are not rules, they are tools.

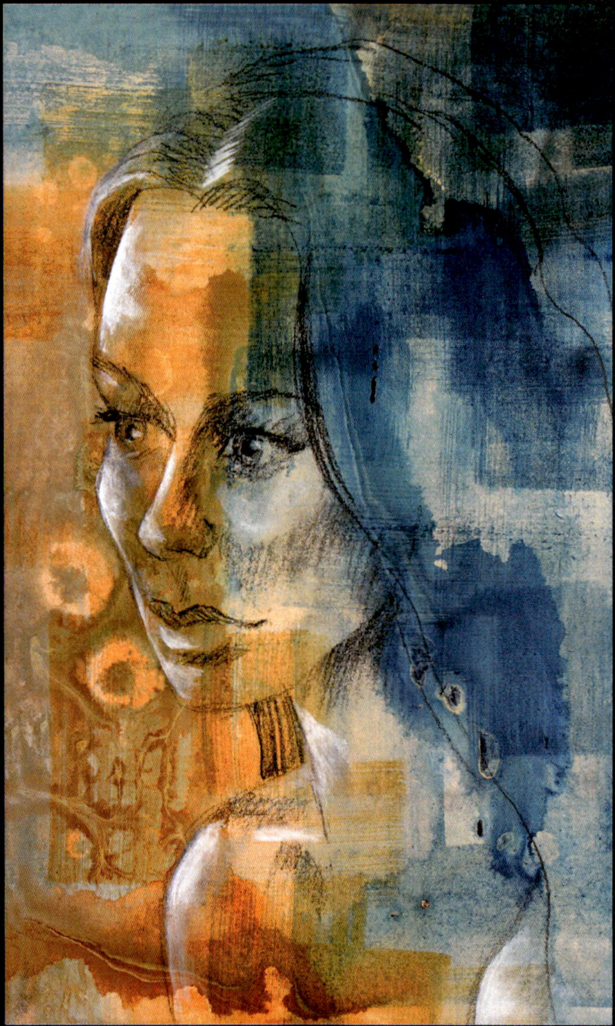

SIMPLE COMPLEMENTARY SCHEMES

Use this page for trying out more harmonious color planning of some Simple Complementary schemes. Map yours on the wheel and add notes under the wheel as to the pigment names, hues,neutrals and chromatic grays/ blacks used.

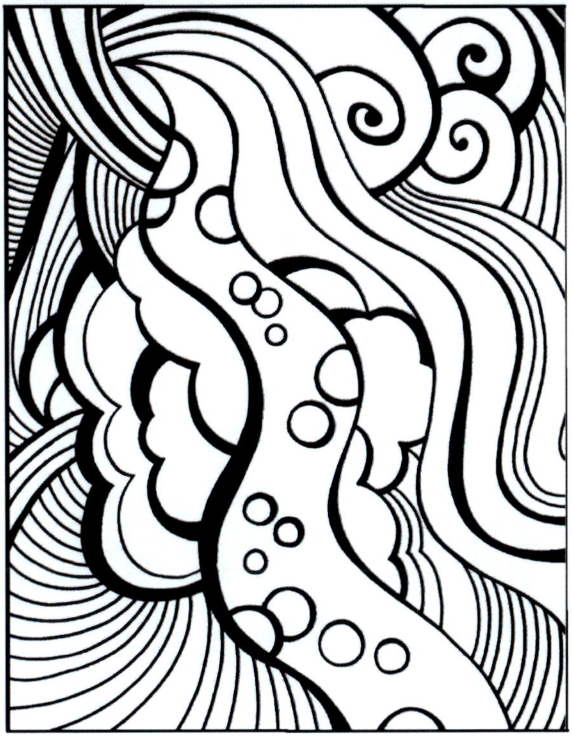

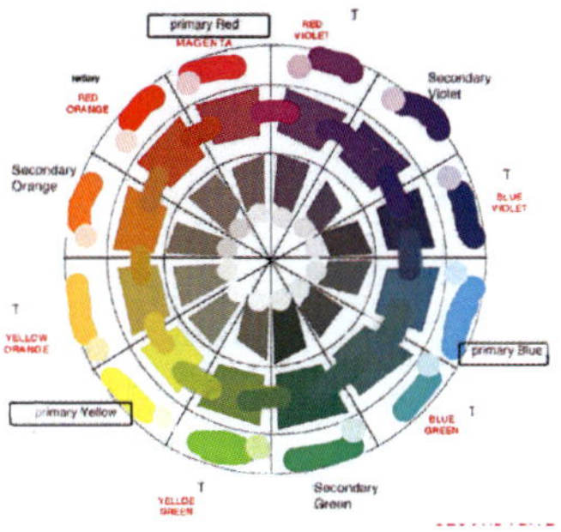

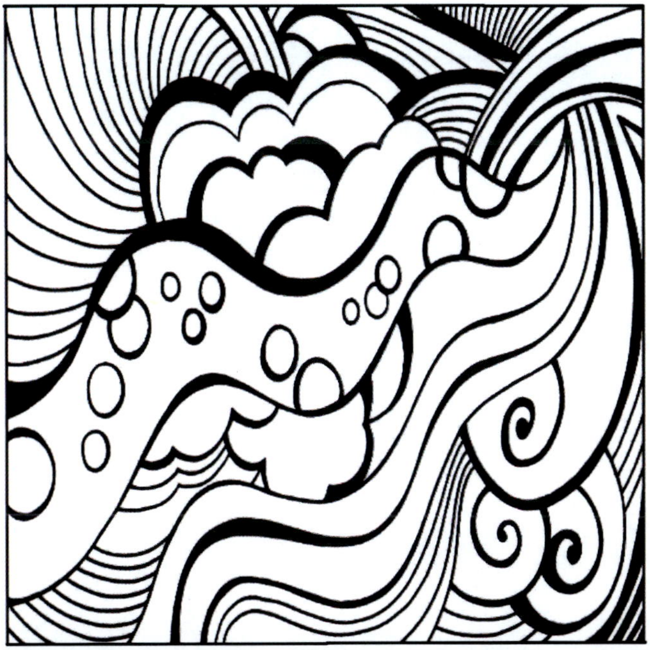

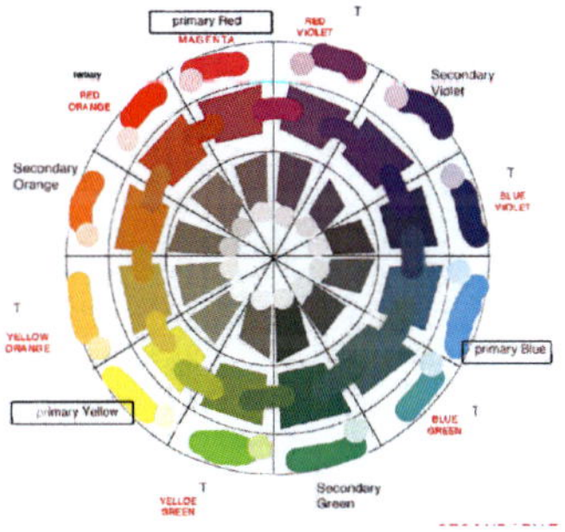

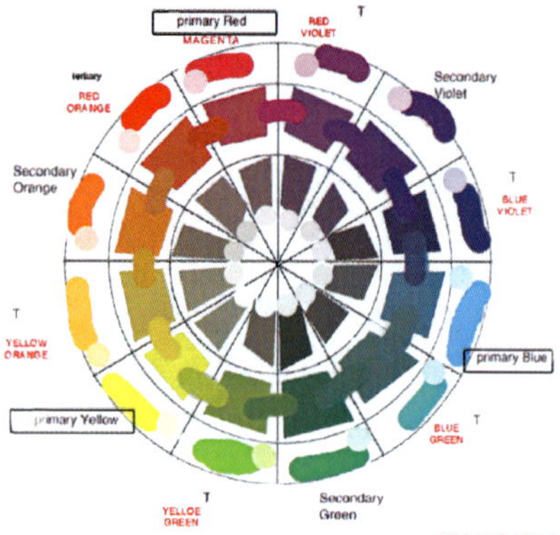
primary Red
MAGENTA
RED VIOLET
T
Secondary Violet
T
BLUE VIOLET
primary Blue
T
BLUE GREEN
Secondary Green
T
YELLOE GREEN
primary Yellow
T
YELLOW ORANGE
Secondary Orange
tertiary
RED ORANGE

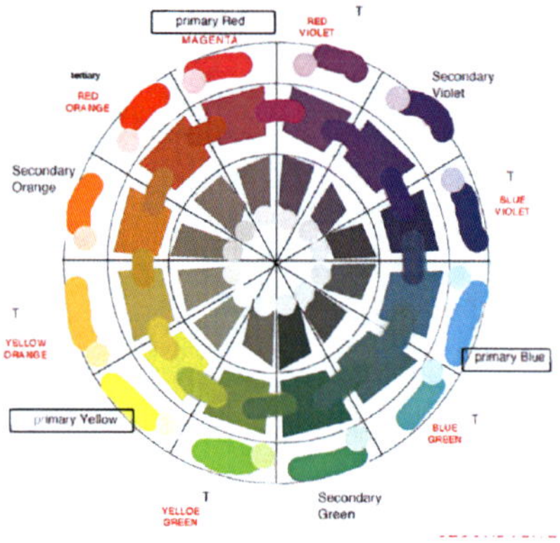
primary Red
MAGENTA
RED VIOLET
T
Secondary Violet
T
BLUE VIOLET
primary Blue
T
BLUE GREEN
Secondary Green
T
YELLOE GREEN
primary Yellow
T
YELLOW ORANGE
Secondary Orange
tertiary
RED ORANGE

SIMPLE COMPLEMENTARY SCHEMES

Use these pages for your own compositional shape sketches and harmonious color planning of some simple complimentary schemes. As before, map them on the wheels and add notes under the wheel as to the pigments, neutrals and chromatic grays/ blacks used. Use your own drawings here.

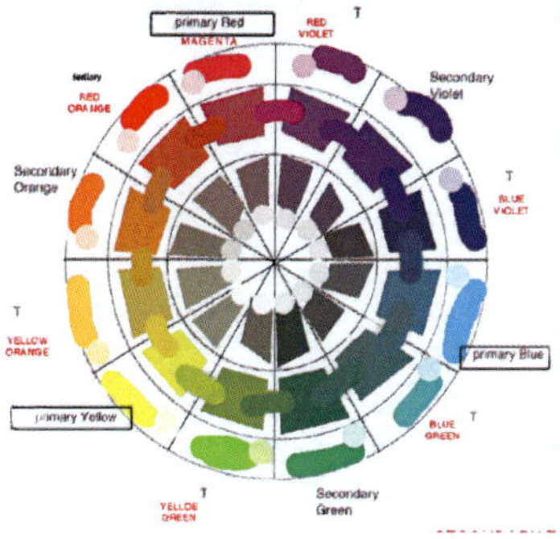

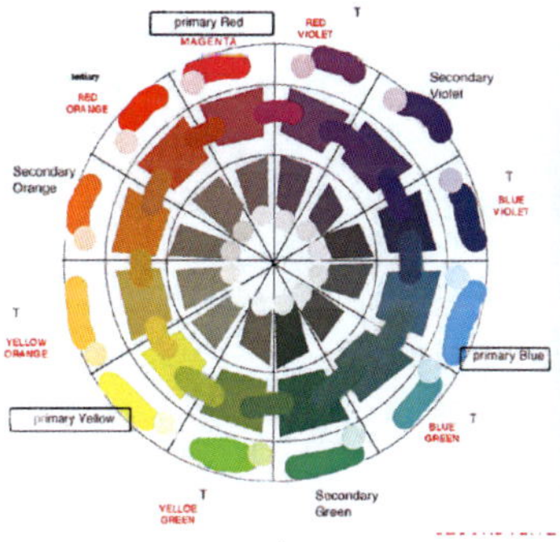

DOUBLE COMPLEMENTARY SCHEMES

Grabbing two neighbors and throwing them in the mix with their opposite two neighbors is the deal here (a bit of an extension of the simple complementary idea).

I have taken my 'Dreamer i' image, scribbled in some blue-violet and some yellow-orange in photoshop as a comparative study of simple complementary compared to the double.

That subtle change in harmony plan gives a whole other mood to the piece (more psychodelic dream...less daydream!)

When you are planning your schemes for paintings, try more than one until you feel for yourself if your choice of color combos are saying exactly what you wanted to express.

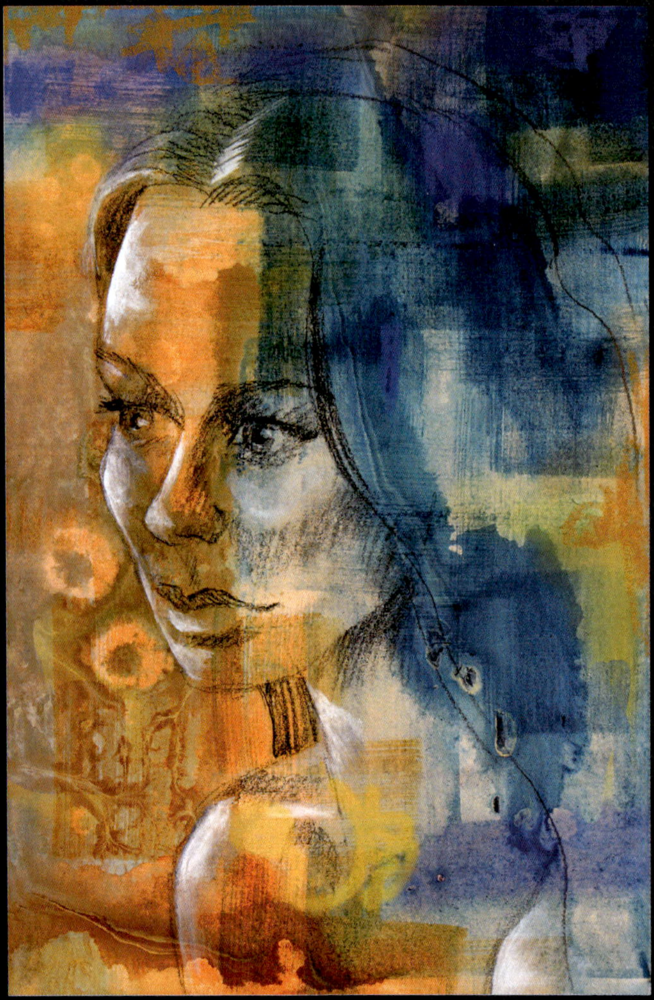

The psychodelic trippy feel was not what I was going for when I created the 'Dreamer' series.

An example to illustrate the benefits of trying a few options while planning your schemes.

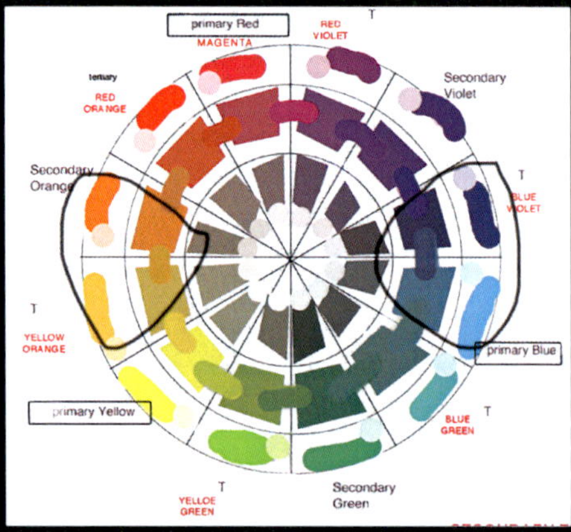

CREATE MORE DOUBLE COMPLEMENTARY SCHEMES OF YOUR OWN

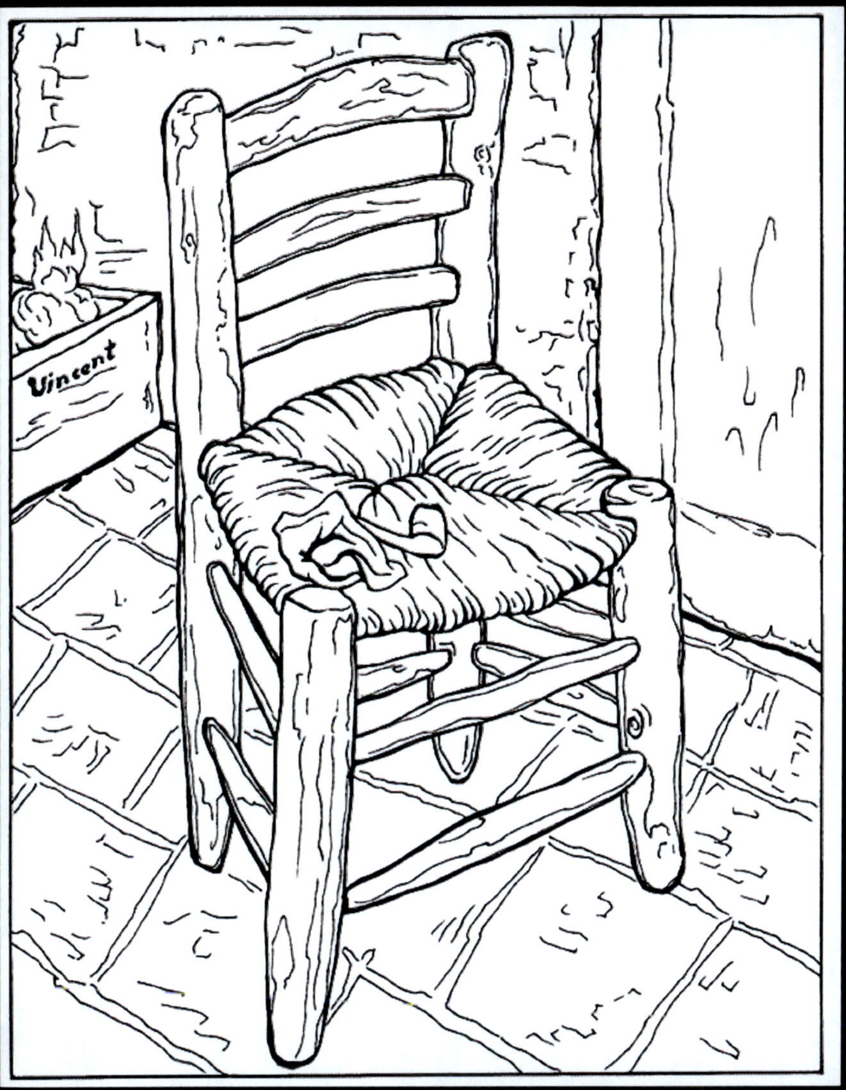

Plan a Double complementary scheme including secondary orange (generally try to make schemes either warm dominant or cool dominant, avoid using any element in competition, in this case temperature. Allow one to dominate).

Circle the two opposite pairs you plan to use.

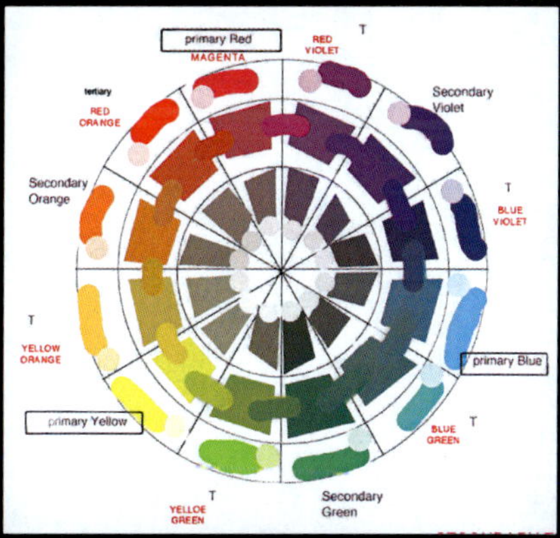

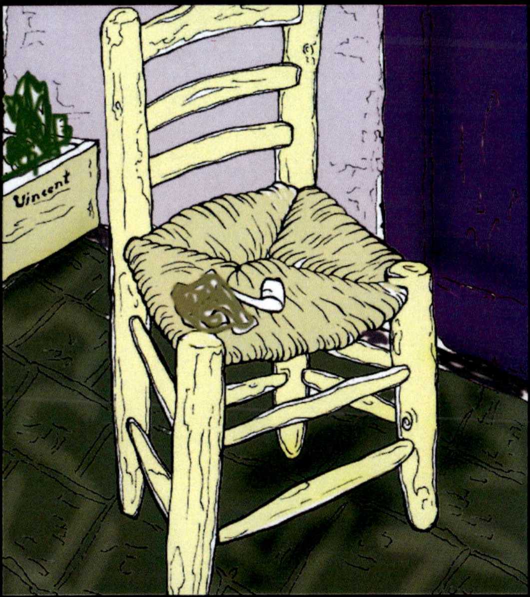

Here is a double complementary scheme with red-violet / violet and yellow/ yellow-green

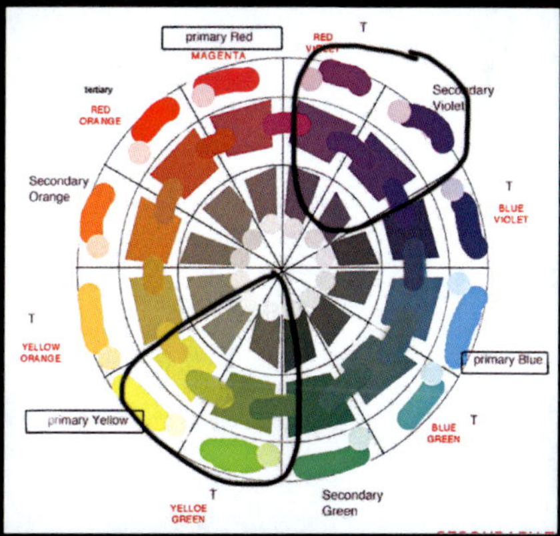

DOUBLE COMPLEMENTARY SCHEMES

Use this page for your own compositional shape sketches and harmonious color planning of some Double Complementary schemes. Like before, map your schemes on the wheels and add notes under the wheel as to the pigment names, hues,neutrals and chromatic grays/ blacks used

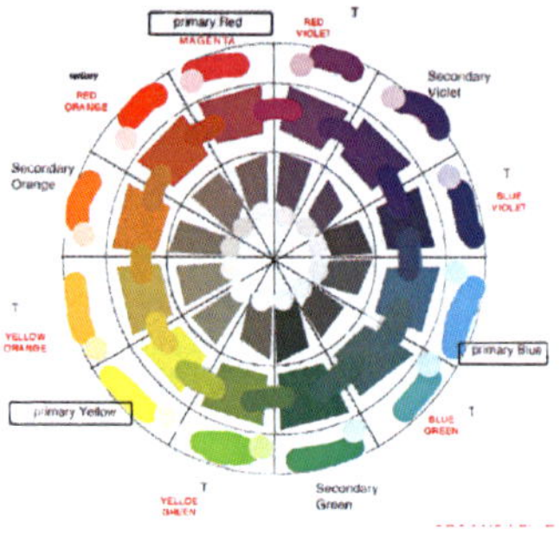

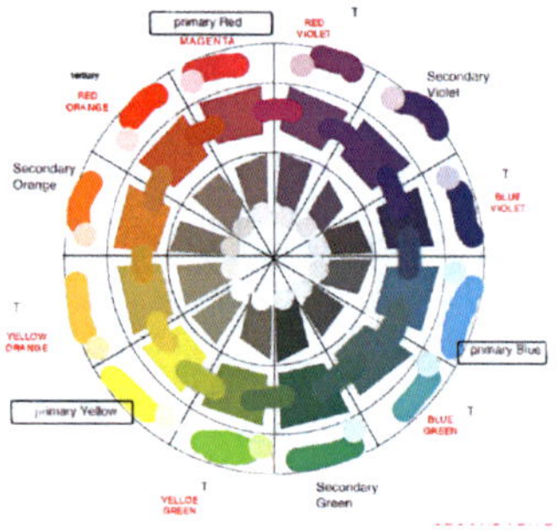

DOUBLE COMPLEMENTARY SCHEMES

Double Complementary schemes are slightly more animated and dynamic than Simple Complementary Schemes (considered to be more stimulating, less relaxing because of the extra subtle relationships combined.)

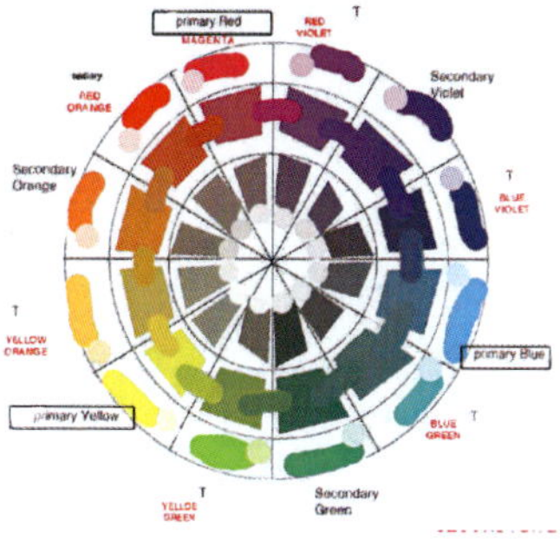

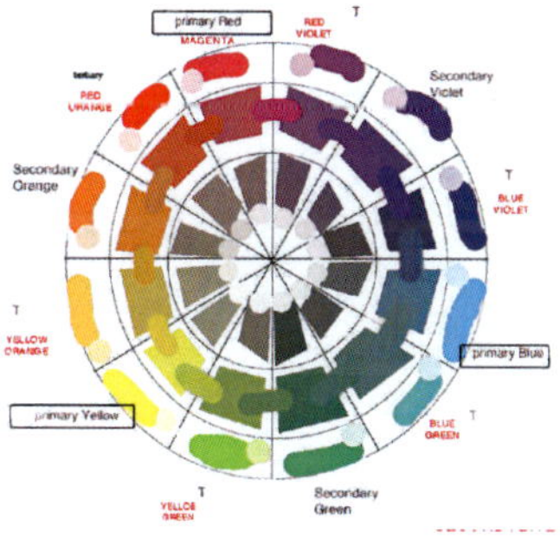

DOUBLE COMPLEMENTARY SCHEMES

Use this page for your own compositional shape sketches and harmonious color planning of some more Double Complementary schemes. Use your own drawings/ sketches.

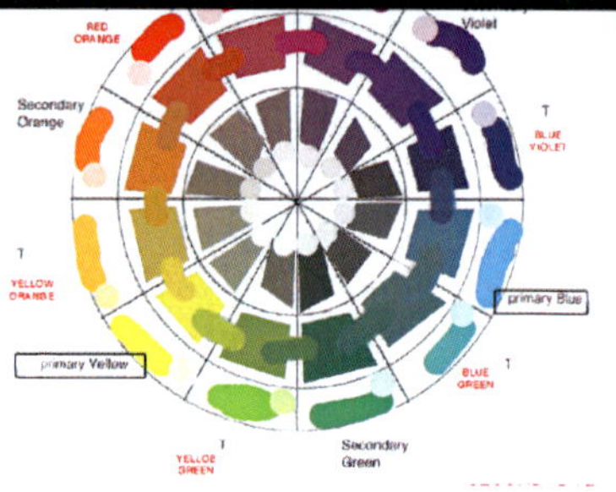

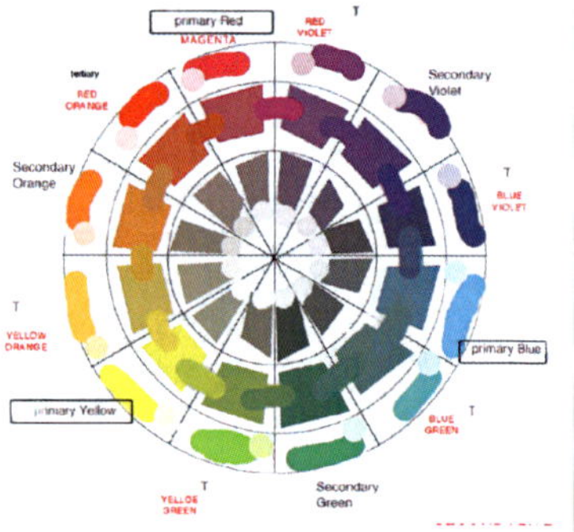

SPLIT COMPLEMENTARY SCHEMES

We could have used Monet's Parliament House series for so many scheme examples, as he designed his color relationships to give the feel for varying times of day. This one employs a Split complementary scheme with yellow sitting opposite both red-violet and blue-violet (very desaturated versions of all due to the late evening lighting effects). Fig 19

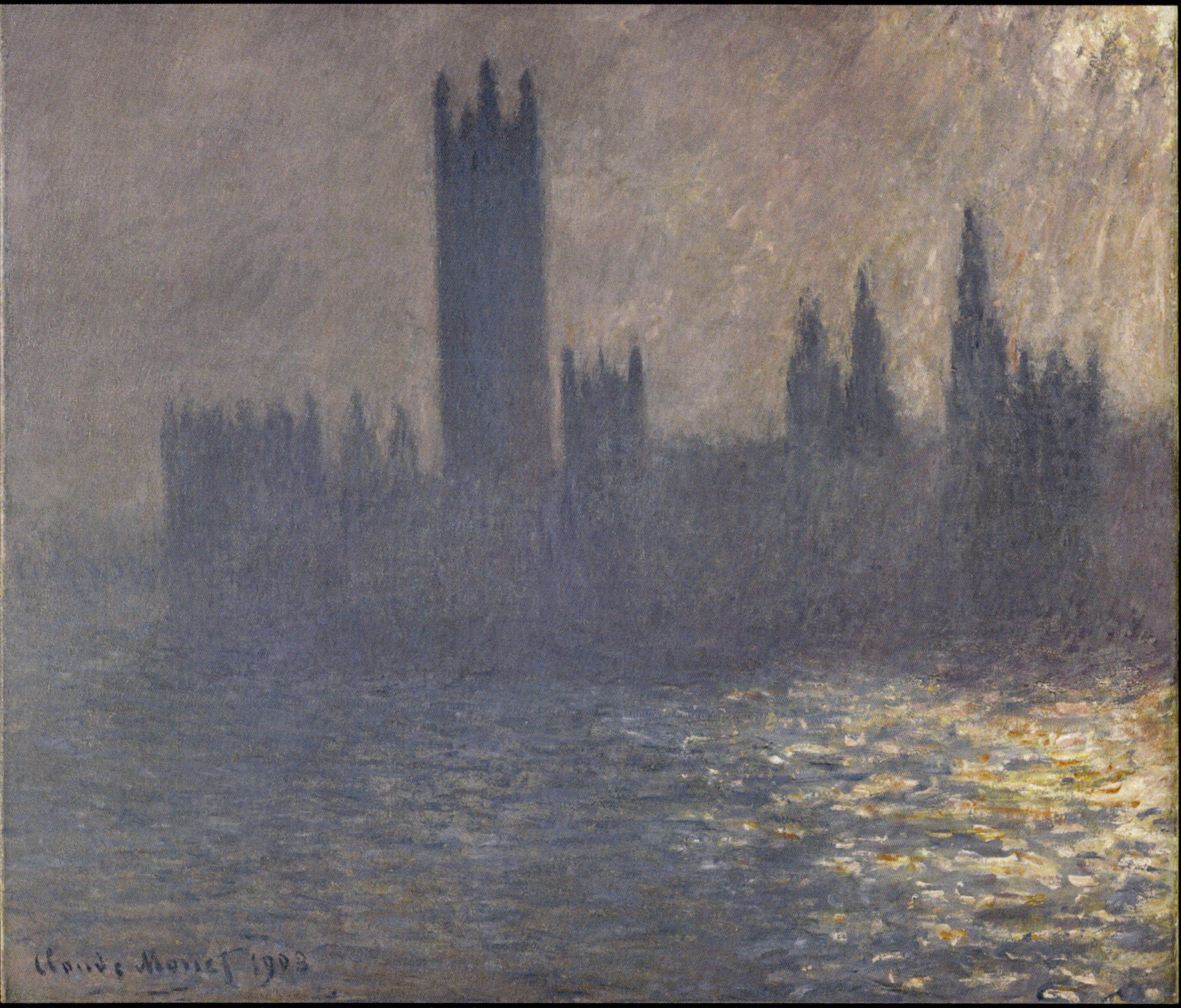

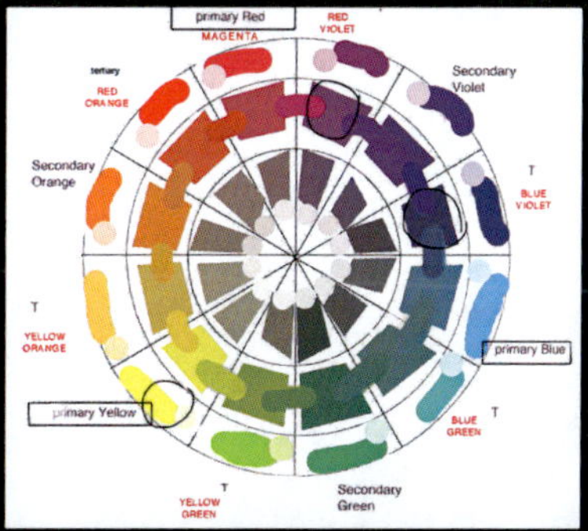

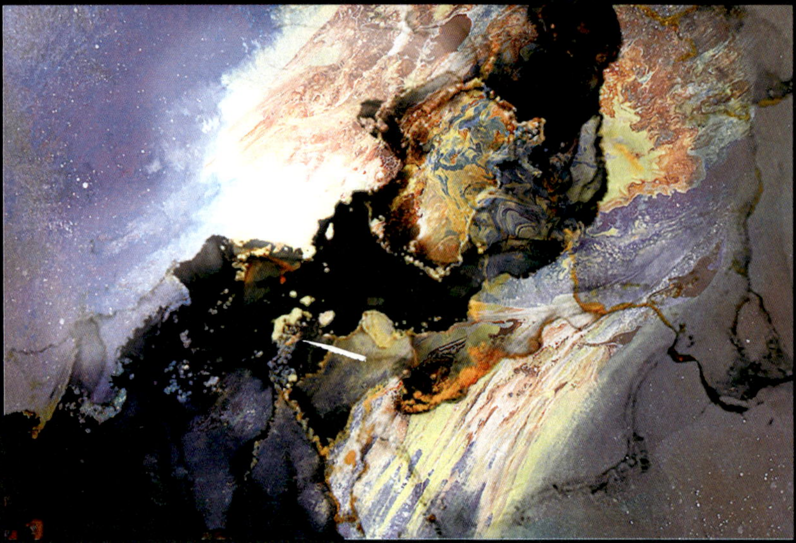

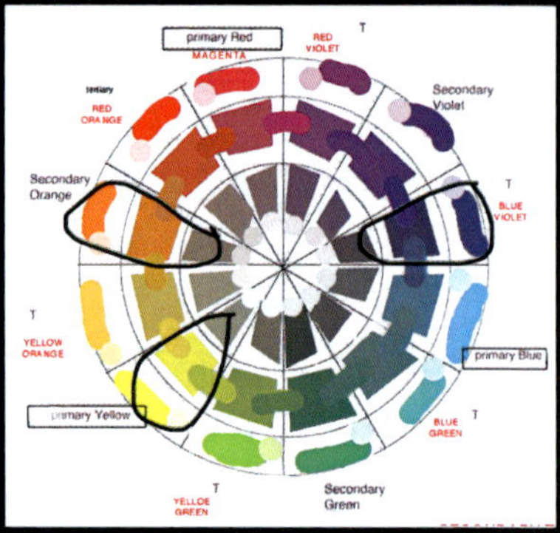

Fig 20 - Try out two more different possible Split complementary schemes for this abstract composition, converted here to a simple greyscale drawing sketch to work on.

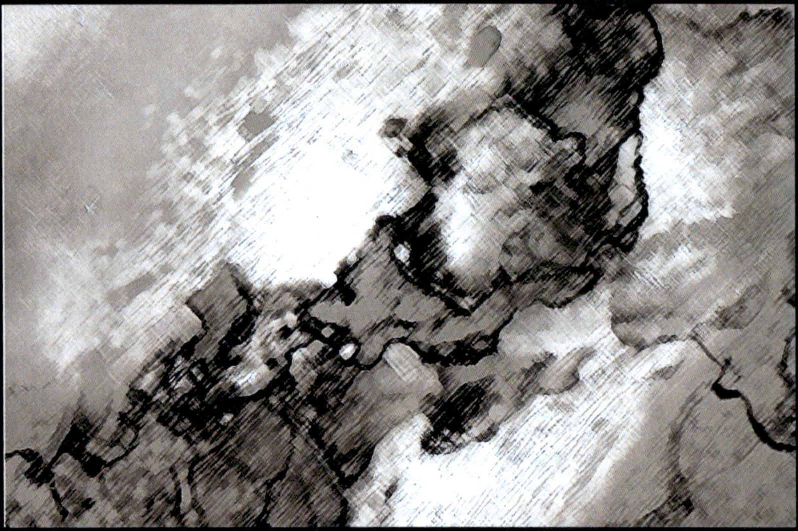

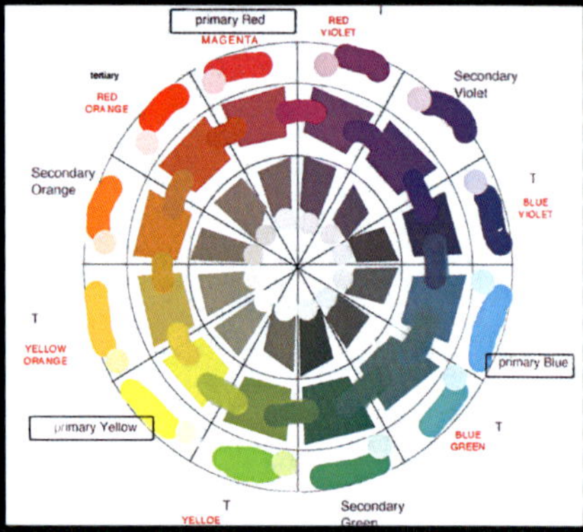

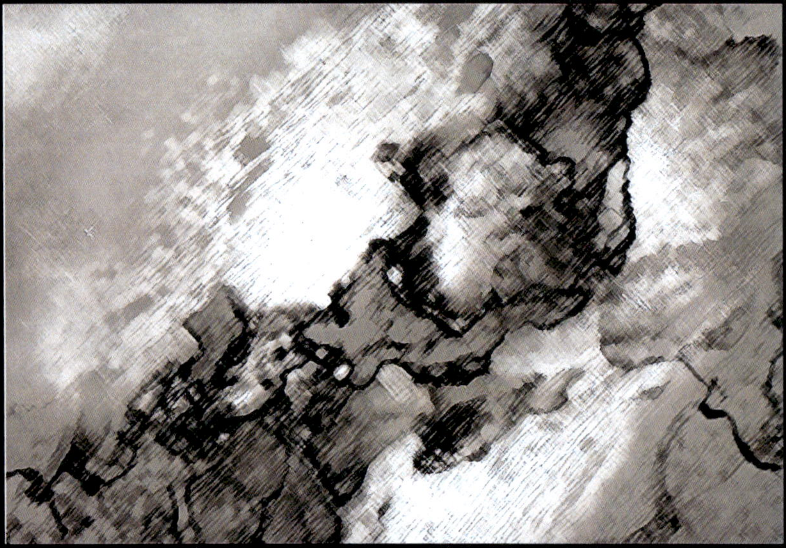

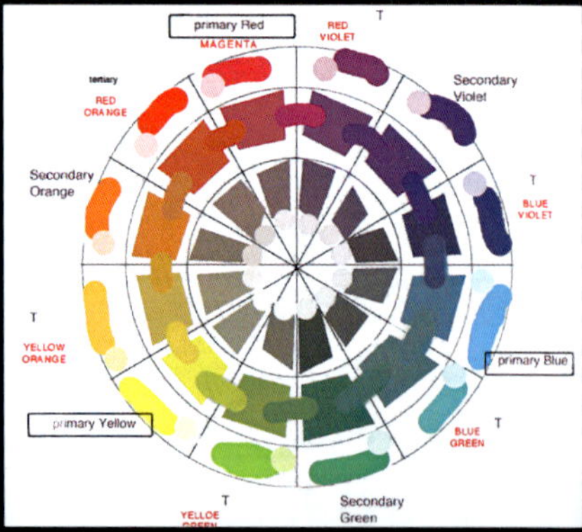

SPLIT COMPLEMENTARY SCHEMES

Use this page for your own compositional shape sketches and harmonious color planning of some Split Complementary schemes for your own drawings or simple compositional sketches.

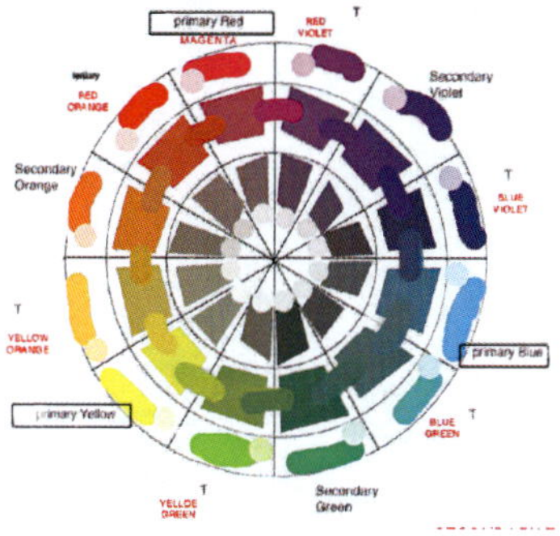

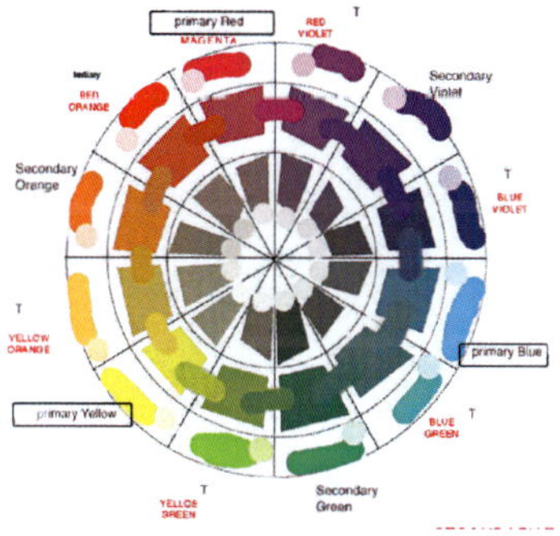

TRY SOME SPLIT COMPLIMENTARY SCHEMES ON THIS ART NOUVEAU DRAWING

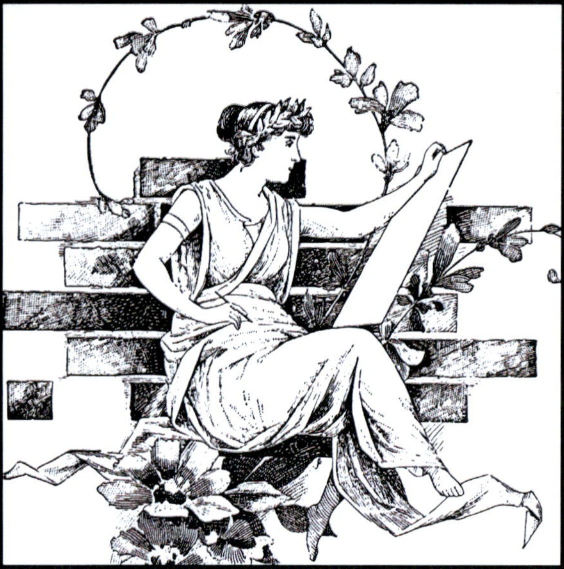

Plan a Split complementary including Primary blue (NB. try to make schemes either warm dominant or cool dominant).

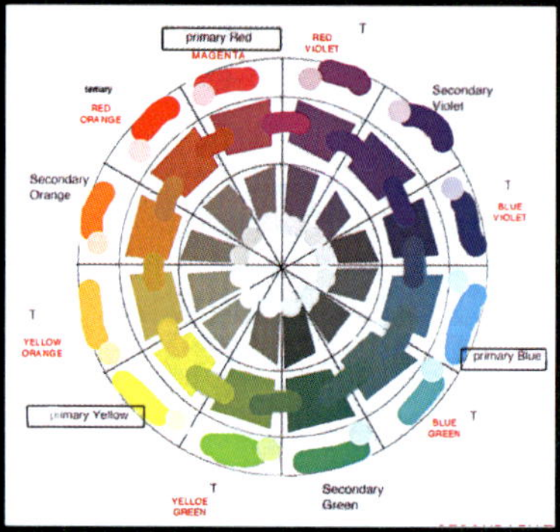

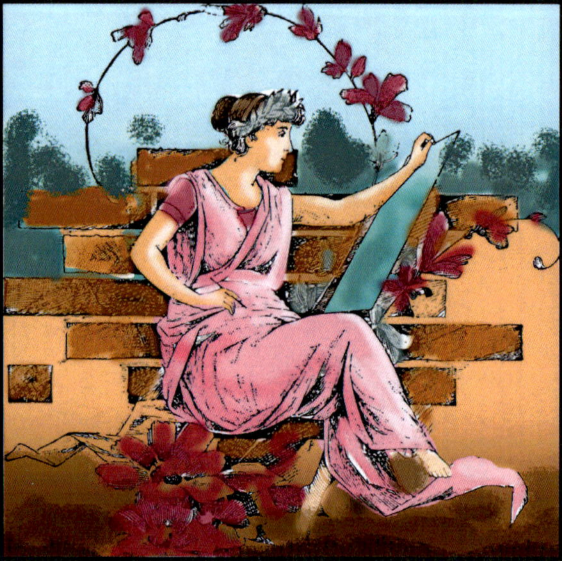

Here I planned a Split complementary including primary red (magenta). I included some tints and neutrals of orange, magenta and blue-green (warm dominates).

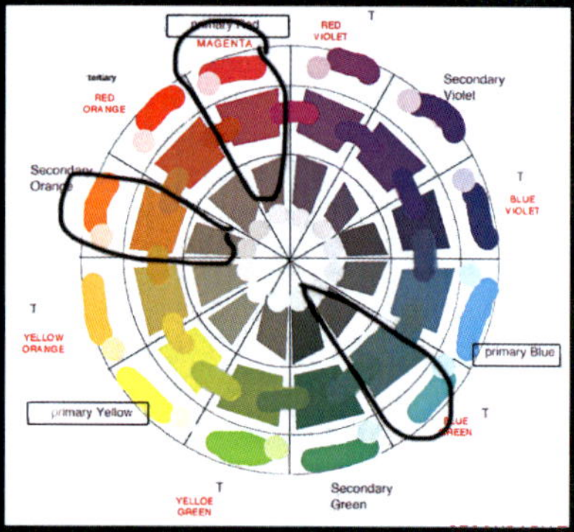

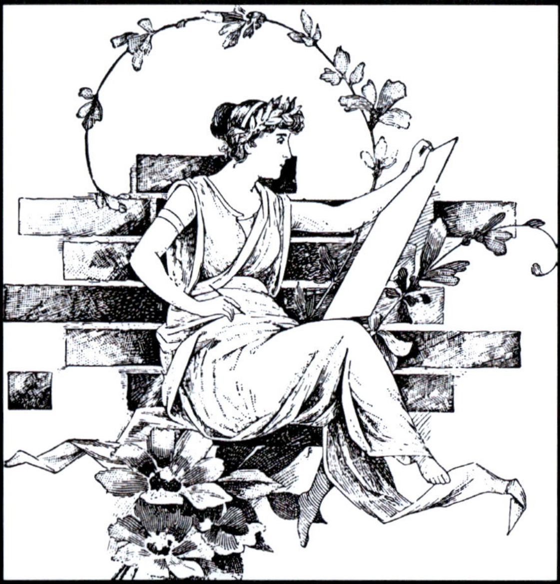

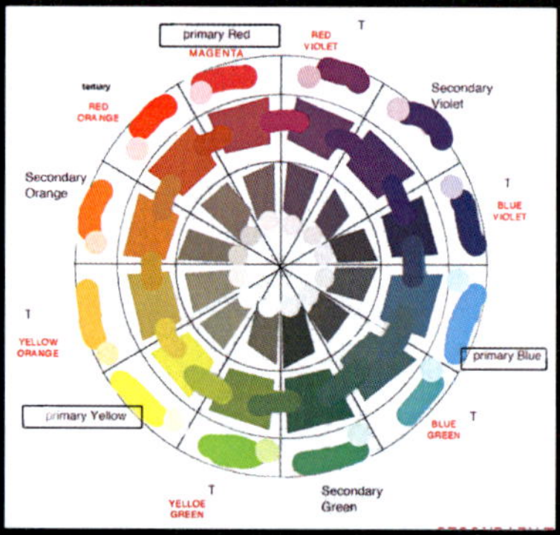

Plan a Split complementary including Primary Yellow.

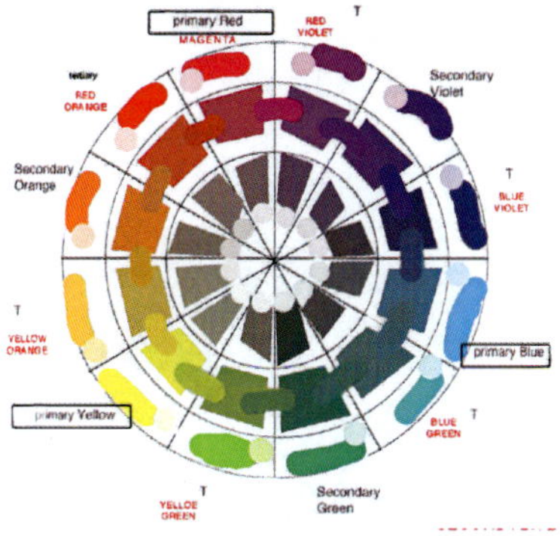
primary Red
MAGENTA
RED VIOLET
T
tertiary
RED ORANGE
Secondary Violet
Secondary Orange
T
BLUE VIOLET
T
YELLOW ORANGE
primary Blue
primary Yellow
BLUE GREEN
T
T
YELLOE GREEN
Secondary Green

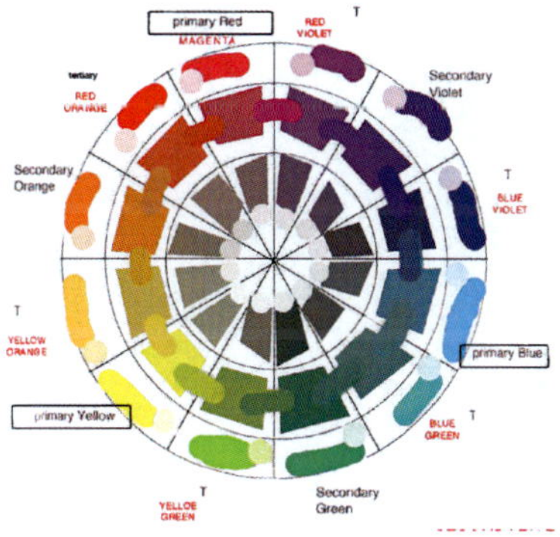
primary Red
MAGENTA
RED VIOLET
T
tertiary
RED ORANGE
Secondary Violet
Secondary Orange
T
BLUE VIOLET
T
YELLOW ORANGE
primary Blue
primary Yellow
BLUE GREEN
T
T
YELLOE GREEN
Secondary Green

ANALOGOUS PLUS COMPLEMENT SCHEMES

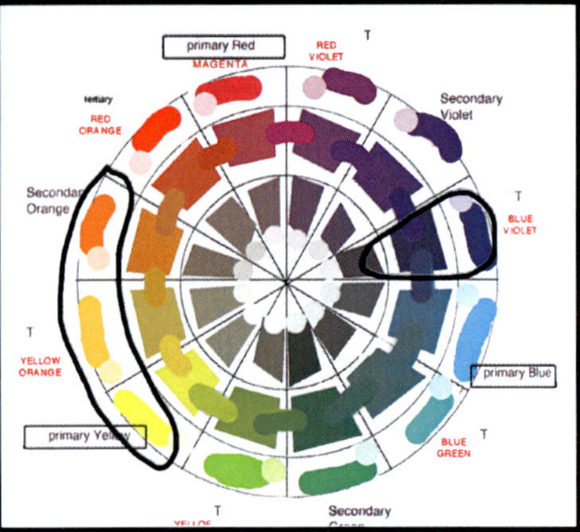

One of the easiest and simplest harmonies, and quite commonly used throughout history is the 'Analogous plus Complement'. Take 3-5 adjacent hues (neighbors) with a complementary color from the opposite side of the wheel. (often but not always they are all warm with a cool complemen or all cool with a warm complement).

Fig 21

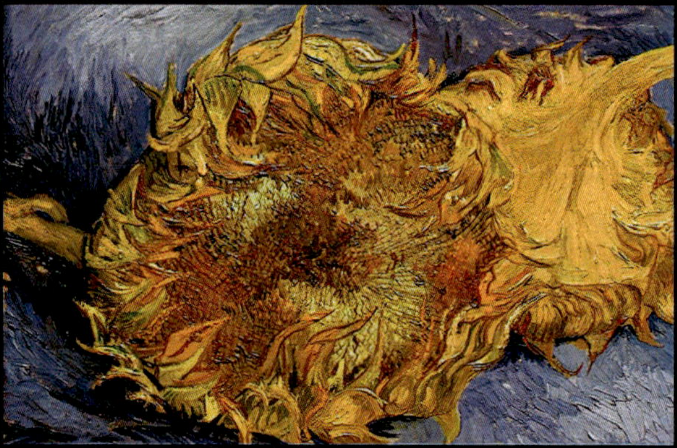

Looking at Vincent Van Gogh's 'The Par-s Sunflowers' from 1887, we see Yellow, Yellow-orange, Orange then a neutral (grayed off) version of Indigo or Blue-violet which sits on the other side of the wheel.

This was a favorite combo for Vincent.

I have seen this image called an example of a split complementary, but the yellow seen mostly is a yellow-orange so I interpret it more as an analogous plus complement as seen in the wheel. The point is, both schemes are harmonious and Vincent used both at times, so it is another example of a reasonably relaxed but effective use of harmonization.

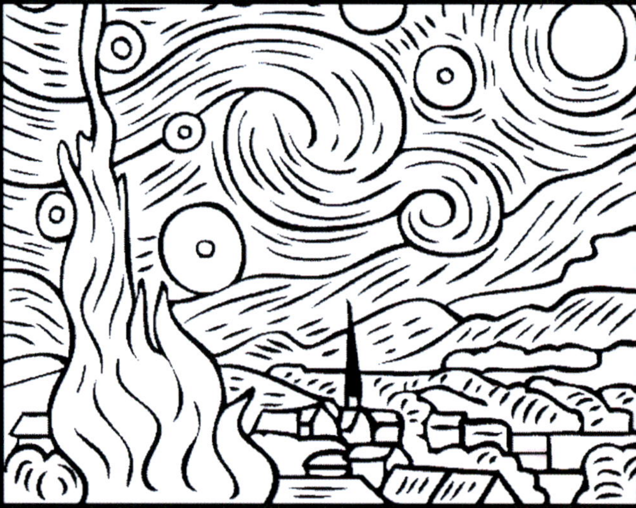

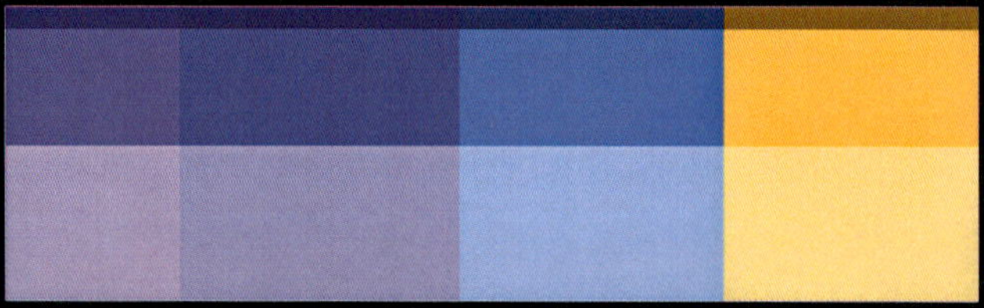

Harmony exercise: Violet, Blue-violet, Blue and Yellow-Orange (3 cool, 1 warm) Use the little line drawing of Starry Night and give it an analogous plus complement scheme with these hues (use your little pointer brush to do a tiny color study.)

PLAN ANALOGOUS PLUS COMPLEMENT COLOR SCHEMES

Use this page for your own compositional shape sketches and harmonious color planning of some Analogous plus Complement schemes for your drawings / designs .

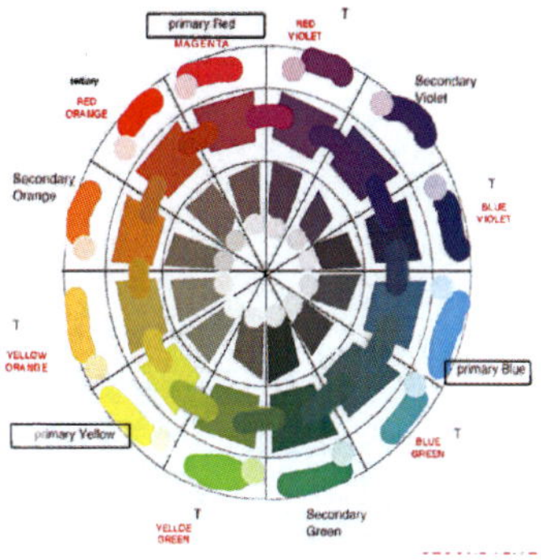

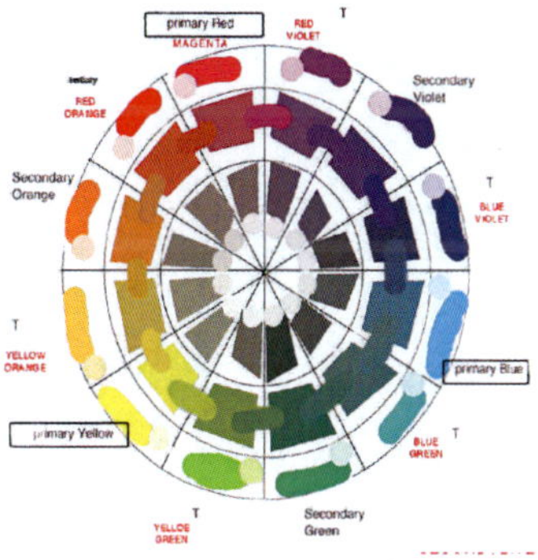

ANALOGOUS PLUS COMPLEMENT SCHEME - EXAMPLE

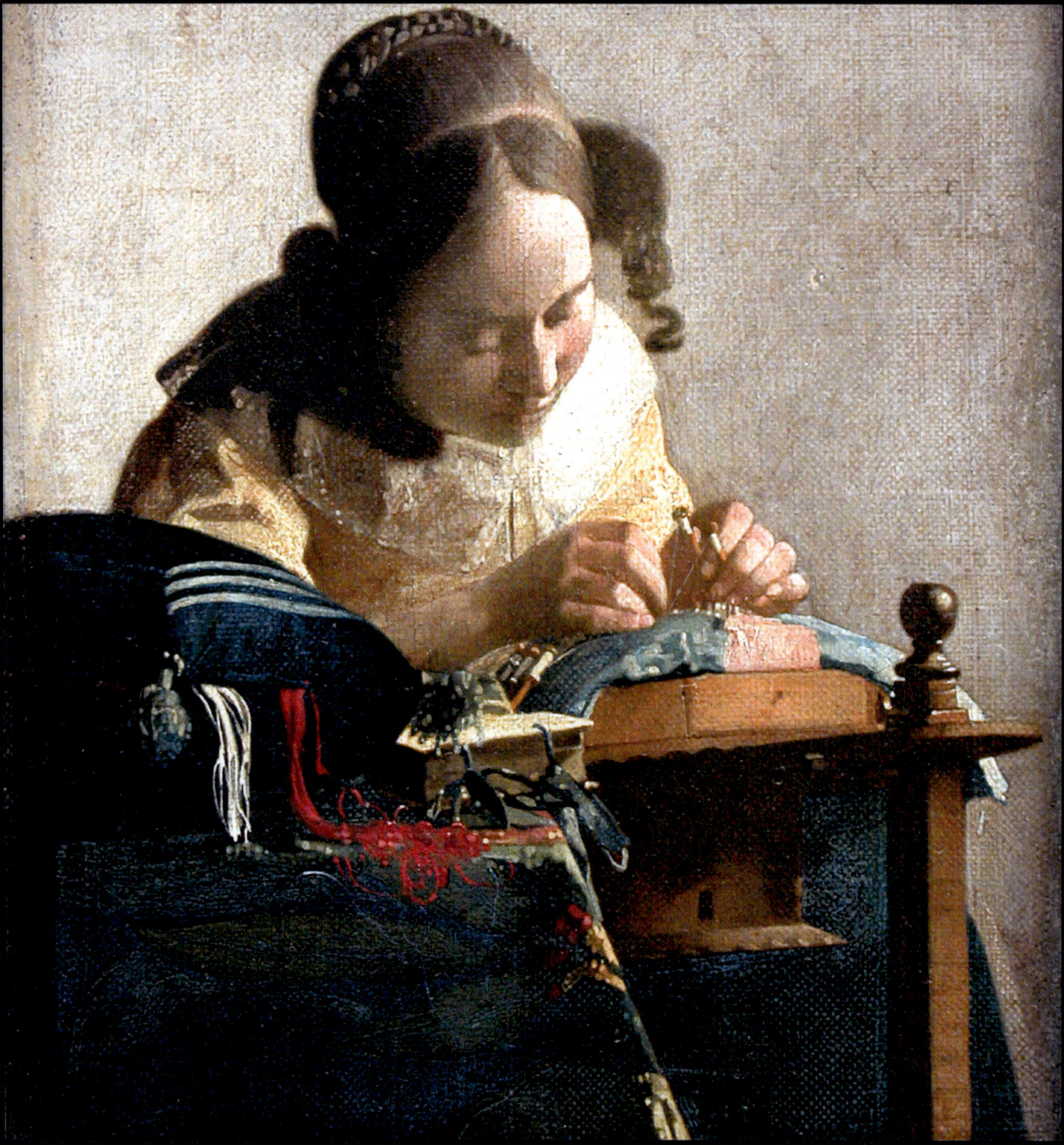

Fig 22

'The Lacemaker'- just 24 × 21 cm

painted by Vermeer in around 1671. Mostly, the warm analogous colors are neutralized and sit opposite various values of the lovely rich blue. (probably 'Azurite' which we don't use anymore due to more stable alternatives in pigment.)

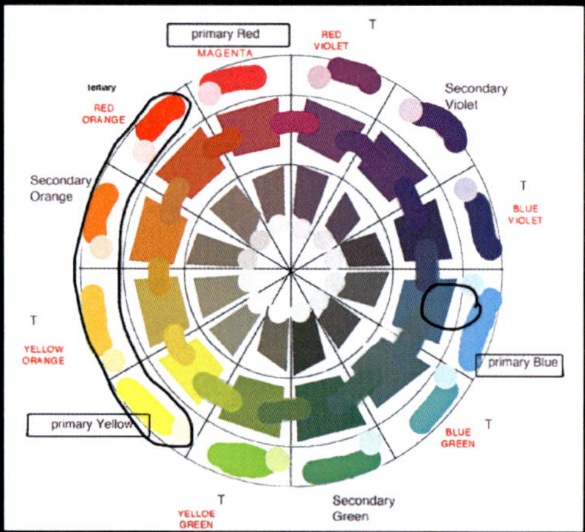

PLAN ANALOGOUS PLUS COMPLEMENT COLOR SCHEMES

Use this page for your own compositional shape sketches and harmonious color planning of some Analogous plus Complement schemes for your drawings / designs .

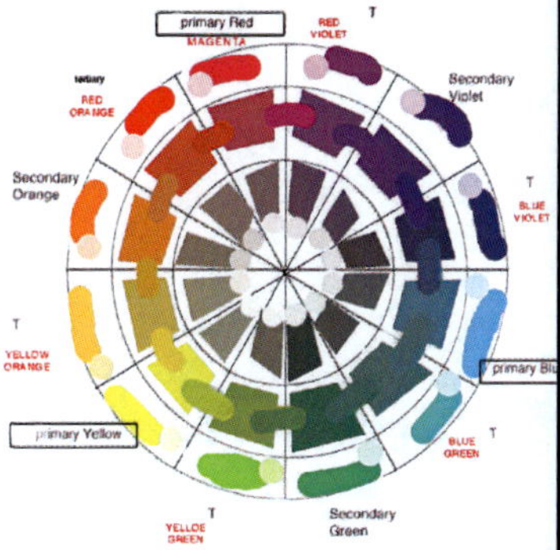

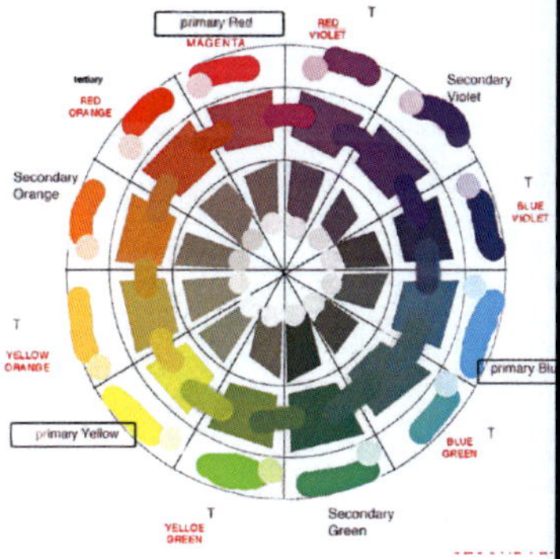

CREATE SOME MORE ANALOGOUS PLUS COMP SCHEMES OF YOUR OWN

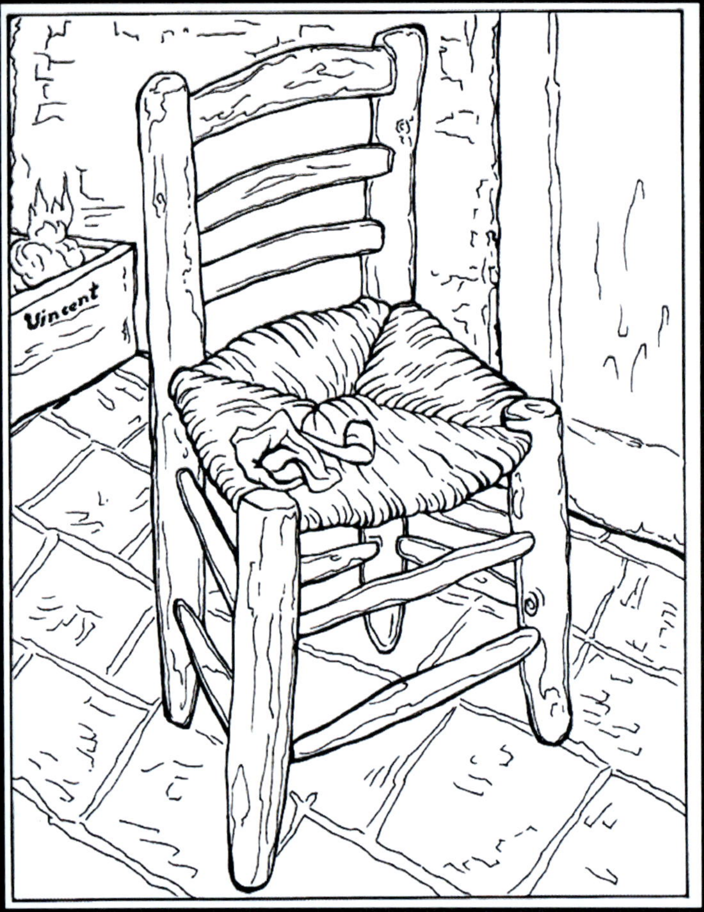

Plan an Analogous plus compliment scheme (generally try to make schemes either warm dominant or cool dominant, avoid using any element in competition, in this case temperature. Allow one to dominate.

Circle the hues you plan to use

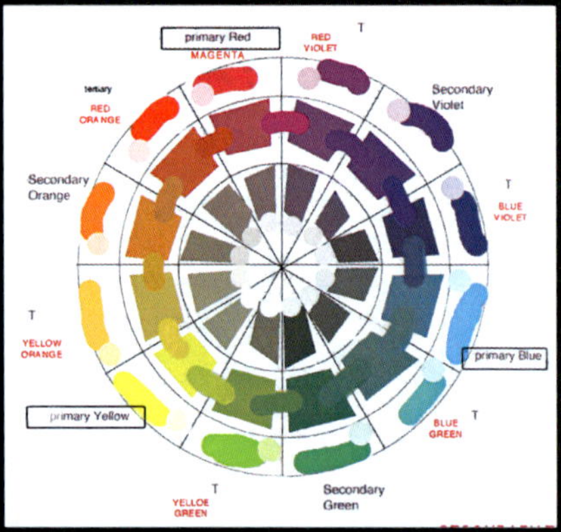

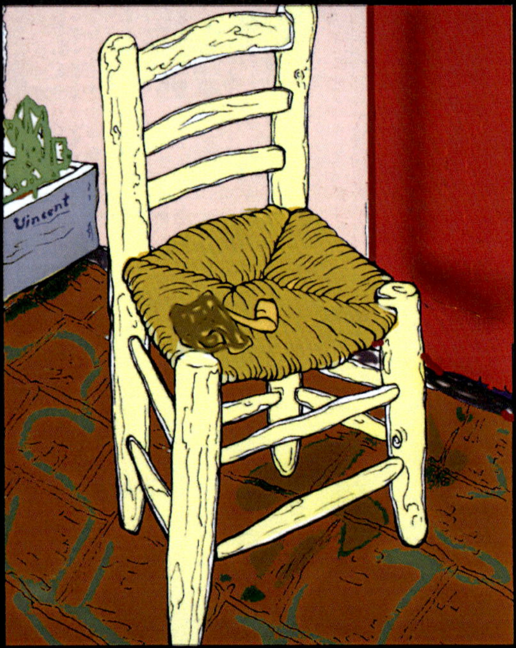

Here is an analogous plus complement with mainly warm hues and a balance of cool.

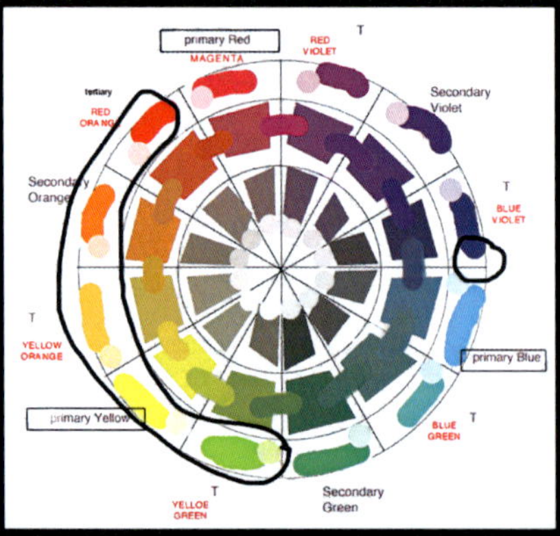

ANALOGOUS PLUS COMPLEMENT SCHEME- EXAMPLE

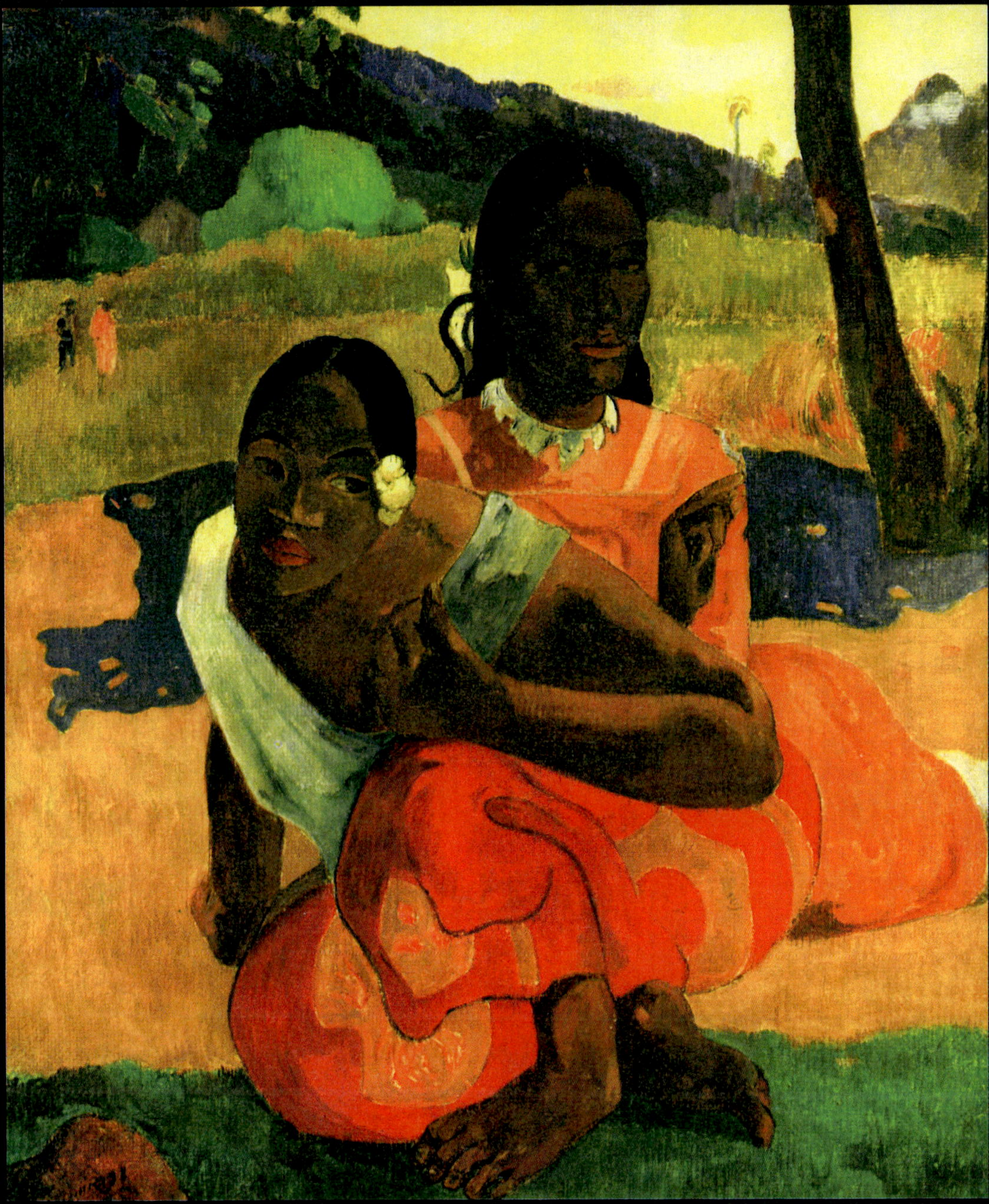

Fig 23

'Nafea Faaipoipo' - 1996 by Paul Gaugin, typical in it's highly saturated hues (similar scheme hues, how different to the previous Vermeer image is it?

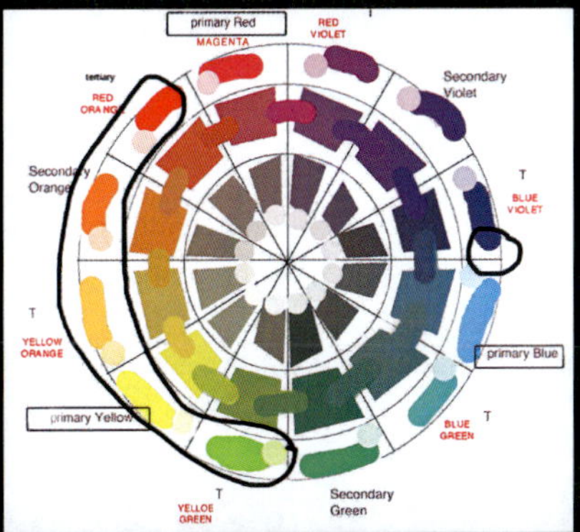

CREATE SOME ANALOGOUS PLUS COMPLEMENT SCHEMES

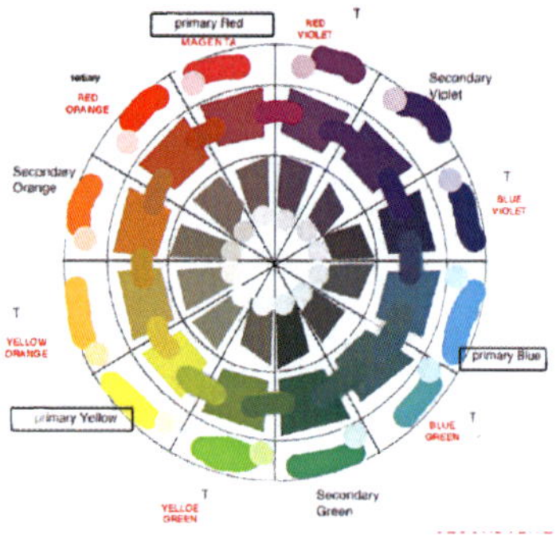

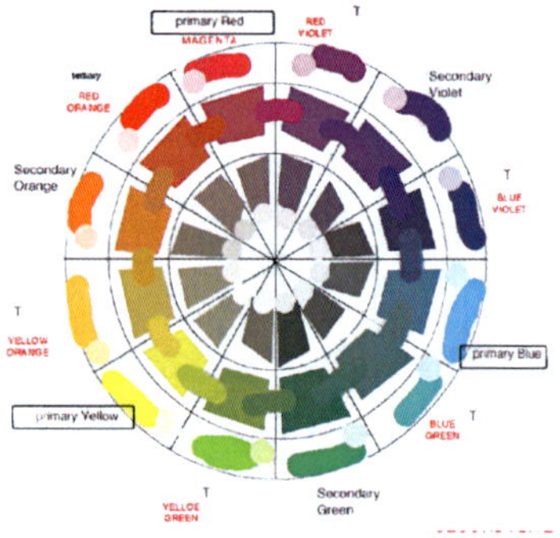

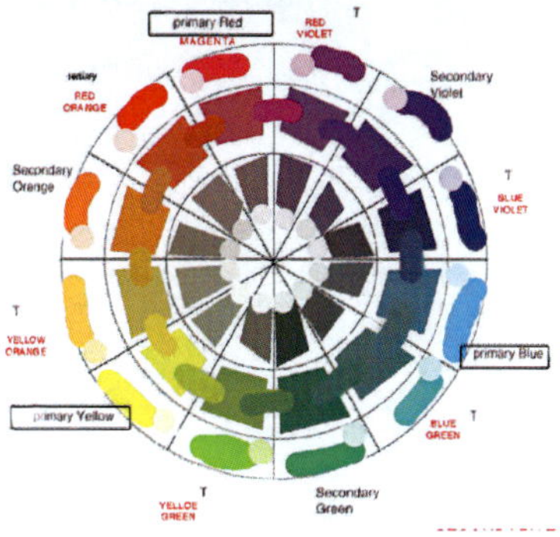
primary Red
MAGENTA
RED VIOLET
T
Secondary Violet
tertiary
RED ORANGE
Secondary Orange
T
BLUE VIOLET
T
YELLOW ORANGE
primary Blue
primary Yellow
BLUE GREEN
T
T
YELLOE GREEN
Secondary Green

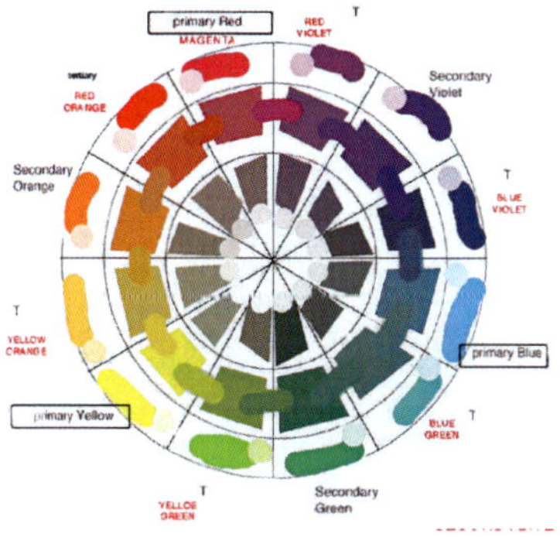
primary Red
MAGENTA
RED VIOLET
T
Secondary Violet
tertiary
RED ORANGE
Secondary Orange
T
BLUE VIOLET
T
YELLOW ORANGE
primary Blue
primary Yellow
BLUE GREEN
T
T
YELLOE GREEN
Secondary Green

DOUBLE SPLIT COMPLEMENTARY SCHEMES - GROUPINGS

In a 12 sector triadic color wheel, there are broadly 6 x 4 possible groupings (with tints, neutrals, chromatic grays and everything in between. All variations would be in the thousands. As you get to know your pigments and their mixes, you can determine your own rectangular relationships (making a 'Spinning scheme selector' really helps with this.)

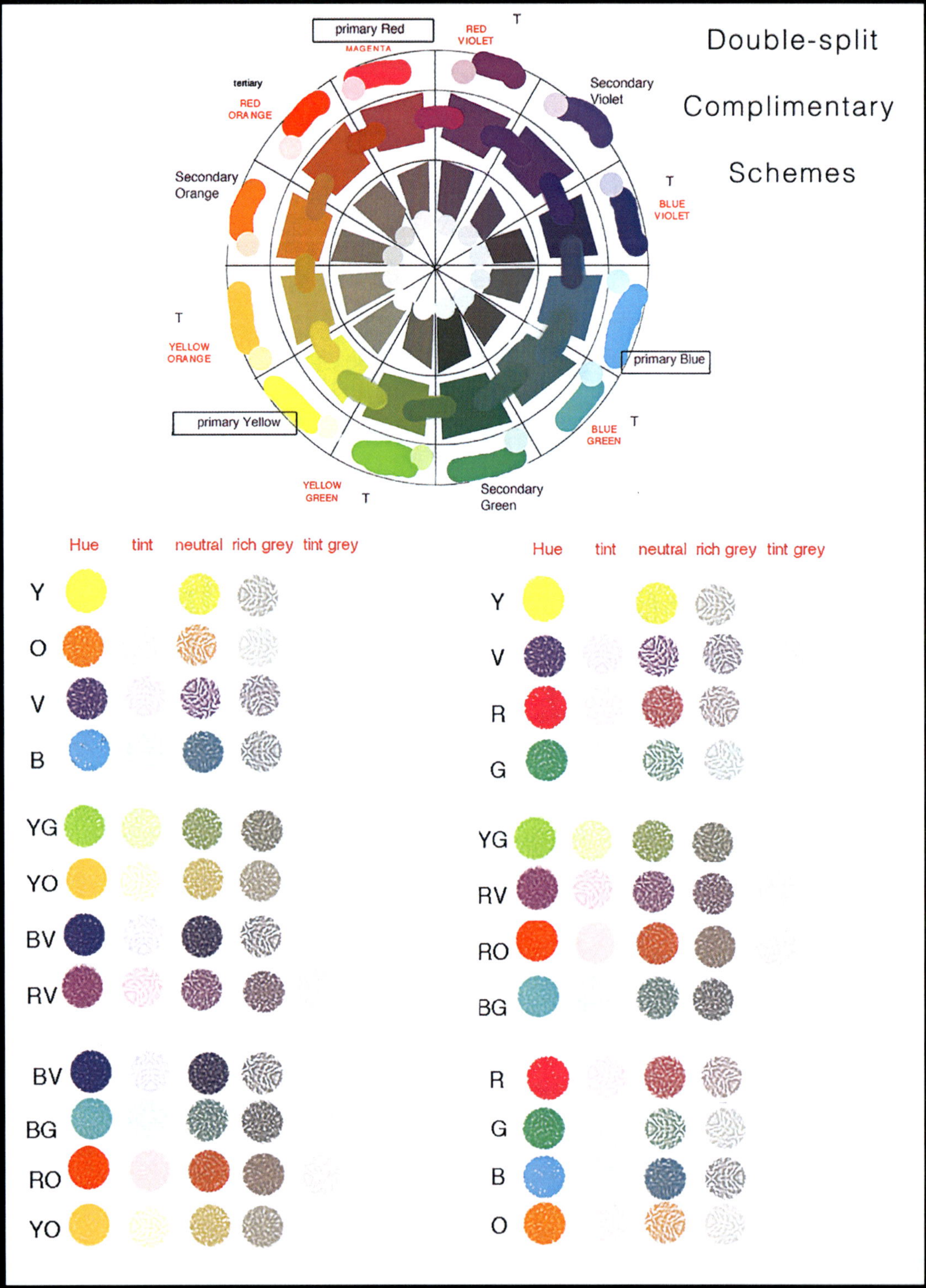

DOUBLE SPLIT COMPLEMENTARY SCHEMES

In this happy little study, Yellow Irises, by Claude Monet, 1924, you can see the beautiful relationship of a double split complementary in all of it's impressionistic splendor

Fig 24

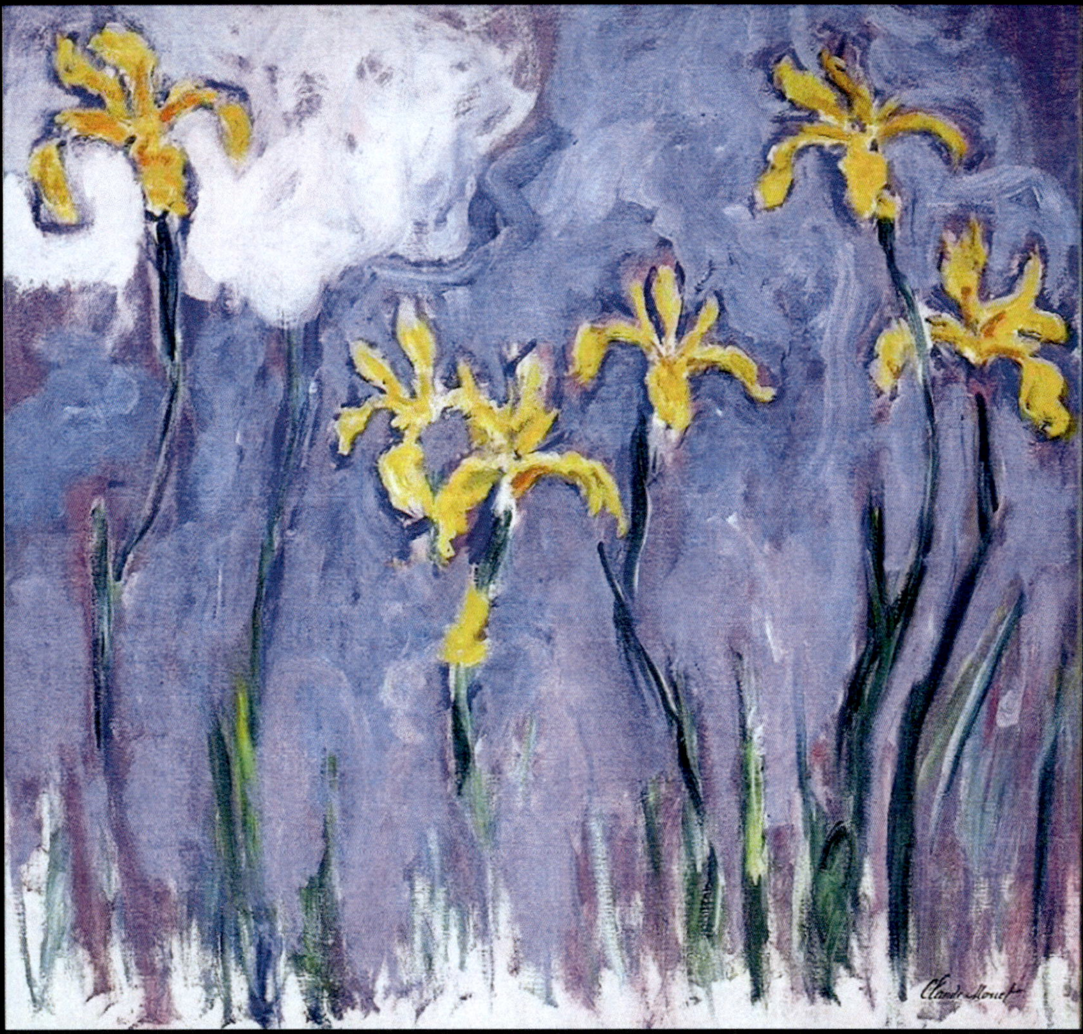

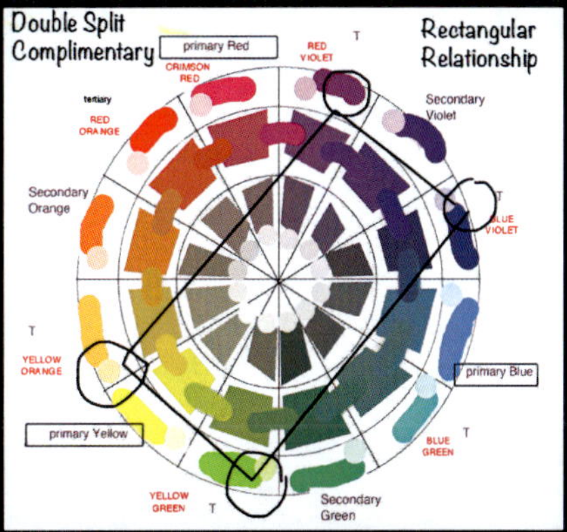

CREATE SOME DOUBLE SPLIT COMPLEMENTARY SCHEMES

Practice your own Double Split harmonious schemes by selecting a combination of 4 colors related by a rectangle (including any tints, neutrals, rich grays and saturated hues (from the one group) then do a comparative study with another grouping.

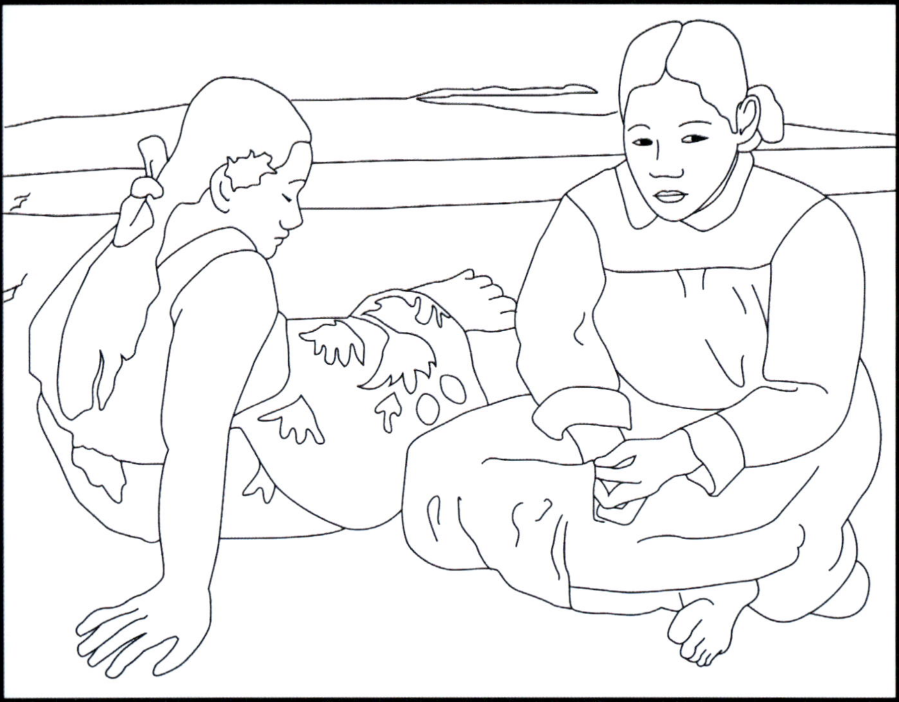

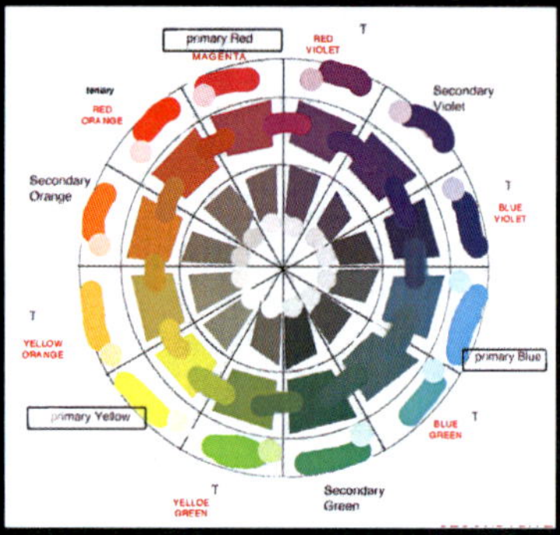

Even though they will not all be saturated hues, the combinations will all still sing with the same harmonious vibe because they are from the same hue partnerships. The desaturated shades can assist you in creating value patterns and 3D form. Look back to the grouping chart and see 6 broad groupings of hues (multiple possibilities exist within each hue sector chosen.)

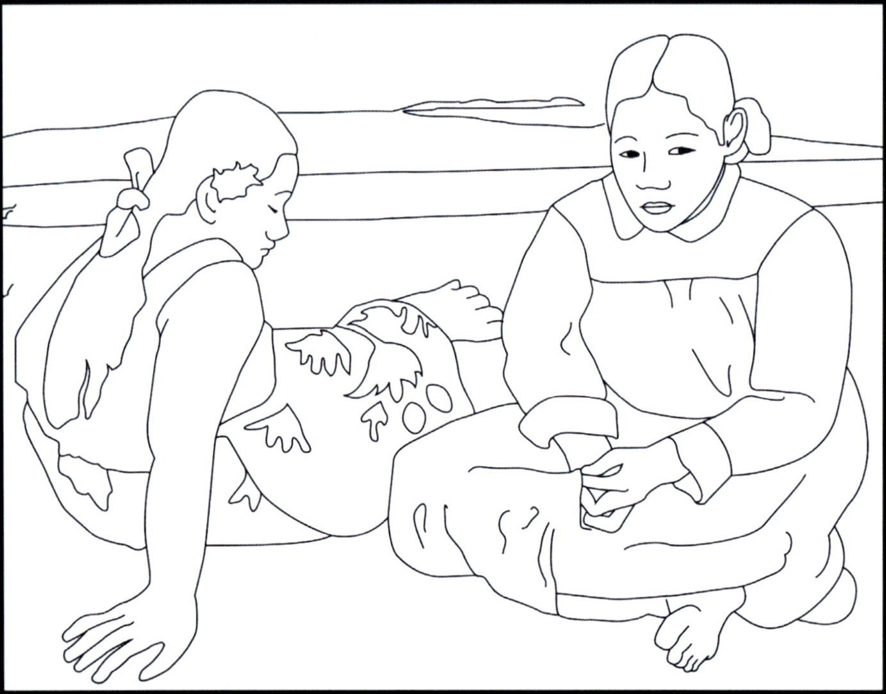

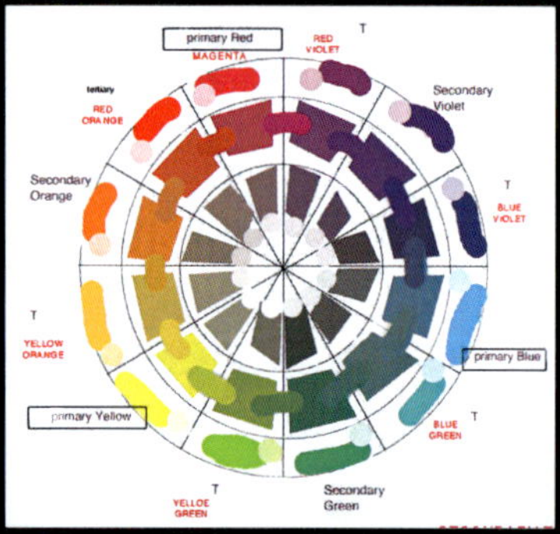

CREATE YOUR OWN DOUBLE SPLIT COMPLEMENTARY SCHEMES

Use these pages for your own compositional shape sketches and harmonious color planning of some Double Split Complementary schemes. Map them on the wheels and add notes under the wheel as to the pigment names, hues,neutrals and chromatic grays/ blacks.used in your study.

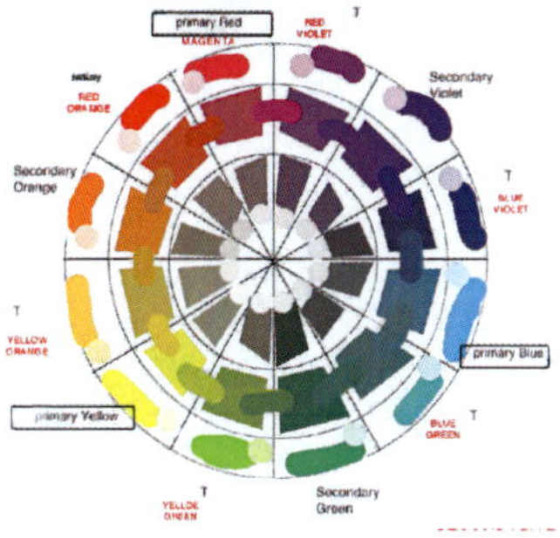

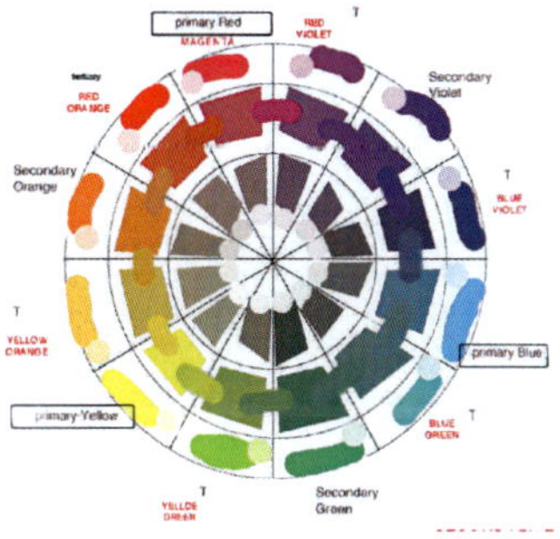

DOUBLE SPLIT COMPLEMENTARY SCHEMES

Create a few more studies with planning for Double Split Complementary schemes.

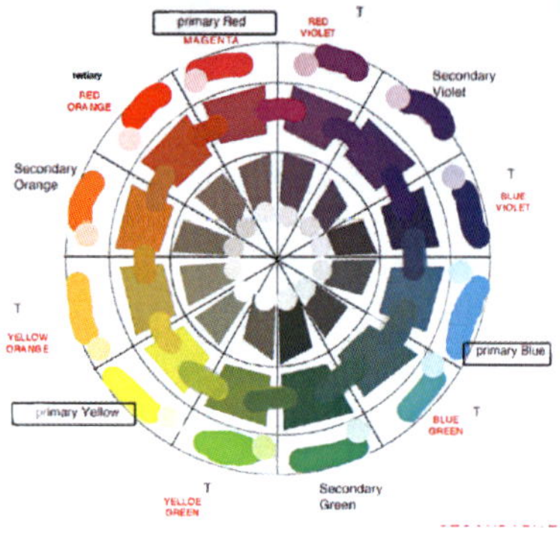

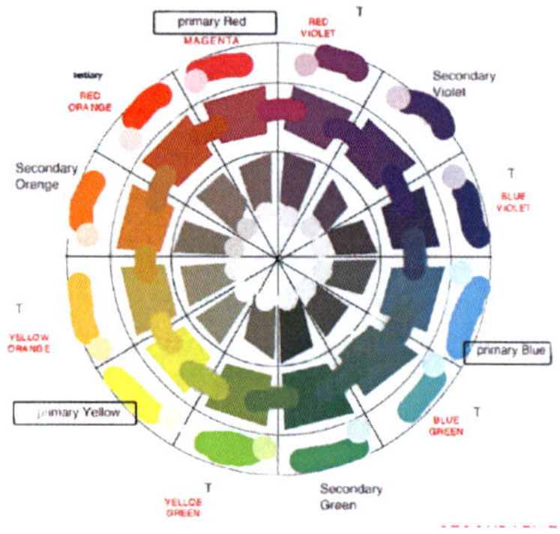

DOUBLE SPLIT COMPLEMENTARY SCHEMES

Create a few more studies with planning for Double Split Complementary schemes.

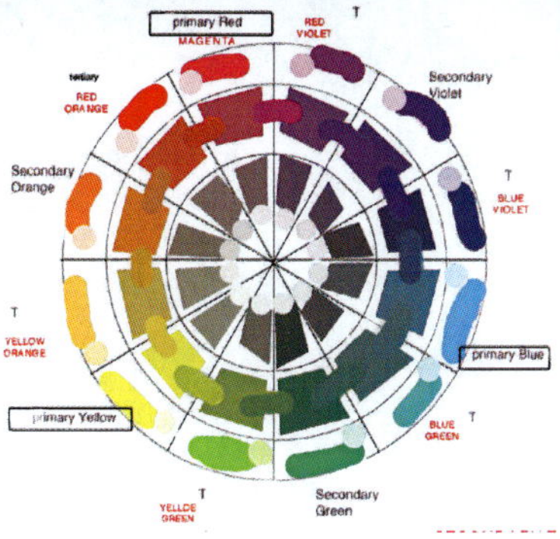

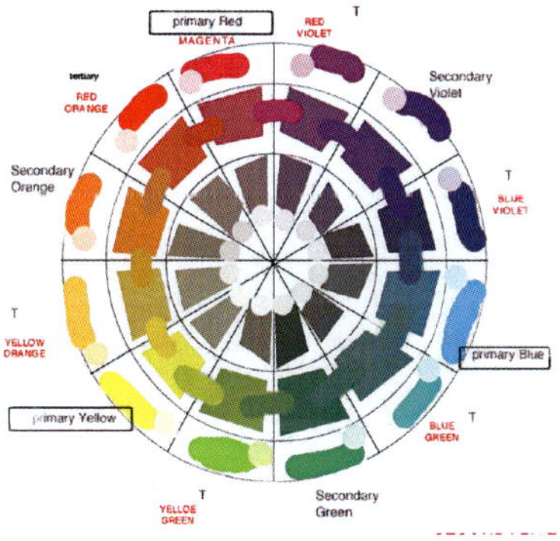

TRIADIC COLOR SCHEMES

The next set of harmonious color schemes to look at here are the triads (a relationship of 3 hues, connected by a triangular arrangement).

Any version of a hue sector is harmonious in these arrangements too as you will see in the case studies. (The rich grays, neutrals, tints as well as the saturated hues). Remember to let one saturated hue dominate, let one temperature dominate and let the rest of the scheme colors sit back and harmonize quietly (neutrals or rich grays)

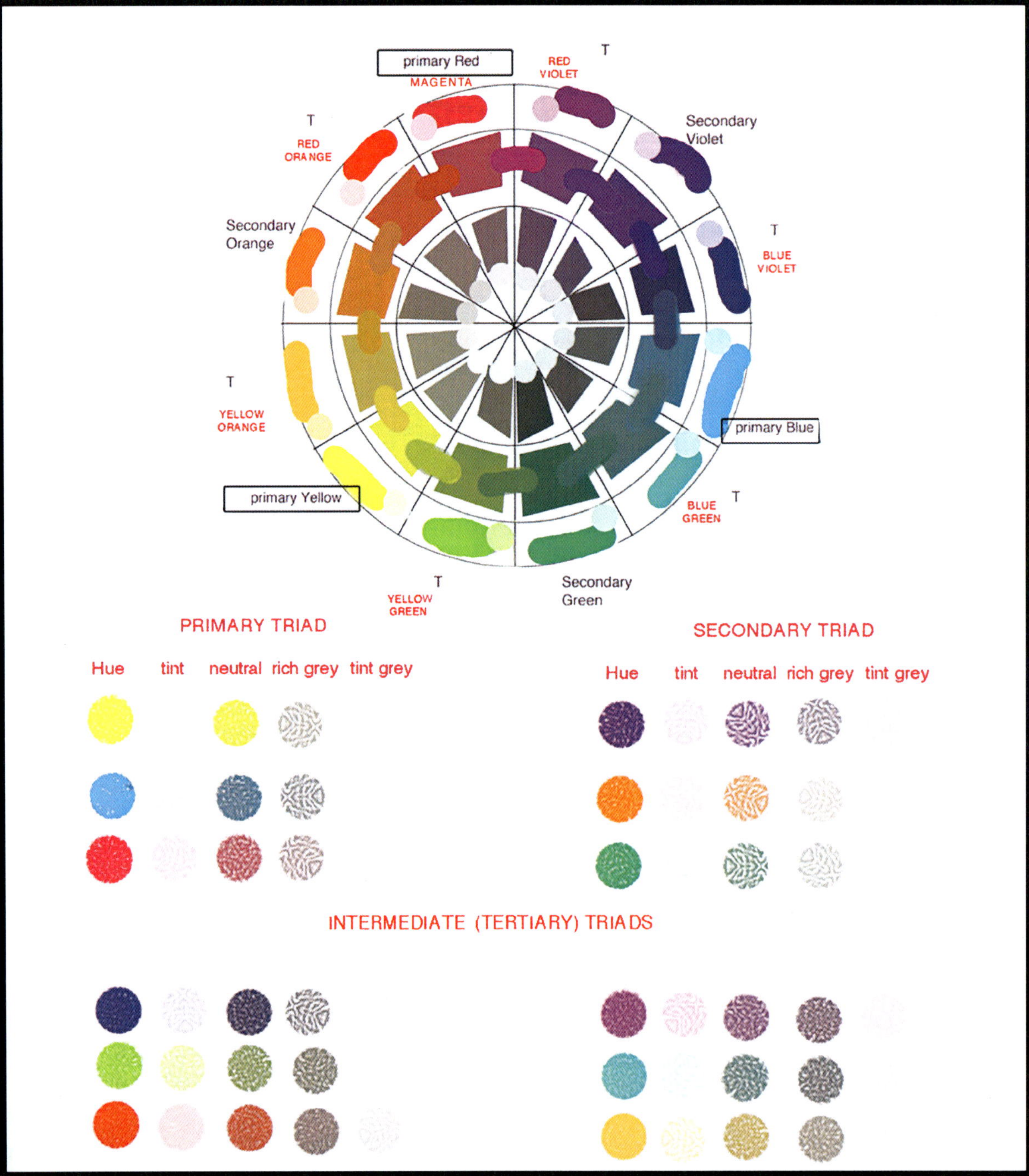

TRIADIC COLOR SCHEMES

Monet has his tertiaries singing here, in a beautiful triadic harmony of Yellow-green, Blue-violets and Red-oranges.

NB. there are other hints of secondary green tint and a cool blue, but the dominant scheme is triadic in nature.

Fig 25

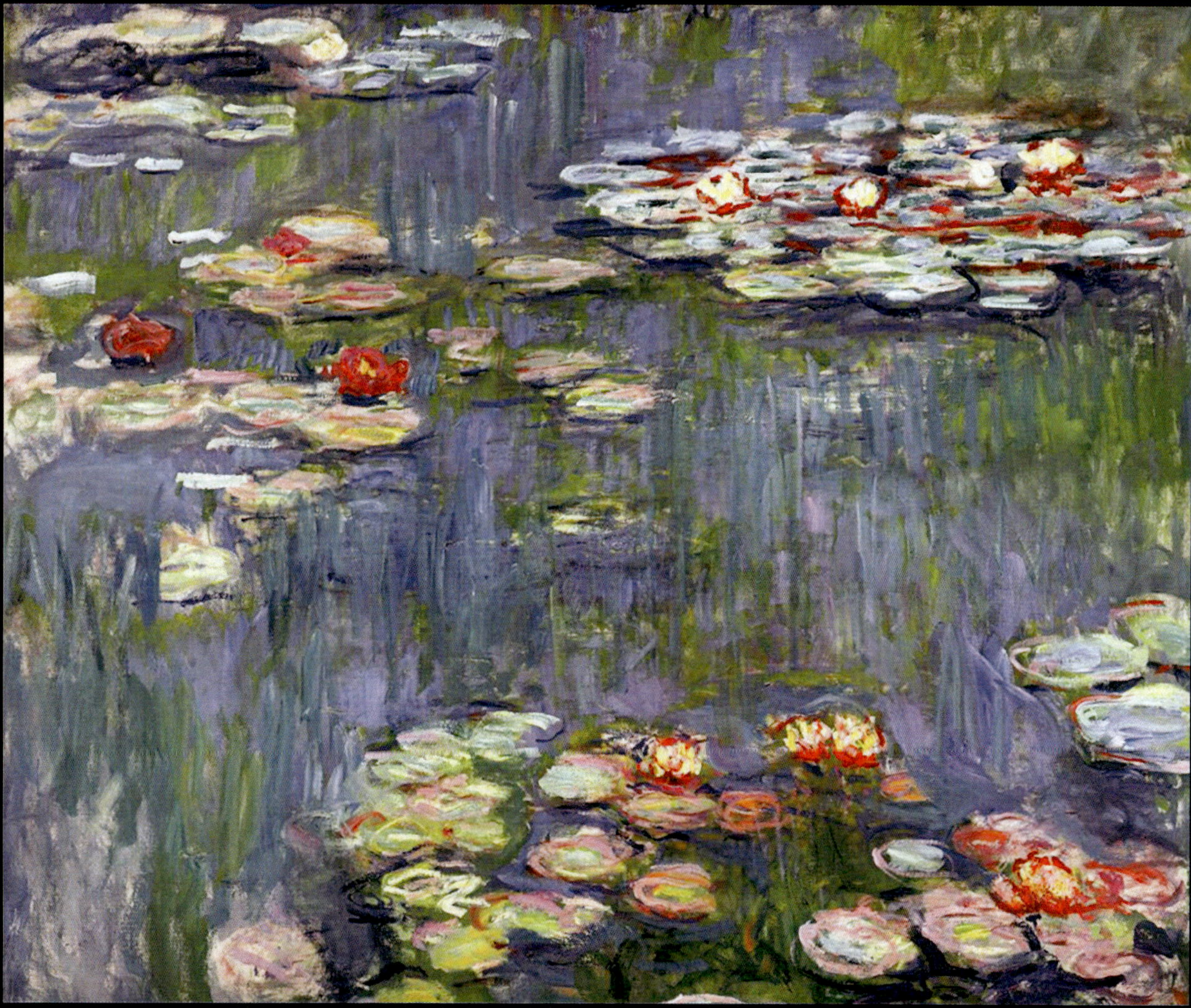

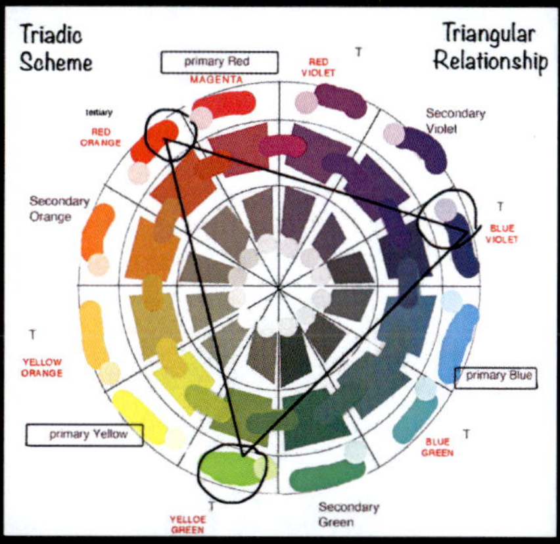

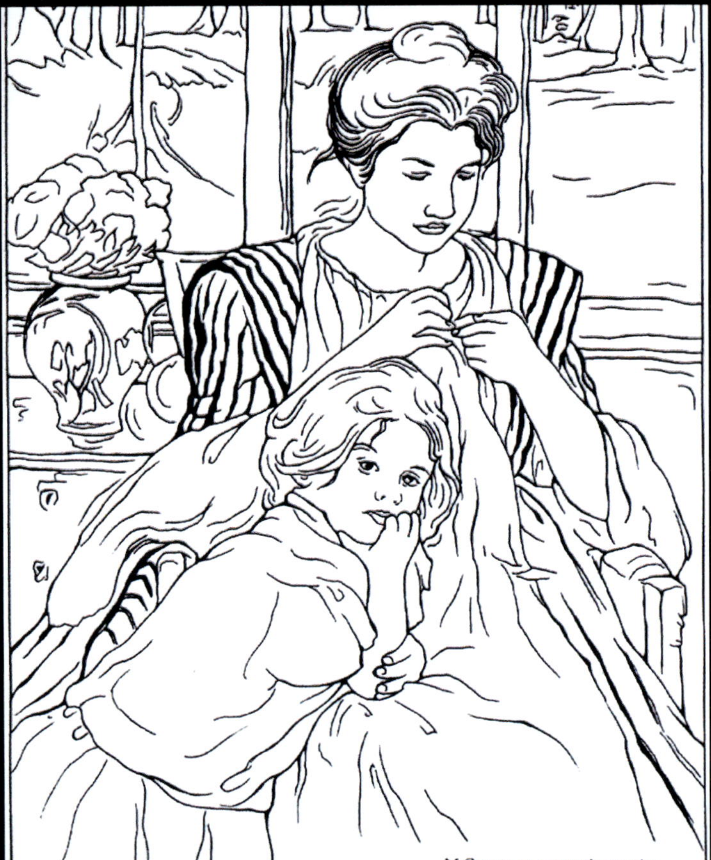

M Cassatt, young mother sewing

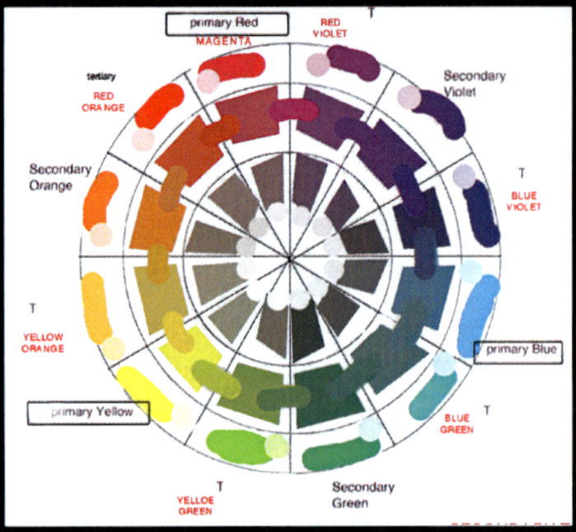

No detail required, just a block in.

Just rough in your color scheme ideas

PRO-TIP: There are skin tones here so start the selection with hues that might fit that and build around those.

(or not! You may feel like 'doing a Picasso' and completely abstracting the color scheme away from naturally expected hues). The exercise here is to try out two different triadic schemes that you feel might suit this composition. Use colored pencils or undiluted acrylic.

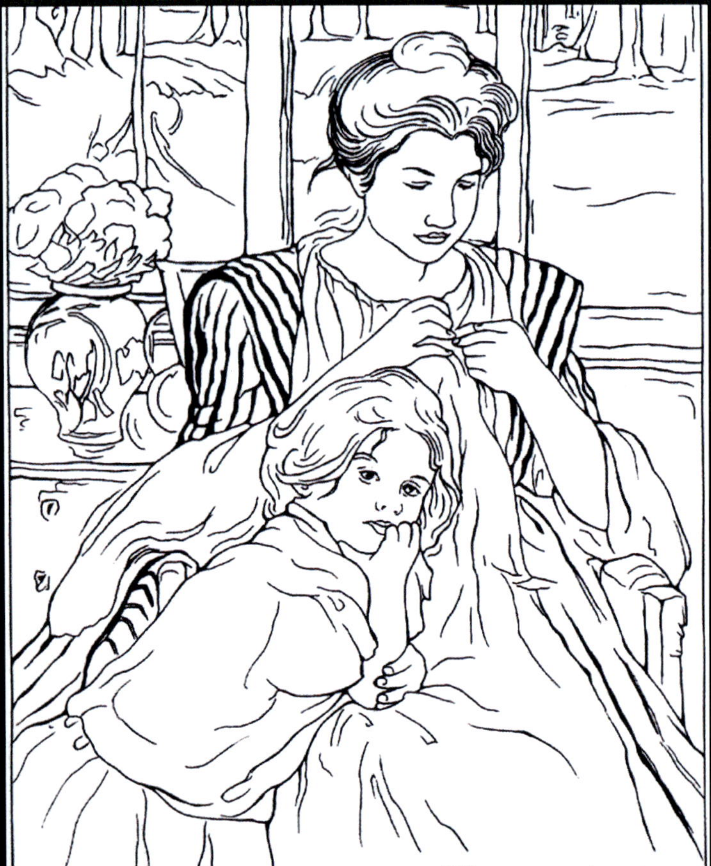

M Cassatt, young mother sewing

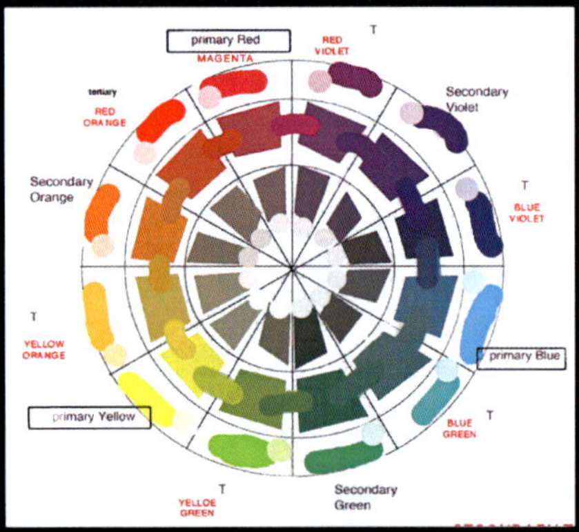

Create a few more studies with planning for Triadic Color schemes

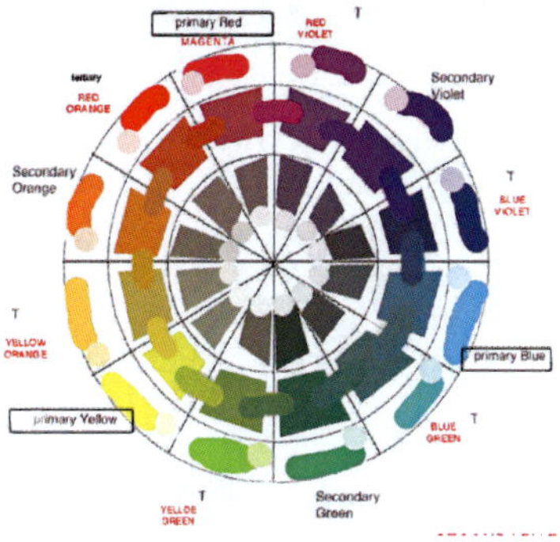

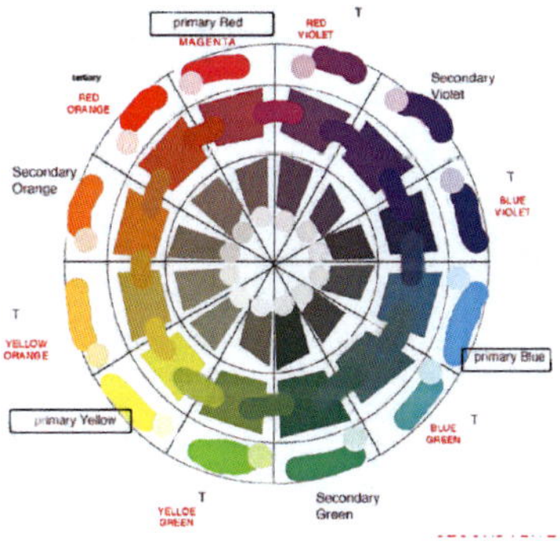

tonal study of this abstract art work. Fig 27

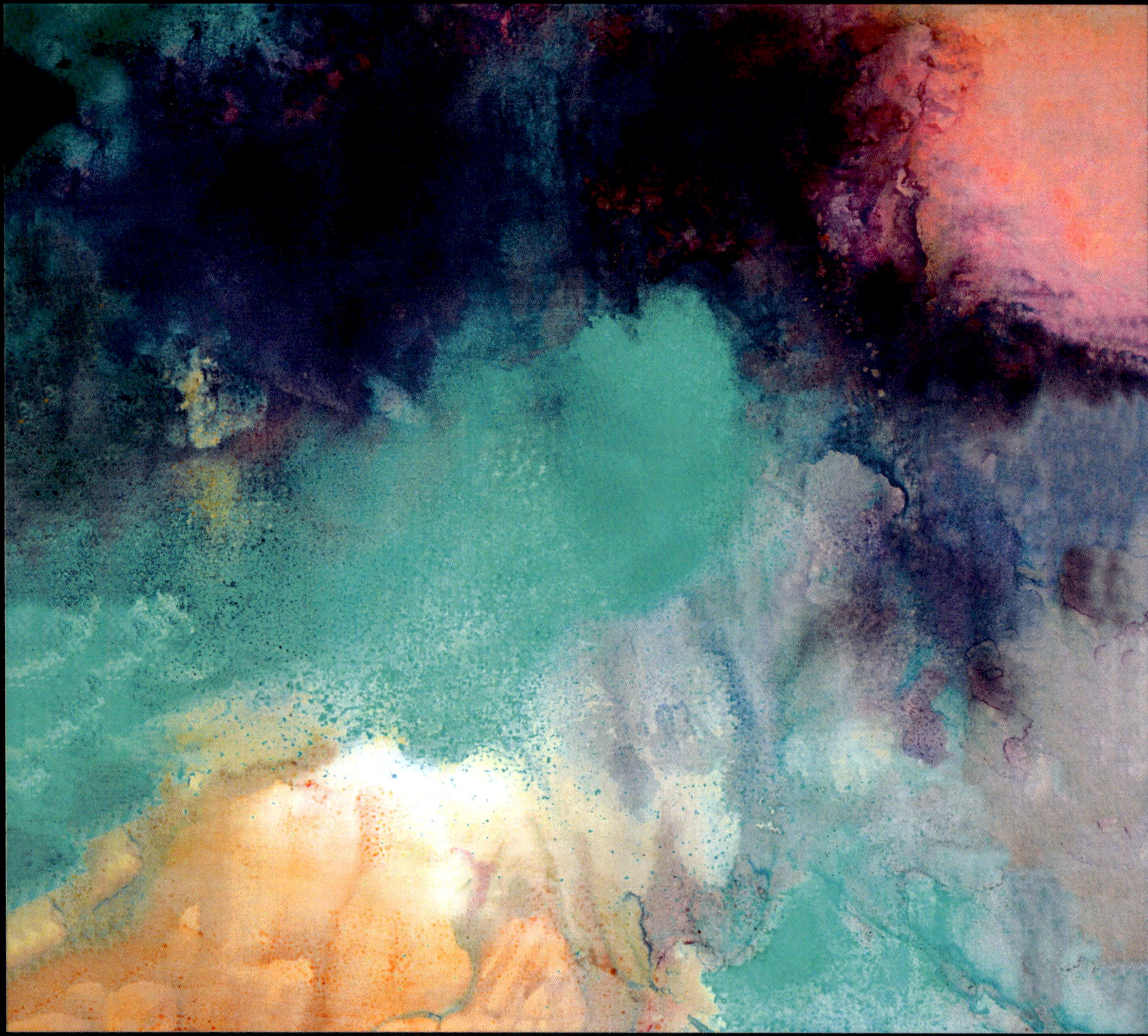

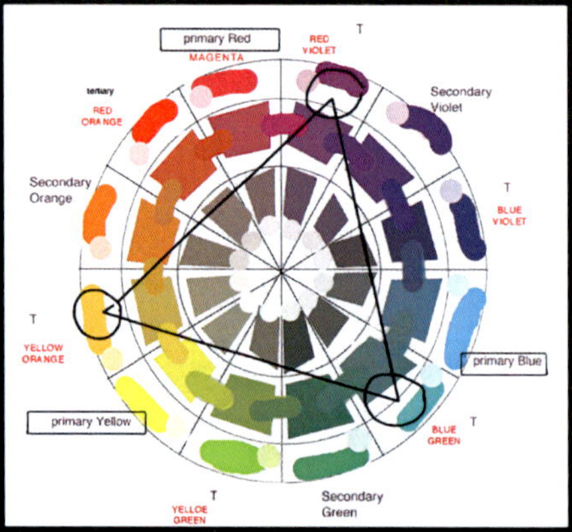

TRIADIC COLOR SCHEMES

No detail required, just a block in. Thanks to John Louis Lloyd for allowing us to use his abstract composition as a value study for color harmony practice. Try to use the value pattern and assign hues accordingly.

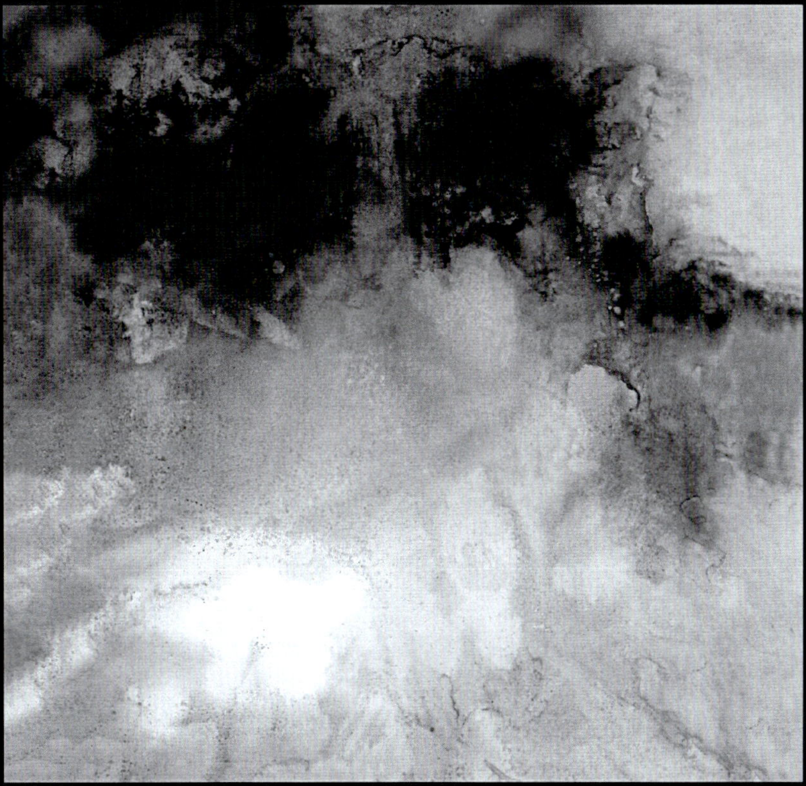

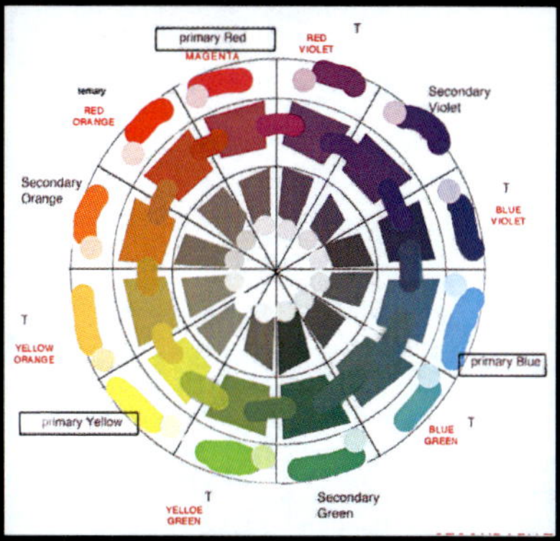

The exercise here is to try out two different triadic schemes that you feel might suit this abstract composition Convert it from a value pattern to two options for a triadic color study.

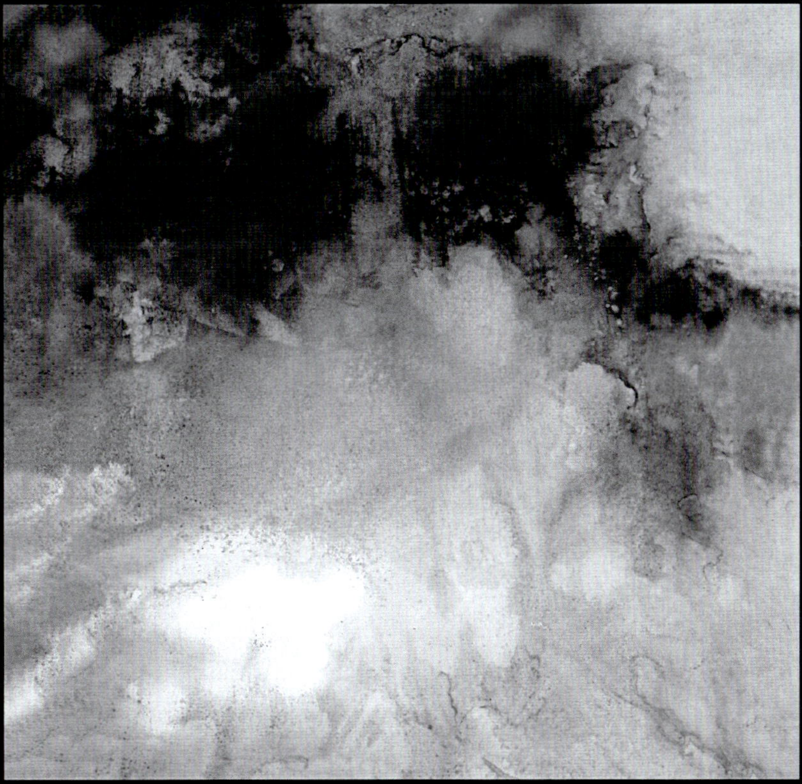

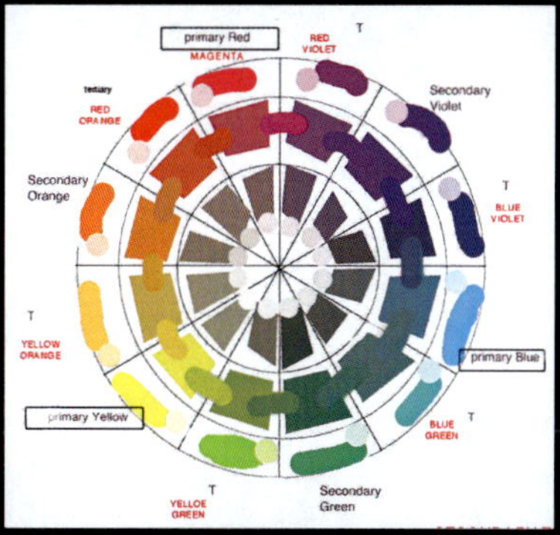

Monet seems to have been going for a triad of Red-violet, Yellow-orange and Blue-green for this sunset behind Parliament House, London. It is 81.3 × 92.5 cm and was created in 1903

Fig 26

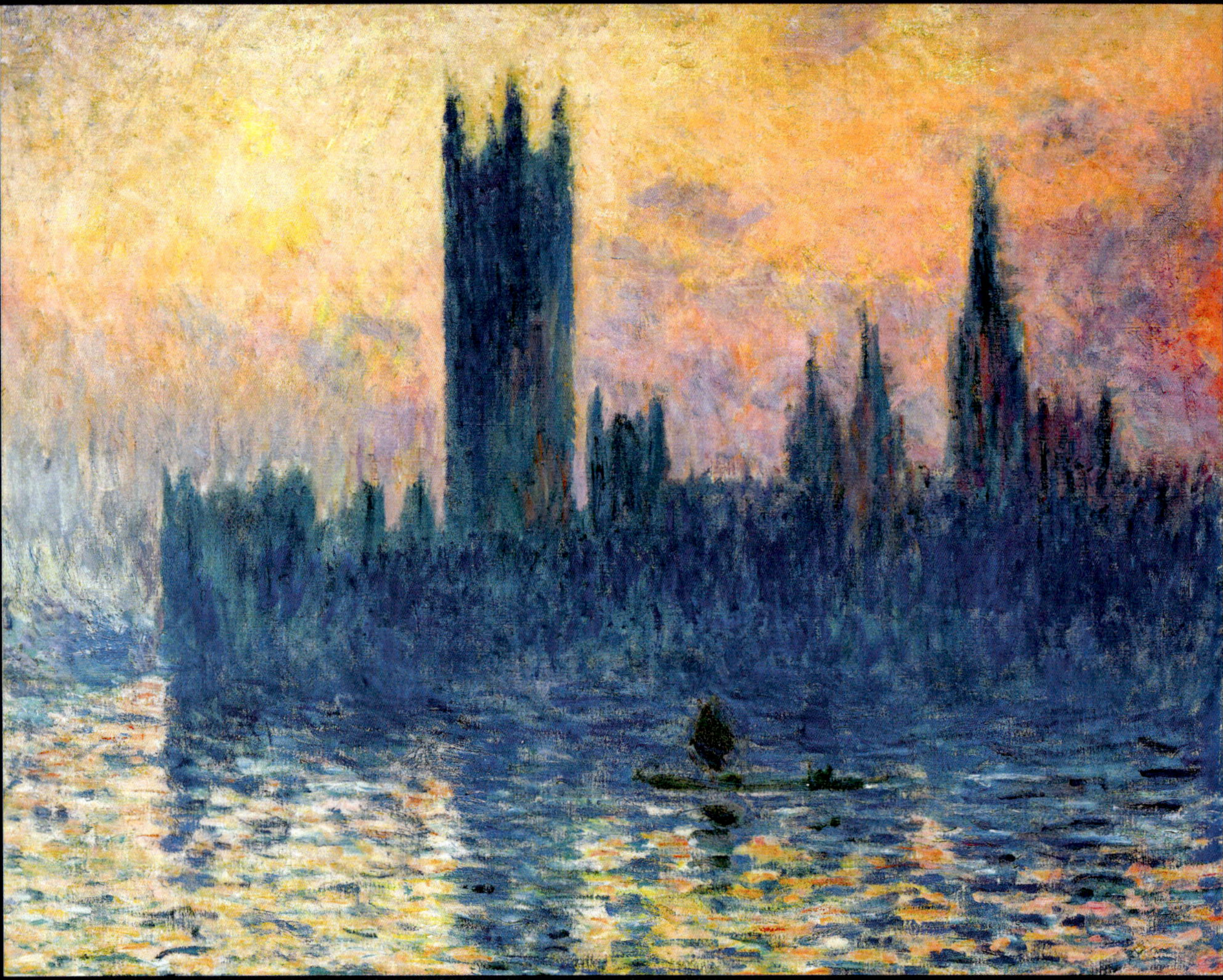

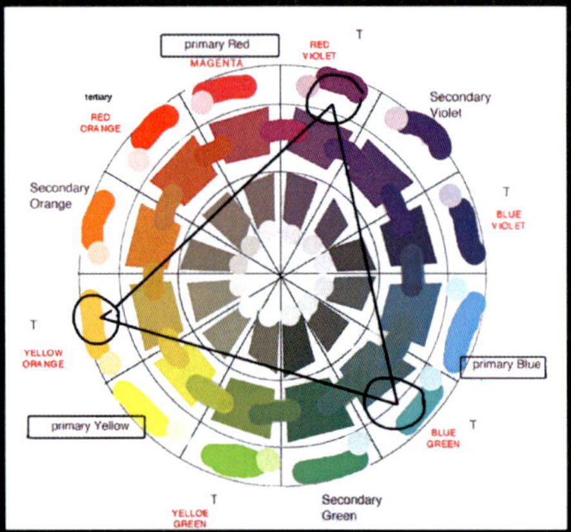

Create a few more studies with planning for Triadic Color schemes

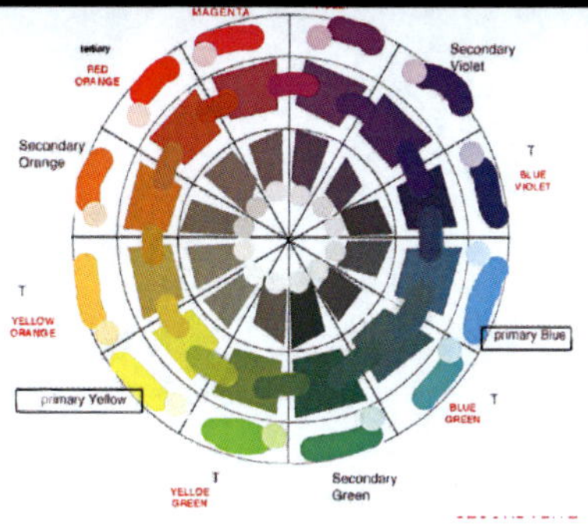

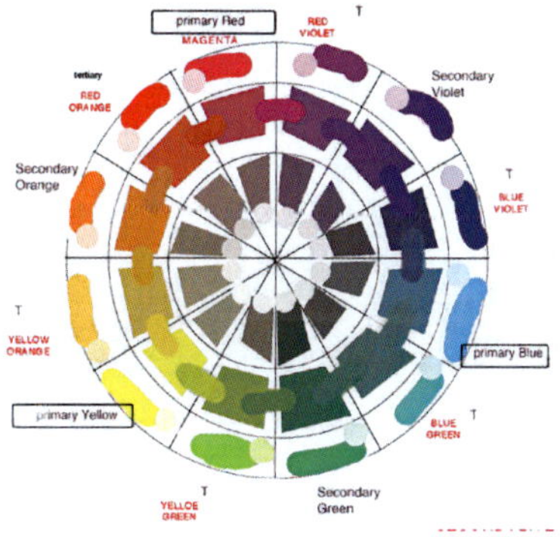

How different does this painting appear to the previous example and yet it has the same triadic relationship of Blue-green, Red-violet , Yellow-orange

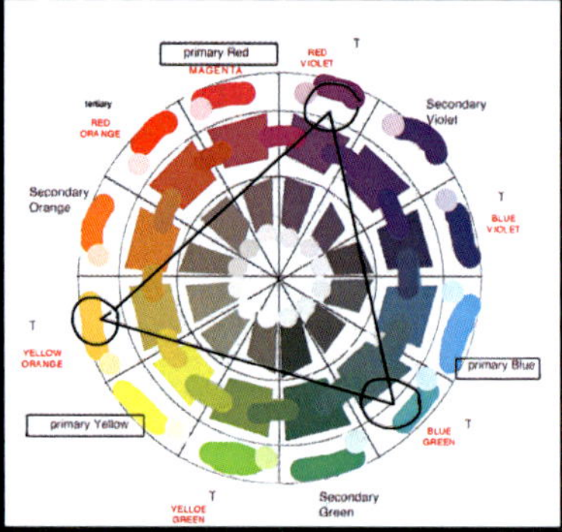

Fig 27

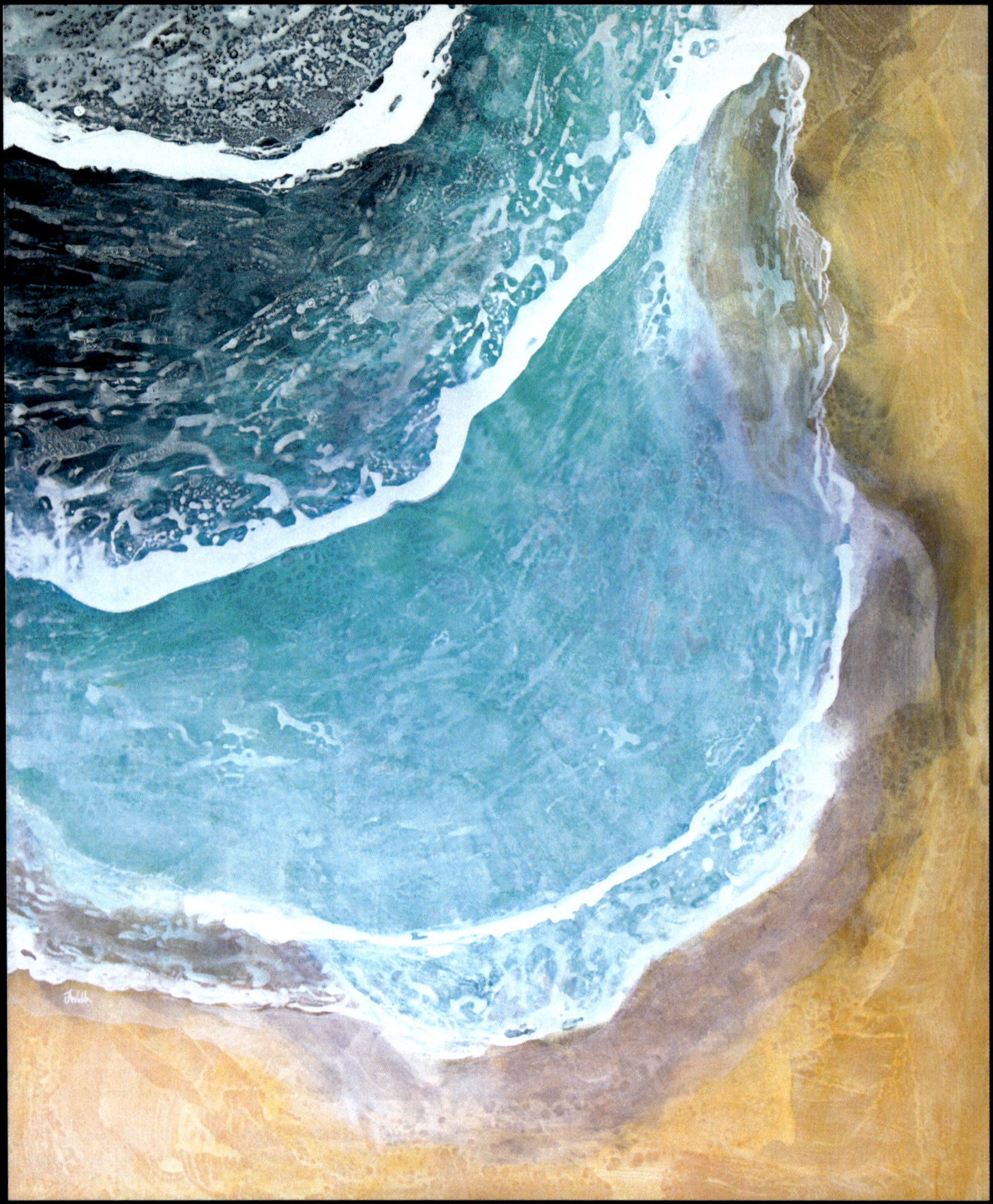

TRIADIC COLOR SCHEMES

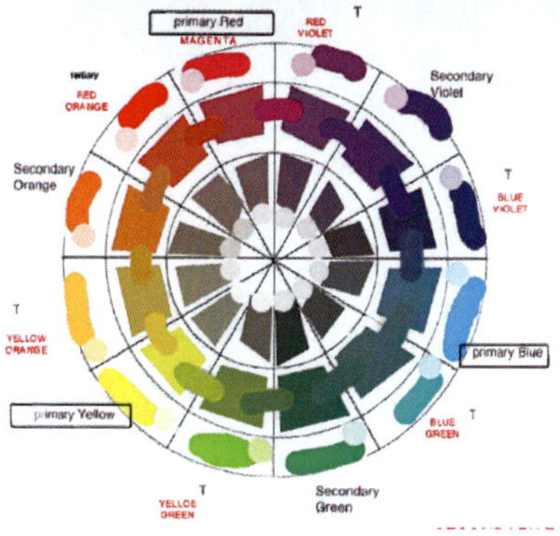

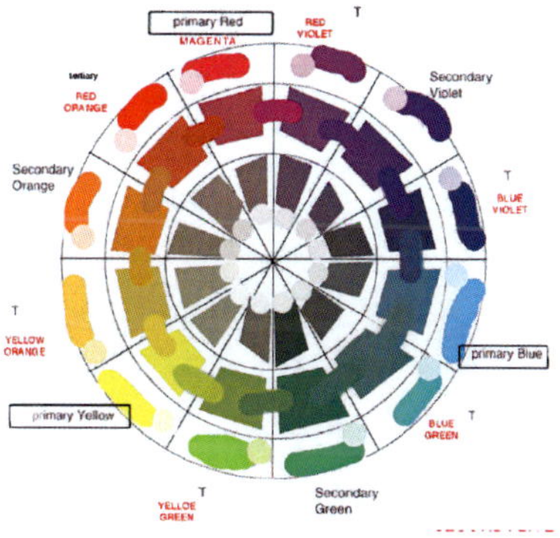

TETRADIC COLOR SCHEMES

These three groupings under the wheel represent square arrangements called Tetrad schemes. Some people put double split schemes and tetrads in the same group but there are some notable differences in the color selections.

TETRAD (SQUARE) SCHEMES BELOW

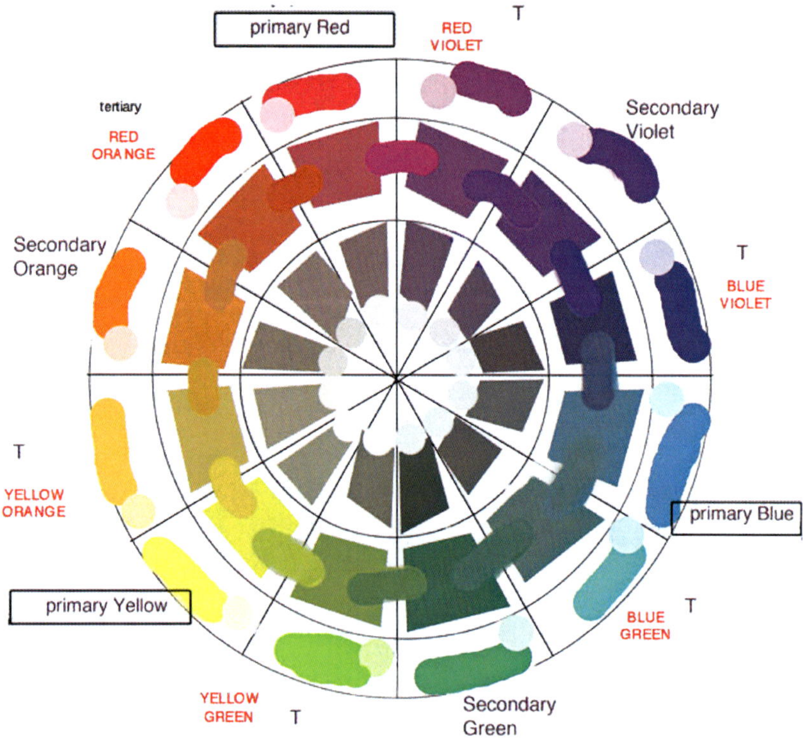

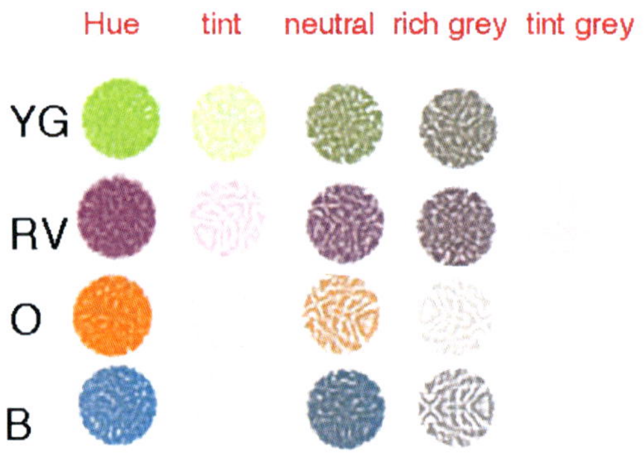

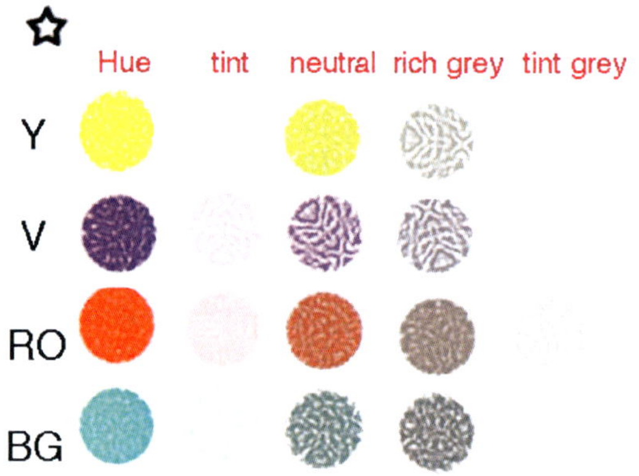

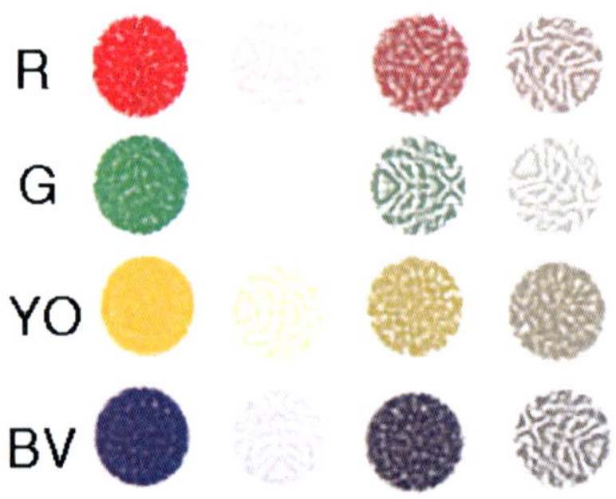

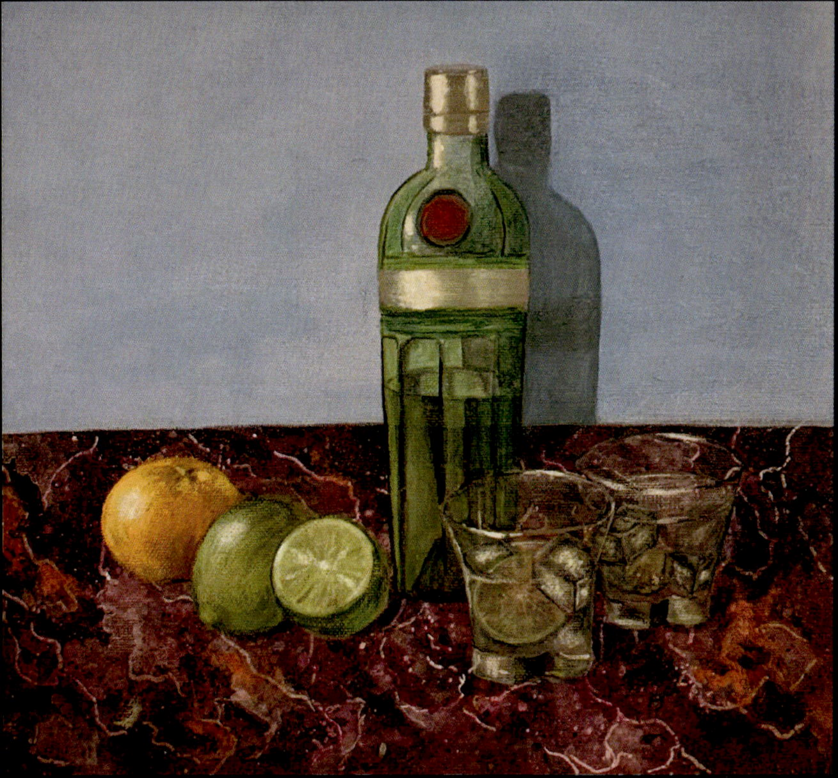

Fig 28

Veronica had an urge to try out a nice harmonious tetrad scheme, as well as an urge to portray her wicked summer habit! (G&Ts)

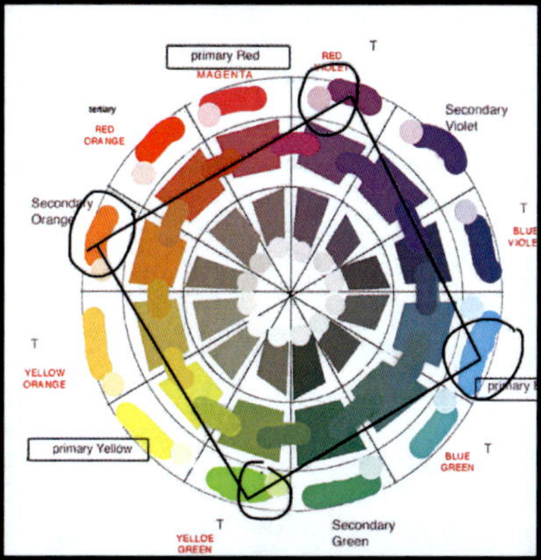

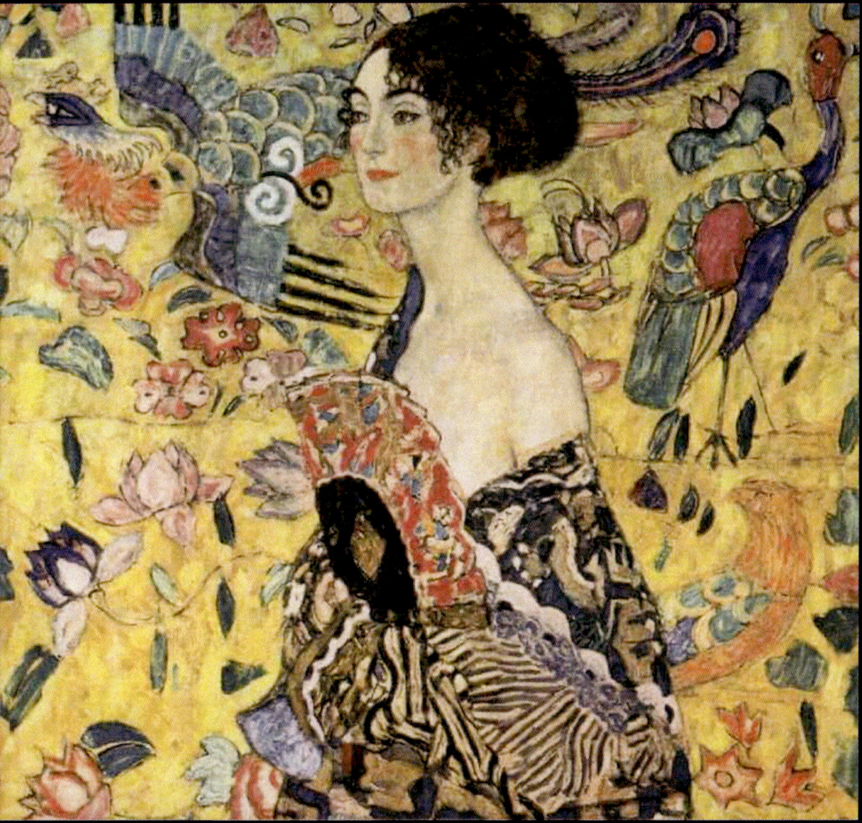

Fig 29 - 'Lady with a Fan' - from Gustave Klimt

This is a lovely example of a tetrad from Klimt, painted in his final year of life.

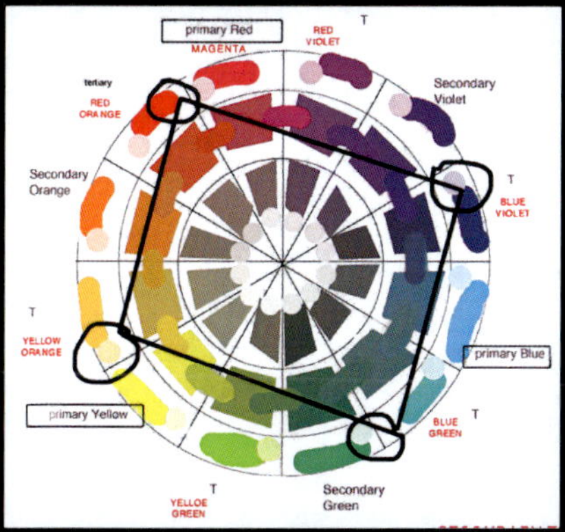

TETRADIC COLOR SCHEMES

Create a few more sketches and studies with planning for Tetradic Color schemes.Try a broad range of combinations across the wheel with the three arrangements of 4 hues shown in the chart of Tetradic groupings. (use tints, neutrals and rich grays as well.)

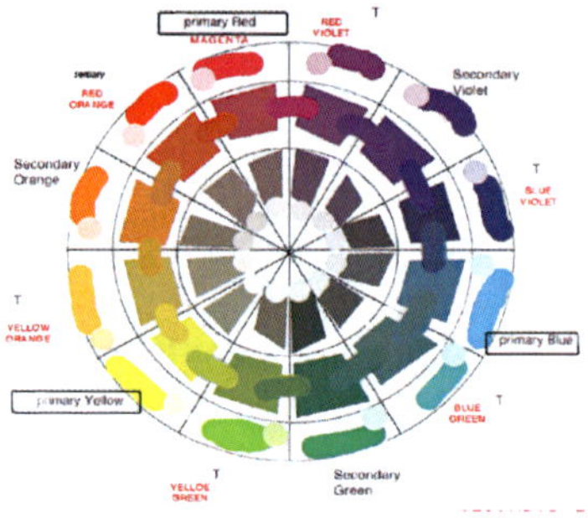

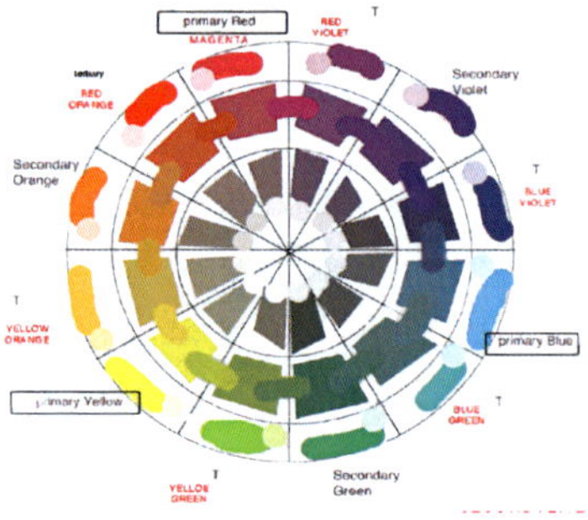

CREATE SOME MORE TETRADIC COLOR SCHEMES

Use this page for your own harmonious color planning of some Tetradic schemes. Map them on the wheels and add notes in the blank section as to the pigment names, hues,neutrals and chromatic grays/ blacks used in your study.

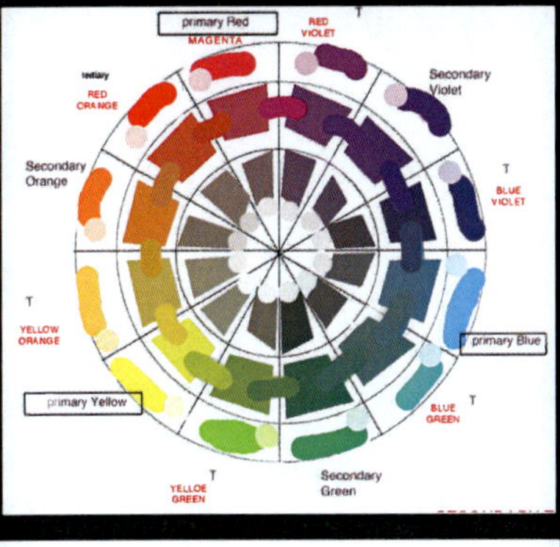

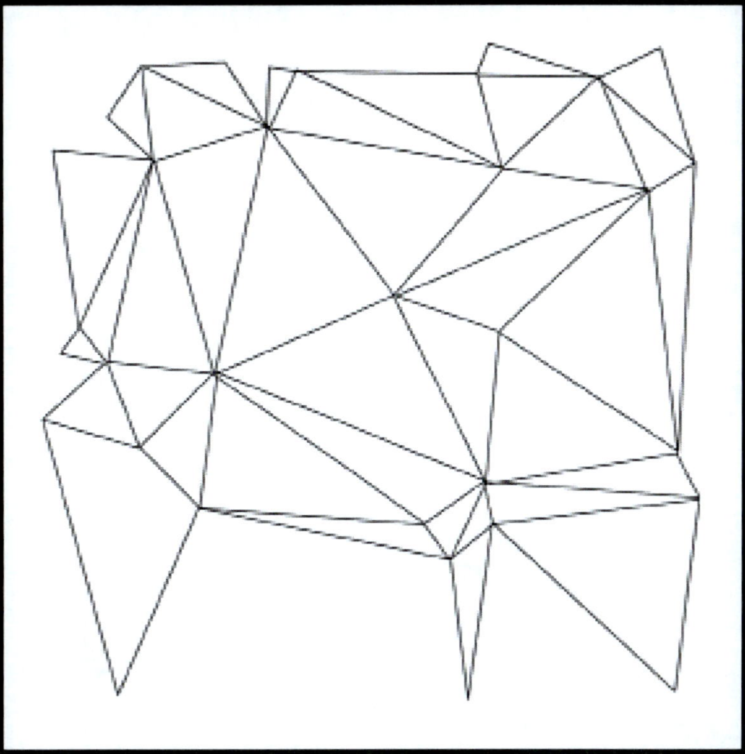

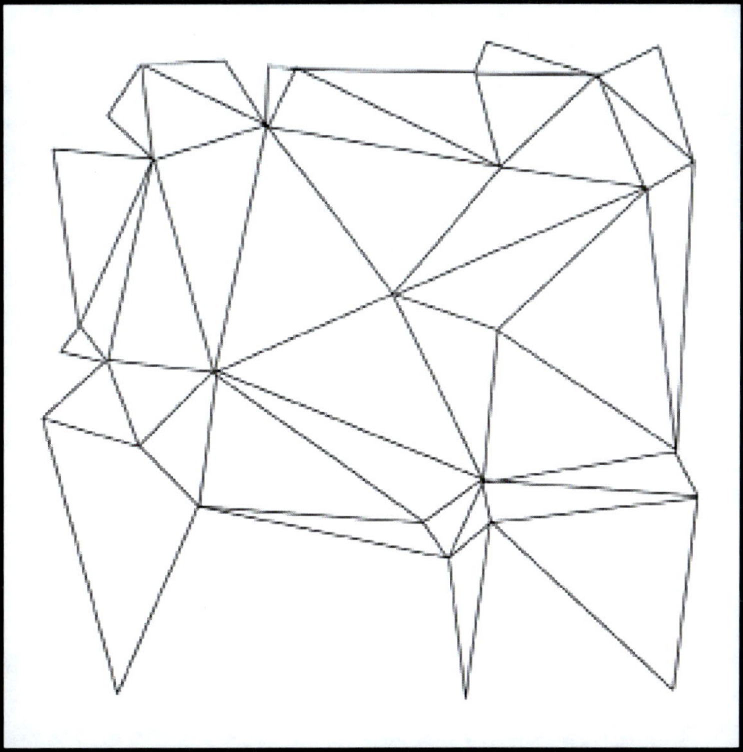

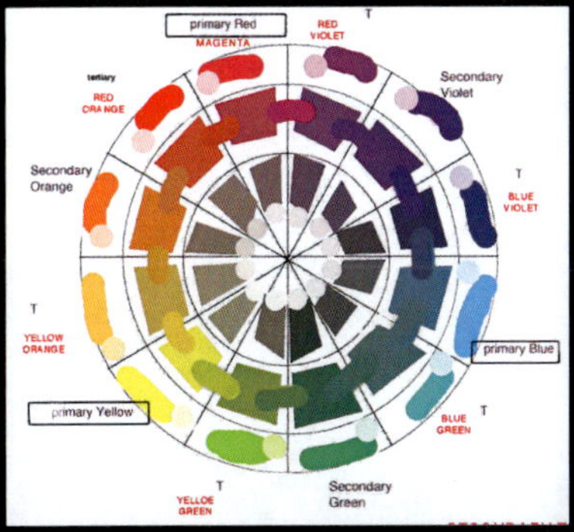

CREATE SOME MORE TETRADIC COLOR SCHEMES

Create a few more sketches and studies with planning for Tetradic Color schemes.

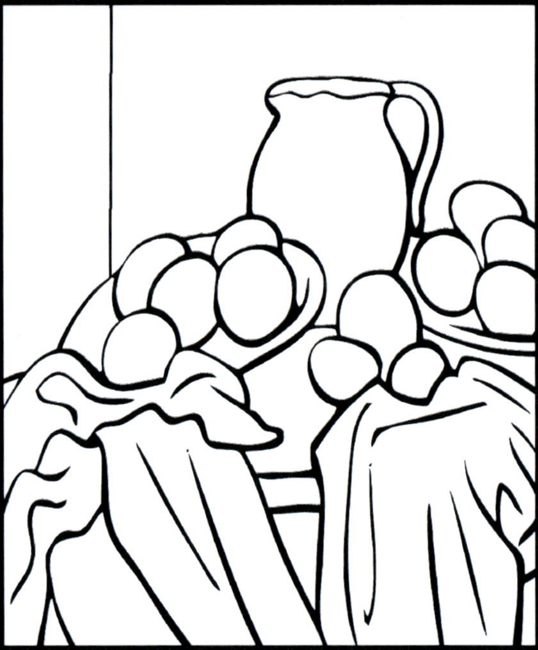

There are many variations of tetrad schemes, but a good way to start (if you are aiming for realism) is to choose one object that strikes you as needing to be a certain hue for your purposes, then work around that.

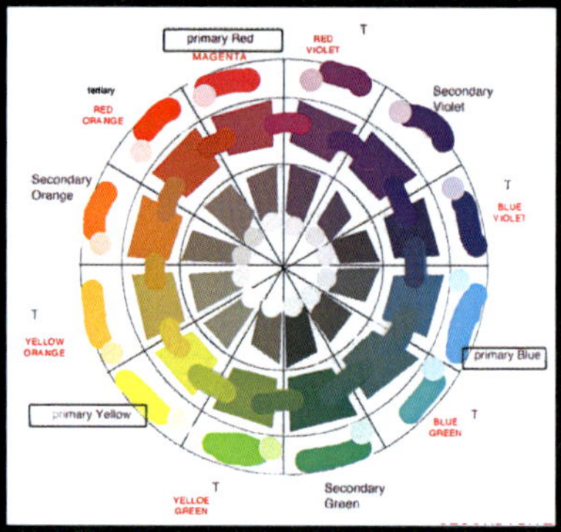

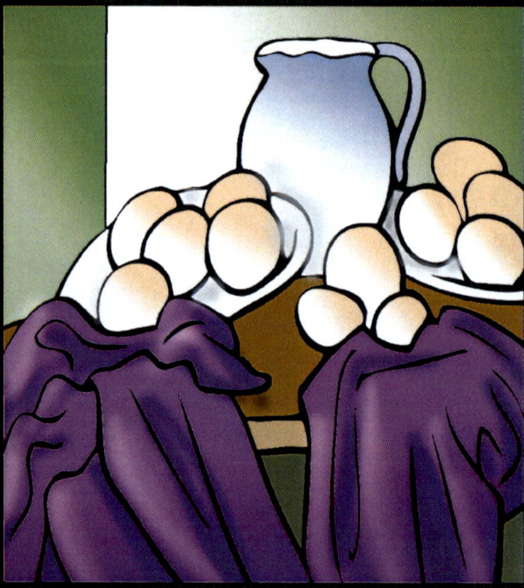

In this digital mockup, I decided to use a neutral tint of orange for the eggs, so that led me to choose blue for the jug and looking at the wheel with my scheme guides I see red-violet and yellow-green form a lovely tetrad with this pair. The red-violet hue is the only saturated choice, otherwise I chose neutrals and tints.

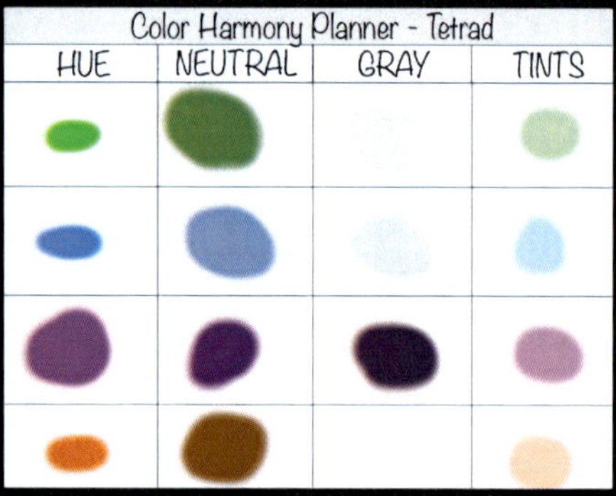

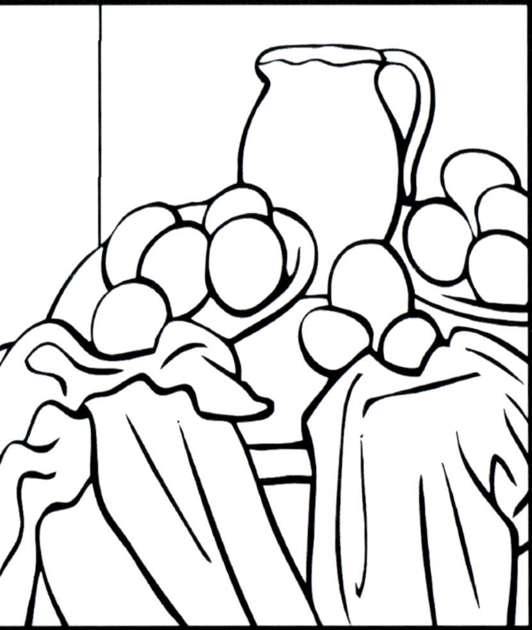

Have a go at two different alternative tetrads, one using yellow-orange, one using red-orange to start.

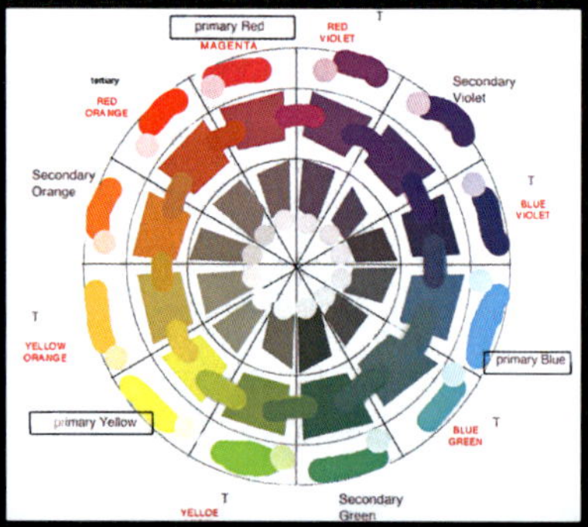

CREATE SOME MORE TETRADIC COLOR SCHEMES

Use this page for your own compositional color planning of some Tetradic schemes. Map them on the wheels and add notes near the wheels as to the pigment names, hues,neutrals and chromatic grays/ blacks used in your study.

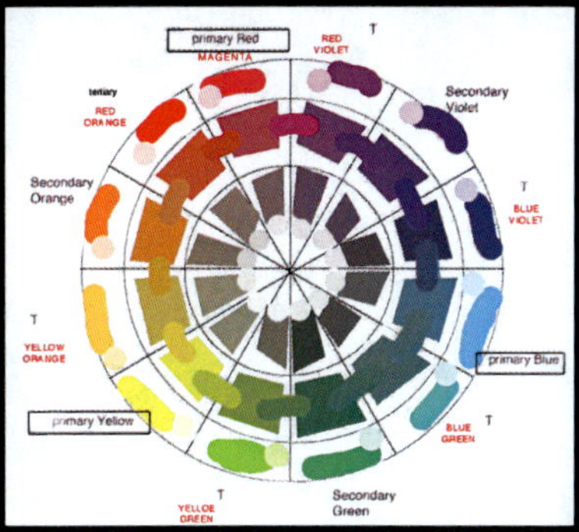

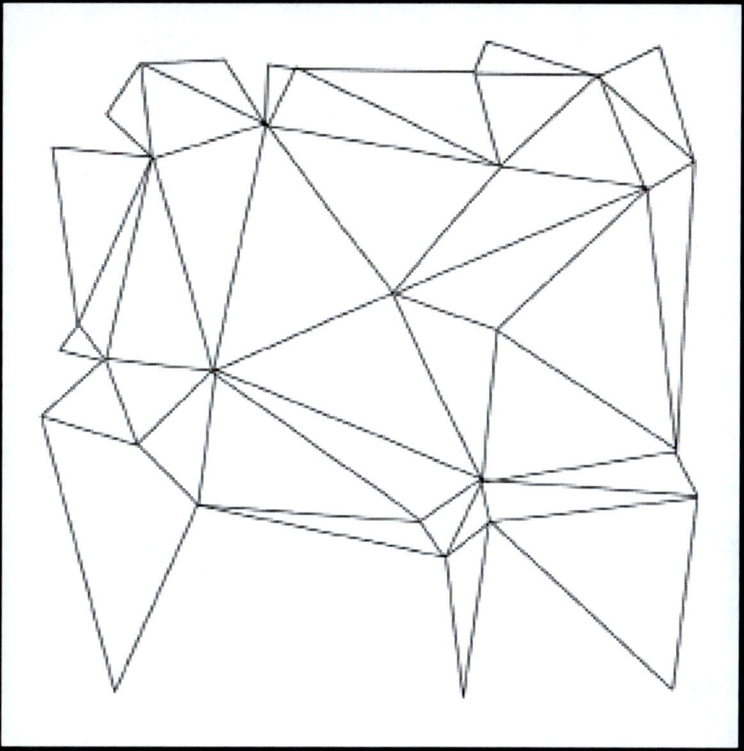

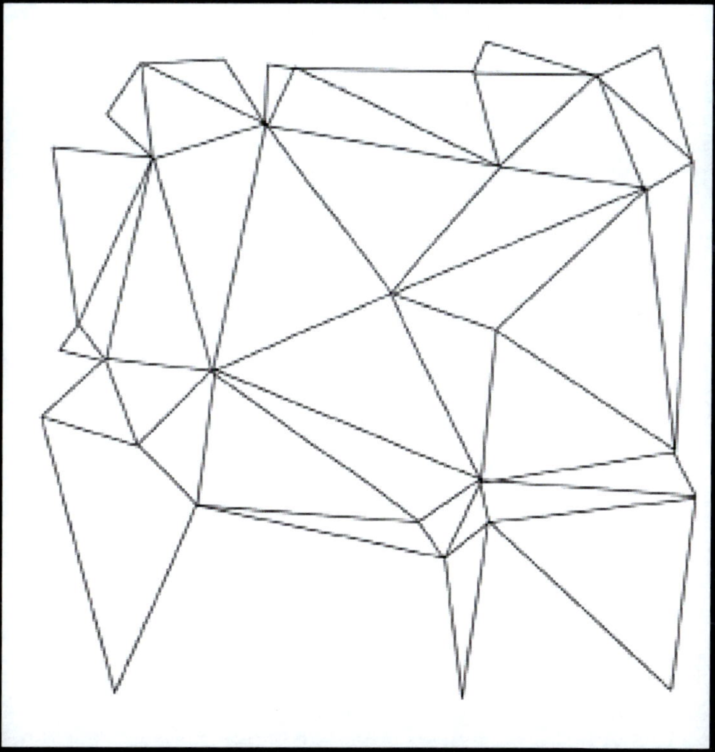

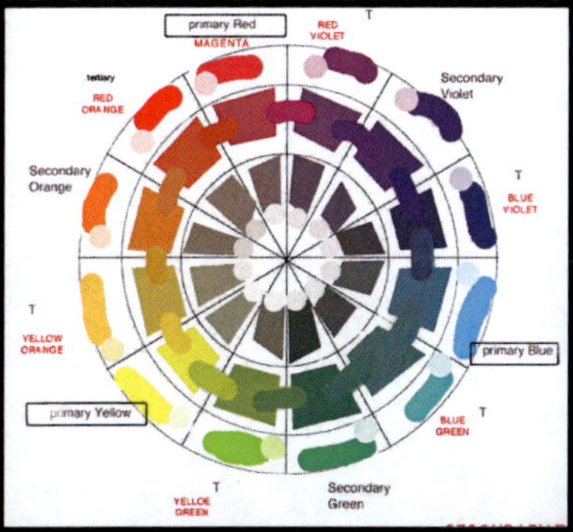

KEEPING A FLEXIBLE APPROACH TO HARMONIOUS SCHEMES

In the previous pages you have read about (and hopefully had a chance to practice implementing) some commonly used color harmonies, arranged in reasonably formal ways to maximize the harmonious relationships in a painting (or a design of any nature).

Your own unique creative expression is still within you and still all yours, and this knowledge of color and how to arrange it (passed on to us by those who studied before us) will serve you well in maximizing and potentiating your unique style. Your intuition will still guide you, but now that your eyes have seen and your brain has interpreted, there is no going back to random accidental use of color. COLOR HARMONY is a powerful tool and you are now wielding it. (Sounds like an old Grandmother witch handing out advice to a graduating trainee in magic!!

Don't be too fussed about analyzing others' schemes. Reverse engineering a color scheme is not as enjoyable as designing a killer one from scratch yourself. You will see schemes you like, and some you dont, let this be your guide in learning and practicing your own.

Another point worth re-iterating is this: if you get an urge for one reason or another to include a hue that does not exactly sit in the formal arrangement you were originally planning for, go ahead, knock it back a bit in saturation (use it in a soft tint or a de-saturated neutral and in amounts that don't influence your dominant scheme. Many successful schemes are not rigidly adhering to the geometrically arranged formats in a robotic and unforgiving way.

As Picasso said " "Learn the rules like a pro, so you can break them like an artist."

Q: I can't afford the top of the range pigments, I am just starting out, on a tight budget, can I learn with a cheap basic acrylics kit?

A: You can still choose wisely and follow the selection suggestions to avoid the many issues that do arise from cheaper multiple pigment mixtures. NB: The best option in this case is to just buy the 6 colors suggested and make everything else yourself as shown. (some of the average kit colors are not helpful at all for learning to mix the 12 hues round the wheel).

Q: Why is black not on the basic list of pigments?

A: To make a 'natural' black, you can use Ultramarine Blue and Burnt Umber. These two each serve another purpose as well to earn a spot on your minimal starting list. A second benefit of mixing blue in to 'gray off' brown is that it forms a quick way of remembering how to balance out browns that you really wanted to be rich grays. (you will see this in the string exercises and color wheel grays). Get some Mars black later if you like, but it is not essential for the color mixing exercises here.

Q: Can I use Cadmium red as my primary?

A: Cadmium reds generally have an orange bias so if you want to crown your cadmium as 'Primary Red Queen', you will need to shift her family members (e.g her complementary green will be a blue-green. In a triad her partners will be more like lemon yellow and warm blue like Ultramarine (like in a Mondrian painting, back when orangish-red was considered the primary red).

Q: I bought two Magenta pigments from different companies, how do I know which is the true Magenta?

A: Other than in the light spectrum (where there is not even a certain wavelength for Magenta), there will possibly never be a 'pure' Magenta in paint but with the Quinacridone pigments for example all you have to look for (if you want to use it as your primary) is a minimal or no bias toward violet or orange. Which one looks like Magenta ink? The ones we look for are PR 122 , PR 202 , PV 19 , PV 42 or PR 202 even PR 176 can do, but they vary from one manufacturer to the other.

FAQS & TROUBLESHOOTING - the same few questions pop up a lot

Q: My primary red paint does not look like the color on my wheel. How do I make that color?

A: If you printed one of our wheel template, if it has color guides, they are made in ink, you are rarely likely to achieve the same vibrancy as Magenta ink. They are there as a hue guide only. It is the same problem with commercialy available wheels often. The colors in this book(printed version) are not exactly like our chosen pigments either. There are many pigments that can be bought and used to fit within the Primary Hue section and they vary in hue degree, value, saturation and transparency. You will not be able to mix a primary red from other pigments. This all makes a good case for always creating your own wheels for your own pigments (and make a new one for a different medium).

Q: I have a cerulean blue in my painting set that I was given as a gift, can I use that as a primary blue?

A: If you wanted to you certainly could call your Cerulean your primary and mix an orange partner that gives a nice shadow color for that particular blue. The reason that Cerulean is not on the basic starter kit of 6 is because it is light in mass tone therefore will be limited in your range of values for blue (basically only mid to light values are possible (without de-saturating to darken). Phthalo Blue is one of the cheaper pigments, you would open up more opportunities with a tube of this added at least.(it is usually a green bi-ased blue in cheapest brands, so your complementary orange will need to be more of a red-biased orange.

Q: I have made a lot of colors I was not wanting to make. How can I use these mishaps?

A: Eventually you may need a brown, a beige or a color that can utilize your 'happy little accident'. Keep a bottle or jar just for adding these and toss in the poor innocent blobs of unwanted color for later use. They can be turned into neutral versions of other colors (eg. a brownish color can nicely neutralize a vibrant green (for landscape). A dull brown can be vamped up with orange or red-orange. Once you know how to mix colors by undertaking the practical exercises, you will have a very good idea of how to utilize the early 'mishaps'.

TERMINOLOGY- Glossary of terms

ACHROMATIC - Means having no color or hue. eg. Blacks, whites, gray made from them are achromatic.(although in ancient times, black and white were considered primary colors and today people still say 'I am wearing the color black'. It is the color you are seeing when you are not seeing color!

ADDITIVE COLOR MIXING - The overlaying of different wavelengths of light eg. red + green = yellow (not to be confused with Subtractive mixing which is what we are doing with pigments, where in most cases red+green would give a kind of brown or gray.)

ANALOGOUS COLORS - Any set of three to five colors that are closely related in hue and found next to each other on the color wheel - such as Blue, Blue-green, Green & Yellow-green.

ASTM -The American Society for Testing and Materials (ASTM) ,established in recent times and tests the lightfastness of artists' color pigments (equivalent to 20 years of exposure in a gallery). ASTM codes are employed by all manufacturers of fine art paints of identify their colors in terms of lightfastness and permanence, as follows:

ASTM I: excellent lightfastness. ASTM II: very good lightfastness. ASTM III: Not sufficiently lightfast.

BIAS - Every pigment has a color bias to some degree. This means that the color has an overlap with a neighboring hue on the color wheel. Even the closest to 'primary colors' in the form of pigment will have a color bias as they can never possess the purity of scattered light. This color bias appears in varying degrees, and affects how the pigment mixes with other pigments and how it looks when it has been thinned with art mediums and applied as a glaze.

BLUE WOOL SCALE - This refers to the UK standard for pigment lightfastness (British Standard 1006), which is used by some artist paint manufacturers instead of (or in addition to) the ASTM codes.

BRIGHTNESS - Brightness is our perception of luminance (visible light energy). It could be of a primary light source or of a light-reflecting or light-transmitting object. (this is relative, like when you compare how you see your laptop indoors compared to if you take it outside in daylight.)

CHROMATICITY - This is commonly known as "colorfulness". Chroma is the amount of identifiable hue in a color.

A color without hue is achromatic and will appear gray. Highly chromatic colors contain maximum hue with few impurities or additives such as white, gray or black. Chromatic blacks or grays are made with complementary partners on the wheel.

***Colorfulness is the "attribute of a visual perception according to which the perceived color of an area appears to be more or less chromatic"

*** Saturation is the "colorfulness of an area judged in proportion to its brightness"

*** Chroma is the "colorfulness of an area judged as a proportion of the brightness of a similarly illuminated area that appears white or highly transmitting"

Definitions from munsell.com

COLOR - (compare with Hue) The appearance of pigmentation of objects, resulting from the light they reflect. Colors are traditionally classified as "primary" (magenta, cyan, yellow),"secondary" or 'Tertiary"- all other colors obtainable by mixing primaries. Depending on their optical effect, they are grouped into warm, cool, and neutral colors. (see Hue - difference).

COLOR PERMANENCE - Describes the lightfastness/permanence of a pigment: ie. it's resistance to fading when exposed to UV light. This depends mainly on the chemical composition of the color pigment. But some colors which are lightfast at full strength lose their resistance when strongly diluted or combined with white.

COLORANT - Any material that imparts color to another material or mixture: includes inks, dyes and pigments.

COLOR SYSTEMS - Different color systems (eg. RGB, CMYK, HSL) are all utilized for different color conditions depending on how the color is created. When using projected light, then RGB (Red-Green-Blue) is the governing system. When colors are mixed with paints, pigments or inks, and applied to paper, then CMY (Cyan-Magenta-Yellow) is the color model. Because these pure pigments are expensive, the color Black (K), is substituted for equal parts of CMY to lower ink costs, producing the CMYK system. Another major color model is HSL (Hue-Saturation-Lightness). This system comprises several variants substituting saturation with chroma, luminance and value etc.

COLOR VALUE - The value of a color is based on the amount of light emanating from it. The brighter the color, the higher it's color value.

COLOR WHEEL - A circular diagram showing the relationships between primary, secondary, tertiary and complementary colors. An indispensable tool for anyone working with color. It is from the color wheel that color schemes are defined. Usually it comprises three primary colors, three secondary colors, and six tertiary colors.(there could sometimes be 12 tertiary divisions.(18 point wheel).

COMPLEMENTARY COLORS - These colors sit directly opposite each other on the color wheel: Eg. yellow and secondary violet, and magenta and secondary green. Each primary color - magenta, yellow, cyan - has it's own complementary color - respectively green, violet, orange. These are secondaries and made by mixing the other two primaries. Every hue on the wheel has a complementary sitting opposite it.

CONTRAST - Contrast is one of the main principles of art. It is the clever juxtaposition of differences (which in effect is an eye magnet). Any of the elements can be utilized to create contrast (also called 'Emphasis' by some).

CONVENIENCE COLORS- These are pigment colors made up of more that one pigment. The names are generally made up by paint manufacturers and are used by others with slightly different mixtures and differing resultant colors. The negative issues that they can give are two-fold. Firstly a favorite color can be fugitive (not lightfast) because one of it's pigment ingredients is not lightfast. Secondly , once another color is added, things can get muddy very quickly. The positive aspect of convenience colors is the time they save you in mixing your favorite tints, shades, neutrals etc. (so make your own in a reasonable quantity, proportionate to your own general needs.)

COOL COLORS - These commonly include colors like green, blue and violet: they are termed cool because they evoke images of cool things like the sea or a winter landscape. (there can also be relatively cooler versions of warm colors.) Temperature is relative.

DESIGN - Planned organization of lines, shapes, forms, colors, textures, and space in a work of art. In two-dimensional art, often called composition.

EARTH COLORS - These are your neutral colors (some are found in the middle ring of the simple color wheel) such as browns, beiges, ochres etc. They are also called neutralized hues or de-saturated (very easy to mix compared to rich grays which need more precise understanding and mixing).

EXPRESSIONISM - A painting movement, originating in the late 1800s to early 1900s which was associated with subjective emotions, somewhat distorted forms and also (commonly) quite vivid colors. These artists used the expressive possibilities of color and line to explore dramatic and emotionally loaded themes.

FAUVISM - This was a short lived colorist painting movement which formed around artist friends in Paris around the turn of the century. Leading the movement were André Derain and Henri Matisse. Meaning "wild beasts", the word Fauves was coined by an art-critic called Louis Vauxcelles to describe the group's wildly colored paintings. (I was a Fauve when I got my first oil paints, straight out of the tube! Wild!)

FUGITIVE - When a pigment fades within a short time it is referred to as "fugitive". Many cheap paints, are made from lower grade, fugitive pigments (refer to p.40-42 on Lightfastness ratings).

GLAZING - Pigments are diluted with medium or water (depending on which painting medium is used) . Best done with an inherently transparent pigment mixture, the applied color can transform the image or part of it without covering anything. A luminescence can be achieved that is not possible with the mixing or overlaying of opaque pigments.

GRAYSCALE- Grayscale is a description of an image with a range of shades of gray without apparent color. The darkest possible shade is black, which is the total absence of transmitted or reflected light. All images on these pages are grayscale images.

GRISAILLE - is a type of monochrome painting done completely in grays, a grisaille may be created for it's own sake, or as an underpainting for a painting (in preparation for glazing layers of color over it). This combo of techniques enabled the renaissance artists a good degree of photo-realism.

HARMONIOUS - In terms of color, there are several commonly accepted and clearly described color schemes that are said to be the most harmonious. They revolve around geometric arrangements of the 12 hue groups. In art, harmony is also associated with elements other than color , but here, in this work book we concentrate mainly on color.

HUE - Commonly used to describe a color, this term actually describes the distinct characteristic of color that identifies for example, magenta from yellow, or from blue. In other words the position of that color around the outside of a color wheel. Hues show the dominant wavelength of light that is reflected from an object.(or at least what our brain perceives through the retina.) Normal vision can differentiate between approximately 10 million different colors (includes tints, shades, neutrals) from these basic hue groups. complementary hue.

IMPRESSIONISM - an art movement in painting that originated in France in the 1860s, and spread throughout the world. They took their name form the insult of an art critic and went on to have great successes, including off-shoots like the Pointillists, Art Nouveau and Fauvism. Impressionism was characterized by an interest in depicting the visual impression of the moment, in daubs of pure hues, especially in terms of the shifting effect of light and color.

INTENSITY - Also see chroma, saturation, this refers to the purity and vibrance of a hue(we place our most intense hues around the outside of our color wheel then show how they de-saturate or become less intense as we add more and more of their exact opposite.

KEY- Think of the first third of a tonal scale as high key (lighter), the third nearer to black as low key (darker) and the mid-third as mid key.

LIGHTFASTNESS - The measure of a pigments resistance to fading when exposed to sunlight. see ASTM and Bluewool Scale to learn more about systems of measuring.

LUMINANCE - is a measure of the intensity of light that reaches the eye. We perceive different luminance in the same object depending on how much light there is in the environment.

MASSTONE - Whether a pigment is opaque or transparent, observing it in a pot or as a thick quantity, the mass tone is seen as dark, mid-tone or light.(see also undertone).

MEDIUM - A liquid vehicle in which we can suspend pigment to thin and spread it. In the case of glazing, the particles become suspended and a smoother result can result. A gel medium is a thicker version which is used (amongst other things) to add more texture to paint.

MONOCHROME - many people think this means black and white however, mono (one), chrome (color) means many tones of one color .A monochrome or monochromatic painting is one created using only one color or hue.(or grays) . See Achromatic.

MUNSELL NOTATION - A complex type of color classification system, invented in 1905 by artist and Professor Albert Munsell. The Munsell notation for a chromatic color is written: HV/C; which stands for: Hue Value / Chroma.. Munsell's system has 5 primaries (we use a 3 primary system with Magenta, Yellow, Cyan (and a separate value scale).

ing them to 'mix' optically in the viewer's eye.

NEUTRALIZE - To de-saturate, make less vibrant, usually by mixing a small amount of the complementary color (eg.a little blue can neutralize orange)

OPAQUE -This is the adjective referring to the coverage ability of a paint, known as opacity. Paints that allow no light to pass through are called opaque, the opposite to transparent (and some are semi-opaque too)

PAINTERLY - Painterly refers to the application of paint in a free, loose or less controlled approach, resulting in the appearance of obviously visible brushstrokes within the finished painting.

PIGMENT LOADING - This is the amount of pigment particles in a paint mixture, as compared to the amount of binder, fillers and other ingredients sometimes added.

PIGMENT NUMBER - Manufacturers generally use Color Index Name Code & number PY = Pigment Yellow; PO = Pigment Orange; PR = Pigment Red; PV = Pigment Violet; PB = Pigment Blue; PG = Pigment Green; PBr = Pigment Brown; PBk = Pigment Black; PW = Pigment White; PM = Pigment Metal

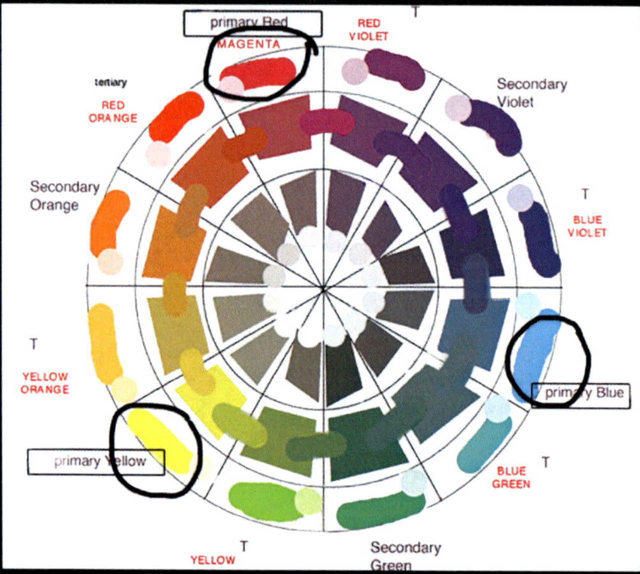

These are the chemical composition numbers given to a pigment by the Color Index International. eg. Burnt Umber PBr 7

POLYCHROMATIC - An image with multiple random colors.

PRIMARY COLORS - These are (in our chosen triadic system) Magenta, Cyan (blue), and Yellow; the colors that can be mixed to produce the secondary and tertiary colors, but cannot themselves be produced from any other mixtures (hence the word primary).

For example, a mixture of primary magenta and blue gives the secondary color violet, which is the "complementary color" of yellow. A combination of primary red and yellow gives orange, the complementary color of blue; while mixing yellow with blue can give us secondary green, the complementary color of Magenta. (see the exercises to come)

Colors seen when sunlight is separated by a prism are known as the spectral colors. These comprise red, orange, yellow, green, blue, indigo, and violet (ROYGBIV). The primary colors for the additive color system are usually limited to red, green, and blue-violet. The primary colors for the modern subtractive color system are cyan, magenta and yellow. Mixing pigments is not like shining a light through a prism!

It needs to be clarified (again and again) that there are many sources still teaching that the spectrum red (light wavelength from around 620 to 750 nm) is your primary. It may well be for many (light) applications but for paint mixing, you will always get brown if you try to desaturate this red (which we call tertiary) with secondary green. If you use secondary green and Magenta (the kind with minimal bias towards orange or violet) you will get a clean chromatic (aka rich) gray. It will become very clear once you start mixing up your own hues.

RICH GRAY - The harmonious gray or shadow color made by adding the precisely mixed complementary color to the one you want a gray for.(as opposed to the dull /achromatic gray made by shading with black.) A dark rich gray is sometimes referred to as a chromatic black.

SATURATION - Sometimes used interchangeably with Chroma, saturation is more a measure of the intensity of a hue. (colorfulness and brightness together)

SCUMBLE - A paint application technique used in many painting media. It involves sparingly 'scrubbing' the paint over another layer to get a more diffuse effect.

SHADE -Shadow. A darker (and thereby less saturated) version of a hue. Some people use the word tone for darkening+desaturating.('toning down') . A commonly used hack was always to use black to create all shades, but the result is a flatter, less harmonious shade than a chromatic shade made with the complementary color (see Rich Gray). Shading with a pencil is adding value or tones.

SIMULTANEOUS CONTRAST - The effect of one color against another and vice versa (colors 'cast' their compliment and can affect our perception of hue, value and chroma (see exercise pages on this phenomena and do your own practical studies to see it in effect). A dark color can make a light color look lighter (as in Chiaroscuro) just as one color affects another.

SPECTRUM - The visible light spectrum is the range of different colors which is produced when light passes through a glass prism or through a drop of water. A rainbow also reveals the colors in the spectrum.

TERTIARY COLOR - These hues are the result of mixing a secondary and a primary. eg. red-orange, blue-green. There are those who use the primary color as the first word and the secondary after. Others insist that the 'adjective' is used first (eg. is it a Red-orange ie.reddish orange or is it an Orangey-red (ie. orangish red). That is only really helpful if you have more than 12 hue sections around the wheel.

TINT - Refers to a color or hue with white added. For example, pink is a name for a tint of red. In watercolor, dilution offers a tint by way of the white showing through more. Tinting also decreases saturation / chroma.

TONE - This word is used confusingly at times, along with value. It is used to describe the lightness or darkness of a color but since color science exploded, it's used more in reference to desaturation + darkening (since Munsell's color 'system' became prevalent (he talks about hue, value and chroma as the 3 dimensions of color.) Chroma and value are linked in this paradigm.

In achromatic drawing however, tone and value are often used interchangeably and this is where the confusion comes in. Tone is measured from 0 - 7, or 1 - 9 (or any number you decide for your tonal scale.ie. you add more tone with charcoal or graphite, it gets darker.)

0 1 2 3 4 5 6 7

Value (per Munsell) is measured in the opposite way - White is 10 and Black is 0. So it is more about light being stronger or brightest at 10 and no light at 0.

This commercial grayscale finder has 1 black to- 10 white (measuring value/brightness not tone)

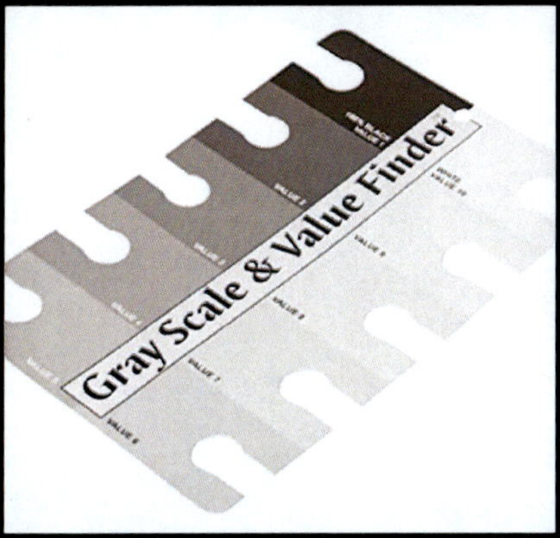

Think about expressions like "Tone it down!" (this may refer to language, volume or indeed to saturation or vibrancy of hue). Both black and white can tone down the saturation of a hue. Another example of crazy old English language having many meanings of the same word!

We align the words 'Key' and 'Value' as most students get that a high key image is lighter and brighter overall and a low key image is darker overall (eg. Chiaroscuro).

Tonal modeling is used to give shape to form and when varied in contrast, helps to give depth to an image. Tonal Value is the relative measure of lightness or darkness.

TRANSPARENT - a transparent pigment has teenier molecules than an opaque pigment so that when you dilute it with water or a glazing medium, everything that is underneath is still seen through the glaze layer, it is simply transformed according to the color you are glazing it with.

UNDERTONE - Undertone – the color produced when you thin and spread a small amount of paint over a white surface. (used at times interchangeably with bias, although this refers more to a leaning to one side of the hue or other)

VALUE (see tone) - The words tone and value have been used interchangeably by some for years (I have used them this way for decades). Some Munsell enthusiasts debate this hotly and use tone interchangeably with saturation/desaturation.

Tonal Value (and Tonal contrast) is a concept within a whole other very important area of study when learning to draw and/or paint, covered in another online module (coming next as a comprehensive practical workbook.) Use the first QR code to join our email list and receive an update as modules and books are launched. (or undertake the online module 'Value, Contrast, Light and Shade'.)

FEATURED IMAGES

Fig 1 - ' The Night Café , Arles' ,oil on canvas, 1888 - Vincent Van Gogh

Fig 2 - 'Cocktail Hour' , acrylics on canvas, 2017 - Tanya Webber

Fig 3 - 'Mantlepiece i' , acrylics on board, 1997 - Jennifer Webb

Fig 4 - 'Three Women', oil on canvas, 1907-8, - Pablo Picasso

Fig 5 - Detail 'Titian Madonna and Child with Sts Catherine and Dominic and a Donor" ,oil on canvas, 1516 - Titian

Fig 6 - 'Picking Flowers' , oil on canvas, 1875 - Pierre-Auguste Renoir

Fig 7 - 'Homage to the Square' series, oil on canvas, 1949-1976 - Josef Albers

Fig 8 - 'Color Study, Squares with Concentric Circles' , Watercolor on paper, 1913 - Wassily Kandinsky

Fig 9 - 'Self Portrait' , oil on canvas, 1889 - Vincent Van Gogh

Fig 10 - 'Beast ii', mixed media on yupo, 2017 - John Louis Lloyd

Fig 11 - 'I had a Dream' , mixed media on canvas, 2018 - Coco

Fig 12 - 'The Tragedy' - oil on canvas, 1903 - Pablo Picasso

Fig 13 - 'Orange, Red, Yellow', oil on canvas, 1961 - Mark Rothko

Fig 14 - 'Waterlilies and Japanese Bridge' , oil on canvas, 1899 - Claude Monet

Fig 15 - 'Starry Night', oil on canvas, 1889 - Vincent Van Gogh

FEATURED IMAGES

Fig 16 - 'Ninfe Bleu' - oil on canvas, 1916-1919 - Claude Monet

Fig 17 - ' The Girl with the Pearl Earring', oil on canvas, 1665 - Johannes Vermeer

Fig 18 - 'Dreamer i' , (Detail) acrylics and graphite, 2018, - Jennifer Webb

Fig 19 - 'The Houses of Parliament', oil on canvas, 1903 - Claude Monet

Fig 20 - 'Glow Beyond vi ,mixed media, 2018, - John Louis Lloyd

Fig 21 - 'The Paris Sunflowers', oil on canvas, 1887 - Vincent Van Gogh

Fig 22- 'The Lacemaker', oil on canvas, 1671 - Johannes Vermeer

Fig 23 - 'Nafea Faaipoipo' , oil on canvas, 1996 - Paul Gaugin

Fig 24 - 'Yellow Irises' , oil on canvas, 1924 - Claude Monet

Fig 25 - 'Waterlilies Pond, Green Reflection', oil on canvas, 1920 - Claude Monet

Fig 26 - 'The Houses of Parliament, Sunset', oil on canvas, 1903 - Claude Monet

Fig 27 - 'Gentle Shore' -, mixed media on board, 2020 - Jennifer Webb

Fig 28 - 'G&T Anybody?', acrylics on canvas, 2020 - Veronica Borrett

Fig 29 - 'Lady with a Fan', oil on canvas, 1918- Gustave Klimt

Fig 30 - 'Regatta at Argenteuil', oil on canvas, 1872 - Claude Monet

Fig 31 - 'The Kitchen Maid'- oil on canvas, 1658, Johannes Vermeer

RESOURCES

HISTORY OF THE SCIENCE OF COLOR

Loeb Classical Library (1936) Aristotle's Minor Works

https://en.wikipedia.org/wiki/Color_theory

Ball, Philip (2003) Bright Earth: Art and the Invention of Color

The Laws of Contrast of Colour - Michel Eugène Chevreul

https://www.nature.com/

https://www.youtube.com/watch?v=iPPYGJjKVco

http://hyperphysics.phy-astr.gsu.edu/hbase/vision/rodcone.html

https://www.eizo.com.cn/global/library/EIZO_DCH_CH1.pdf

https://en.wikipedia.org/wiki/Josef_Albers

https://edu.rsc.org/feature/the-battle-for-magenta/2020242.article

https://arstechnica.com/science/2009/02/yes-virgina-there-is-a-magenta/

RESEARCH ON PIGMENTS AND LIGHTFASTNESS

http://www.artiscreation.com/Color_index_names.html

MacEvoy, Bruce. Color Vision Handprint : Colormaking Attributes

https://www.handprint.com/

https://www.kimcrick.com/

THE COLOR PURPLE'S HISTORY

https://www.bbc.com/culture/article/20180801-
tyrian-purple-the-regal-colour-taken-from-mollusc-mucus

https://www.artsandcollections.com/a-history-of-the-colour-purple/

https://www.sciencealert.com/does-colour-really-affect-our-brain-and-body-a-professor-of-colour-science-explains

https://en.wikipedia.org/wiki/Color_psychology

https://99designs.com.au/blog/tips/color-meanings/

https://www.verywellmind.com/the-color-psychology-of-purple-2795820

ART THEORY AND PRACTICAL COURSES ONLINE

https://melbourneartclasses.com.au/online-art-classes/

Scan the QR code to get to the extra printable templates and online materials to assist creating your own color bible, for current and future media that you decide to work in.

The first person I always acknowledge is my father who bought me my first oil paints at age 11 yrs and later told my friends at my 21st that he always knew that I was a born creative since he saw me drawing on the wall from my cot with the only materials available to me. (Nope, naa, don't think about that for too long!) I took this as a lovely sign of fatherly pride and encouragement! My mother in her greater wisdom, sent me out to the shed (barn) and banned the study of art at school. So I have to thank her even more as this put the creative fire in my belly for life. Steering me towards a 'real career' allowed me to develop autodidactically as an artist, finding my own teachers and mentors.Thanks Mum, love you.

Next, I have to cite the first direct impetus in my creative development who was actually my Math teacher Phil Dean, who invited me at the age of 13 to his home to learn how he made frames for his wife Jan, an exhibiting artist.This resulted in an invitation to exhibit my paintings with her colleagues, a huge honor at such a young age. Thanks to both of you, you inspired me later in teaching as well, with your amazing patience and dedication.

I maintained my private autodidactic art studies throughout two concurrent health field careers and ended up living as an artist in another country (Brazil) before daring to follow the same path in my own country (Australia). I was asked to take some private students by the local high school art teacher and so began my path into passing on what I had spent decades diligently learning in my travels and autodidactic studies. I learned by consuming every source available on every subject that I knew I needed and distilling the results into my own work and a curriculum (pre-internet it was books, videos and other artists' mentoring), many who said they had undergone art degrees with less practical knowledge acquired back then, than I had discovered the long hard way. I believe we can always learn more, so I never stop.

Thanks to my supportive Port Art colleagues, and to my sons, Ari and Kade who support and inspire me in their own way.

A nod goes out to every single group and private student who has passed through our studios, as it is for you that I continue to seek, expand and develop my own learning and yours. There is nothing greater than working in an environment of creativity and communal thirst for knowledge and skill.

Lastly, I acknowledge all artists, past and present who dared to be unique, truly creative and learned from each other while making it their own. I also want to truly acknowledge and honor the original (First Nation) Australian artists who have created meaningful art with the materials available to them from over 40, 000 years ago.

Thanks from the heart to all of you. xx J.W.

FAVORITE QUOTE 'I am still learning' Michaelangelo

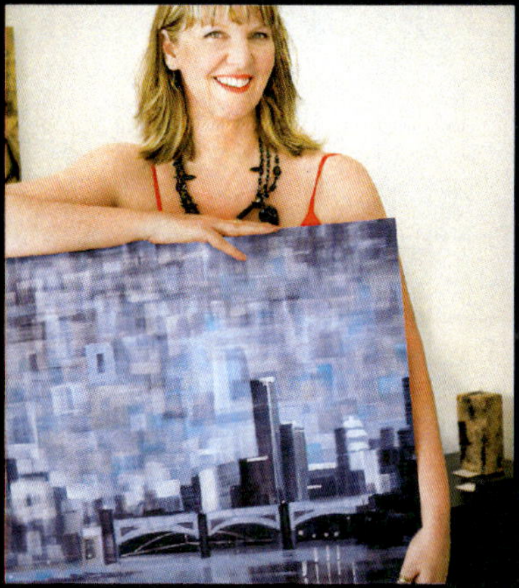

Manufactured by Amazon.ca
Acheson, AB

11242497R00107